Mixed Emotions

Mixed Emotions

Anthropological Studies of Feeling

Edited by Kay Milton and Maruška Svašek

Oxford • New York

First published in 2005 by
Berg
Editorial offices:
1st Floor, Angel Court, 81 St Clements Street, Oxford, OX4 1AW, UK
175 Fifth Avenue, New York, NY 10010, USA

Berg is the imprint of Oxford International Publishers Ltd.

Library of Congress Cataloguing-in-Publication Data
Mixed emotions : anthropological studies of feeling/edited by Kay Milton and
Maruska Svasek.
   p. cm.
Includes bibliographical references and index.
ISBN 1-84520-078-0 (hardcover)—ISBN 1-84520-079-9 (pbk.)
1.   Emotions—Cross-cultural studies. 2.   Ethnopsychology. I. Milton, Kay, 1951-
II. Svasek, Maruska.

BF531.M59 2005
152.4—dc22   2005005535

British Library Cataloguing-in-Publication Data
A catalogue record for this book is available from the British Library.

ISBN-13 978 1 84520 078 7 (Cloth)
ISBN-10 1 84520 078 0 (Cloth)

ISBN-13 978 1 84520 079 4 (Paper)
ISBN-10 1 84520 079 9 (Paper)

Typeset by Avocet Typeset, Chilton, Aylesbury, Bucks
Printed in the United Kingdom by Biddles Ltd, King's Lynn

www.bergpublishers.com

Contents

Notes on Contributors

Peter J. Bowler is Professor of the History of Science at Queen's University Belfast. He specializes in the history of biology, especially theories of evolution, on which he has published several influential books. His other publications include *The Fontana History of the Environmental Sciences* (Fontana 1992) and *Reconciling Science and Religion: The Debates in Early Twentieth Century Britain* (University of Chicago Press 2001).

Paloma Gay y Blasco is a Lecturer in Social Anthropology at the University of St Andrews. She conducted her doctoral research on Spanish Roma and has published a book, *Gypsies in Madrid* (Berg 1999), based on this work. She has also published papers on issues of ethnicity, resistance, sex and gender, and feminist anthropology. Her current interests include memory and forgetting and the state-planned isolation of minorities. She is working on a textbook on how to read ethnography.

Tracey Heatherington is an Assistant Professor at the University of Wisconsin Milwaukee. She has conducted research on environmental issues, political practice and the anthropology of the senses. She has published articles in *Social Anthropology* and *Ethnology*, and is currently working on a book arising out of her fieldwork on political ecology in Sardinia.

Lisette Josephides is a Reader in Social Anthropology at Queen's University Belfast. She has conducted long-term fieldwork in Papua New Guinea and has produced many publications on the area. She is currently in the process of completing revisions to *The Production of Ethnography*, her latest book. Her current research interests are morality and international human rights.

John Knight is a Lecturer in Social Anthropology at Queen's University Belfast. He has carried out field research in mountain villages on the Kii Peninsula in western Japan, and has written on a variety of topics to do with rural Japan. His research interests include human–animal relations and he is editor of *Natural Enemies: People–Wildlife Conflicts in Anthropological Perspective* (Routledge 2000) and *Animals in Person* (Berg 2005).

Karen D. Lysaght is a Post-Doctoral Fellow at the Centre for Social and Educational Research at the Dublin Institute of Technology. She completed her doctoral thesis in 2000 on Loyalist paramilitarism and party politics in inner-city Belfast. She has since completed research on the relationship between space and violence, focusing in particular upon sectarian and homophobic incidents. She has publications on violence, sectarianism, space, gender and sexuality.

Kay Milton is Professor of Social Anthropology at Queen's University Belfast. She has conducted research on environmental anthropology since the mid-1980s, which has led to a current interest in theories of emotion and motivation. Her publications include *Environmentalism and Cultural Theory* (Routledge 1996) and *Loving Nature: Towards an Ecology of Emotion* (Routledge 2002).

Paul Sant Cassia is Reader in Social Anthropology at the University of Durham. He has conducted research on various topics in Cyprus, Greece, Tunisia and Malta, and is currently researching the politics of *patrimoine* in Pezenas, France. He is the author of *The Making of the Modern Greek Family* (with Constantina Bada) (Cambridge University Press 1991) and of *Bodies of Evidence* (Berghahn 2004) dealing with the problem of missing persons in Cyprus. He edits the journal *History and Anthropology* (Routledge).

Maruška Svašek is a Lecturer in Social Anthropology at Queen's University Belfast. Her main research interests include border issues, emotions, politics and visual art. She has published numerous papers and co-edited several special issues of the journal *Focaal: European Journal of Anthropology* on these themes. She is currently working on a book on the anthropology of art, to be published by Pluto, and is the editor of *Postsocialism: Politics and Emotions* (Berghahn 2005).

Elizabeth Tonkin is Professor Emerita of Social Anthropology at Queen's University Belfast. She has a long-standing interest in verbal arts, performance and participatory anthropology. Her regional focus is on West Africa, especially Liberia. Her many publications include *Narrating our Pasts: The Social Construction of Oral History* (Cambridge University Press 1992) and (as co-editor) *History and Ethnicity* (Routledge 1989).

Harvey Whitehouse is Professor of Anthropology at Queen's University Belfast. He is currently testing and developing a theory to explain recurrent features of religion in terms of underlying psychological causes. His many publications include *Inside the Cult* (Oxford University Press 1995), *Arguments and Icons* (Oxford University Press 2000) and *Modes of Religiosity* (AltaMira Press 2004).

Introduction: Emotions in Anthropology

Maruška Svašek

The purpose of this book is to introduce students and other readers to some of the latest anthropological work on emotions. It presents a snapshot of anthropology's current contribution to this important interdisciplinary field. Emotions have always been intrinsic to the production of anthropological knowledge. As in any field of inquiry, emotions shape fundamental concerns and affect the development and design of research projects. They play an essential role in fieldwork encounters, they affect how those encounters are translated into ethnographic accounts, and they influence the theoretical debates that characterize and define the discipline. In these roles, emotions have often gone unrecognized, or even been suppressed – to admit to an emotional component in academic discourse would be to undermine its scientific status, in the context of a perceived opposition between emotion and reason (see below). Occasionally through the history of the discipline, and increasingly since the 1970s, emotions have become a more widely accepted object of analysis, and have been explicitly addressed in both ethnographic and theoretical work (see, for example, Lutz and White 1986; Lutz and Abu-Lughod 1990; Leavitt 1996; Overing and Passes 2000; Milton 2002; Svašek 2002, 2005).

The disciplines of psychology and sociology have undergone similar revolutions, generating a vibrant interdisciplinary debate about the study of emotions in social science, which also draws on insights from the biological sciences. A sample of anthropological contributions to this debate is presented in this volume. The chapters cover a range of theoretical issues – the 'natural' or 'cultural' nature of emotions, their constitutive role in political discourse and social and cultural identity, their relation to memory and their influence in fieldwork – and present material from diverse geographical and cultural areas, including Europe, Africa, Japan and Papua New Guinea.

The aim of this introduction is to show where contemporary anthropological understandings of emotion have come from, by providing a brief and selective pedigree of the study of emotions in anthropology, which mainly focuses on developments in Britain and the United States. I shall begin by examining a number of philosophical assumptions about the nature of 'instincts', 'passions' and 'affects' that influenced the early development of anthropological thought. I shall then show how anthropological interest in the emotions diverged during the early decades of the twentieth century, with a focus on Freudian ideas in Europe and the development of 'Culture and Personality' theory in North America. In these early approaches the focus on emotion was indirect, the main object being to understand the categories and types of actions and institutions that appeared to characterize particular societies and cultures. From the 1970s onwards, anthropologists began to focus more directly on emotions, questioning their nature (as innate, universal human characteristics or cultural constructs) and addressing their role in social life. The main part of this introduction will discuss the perspectives that have dominated this recent period: cultural relativism and constructionism, which lead to an emphasis on discourse (as distinct from culture) as the main object of analysis, followed by a counter-emphasis on embodiment, sensory experience, and renewed interest in naturalistic approaches to emotion and critical psychoanalysis. The introduction ends by examining briefly the role of emotion in fieldwork.

'Reason' versus 'Passion': The Myth of Rationality

The image of anthropology as a purely rational, and thus a non- or even anti-emotional scientific enterprise, was one of its key defining principles when the academic discipline was established in the late nineteenth century. Tylor, one of the founders of academic anthropology in Britain, emphatically argued that rational thinking was vital to the development of scientific knowledge (1913 [1881]: 336). The claim to dispassionate reason as the generator of objective truth reproduced a distinctive Western discourse of emotivity, which defined emotions as wild, bodily passions, that should be kept under strict control by the force of mental power. Oppositional thinking in terms of 'reason versus passion' and the related 'mind–body' dichotomy was deeply rooted in philosophy. Plato (c.429–347 BC), for example, used the metaphor of a charioteer controlling a pack of wild horses to argue that passions needed to be tamed by reason. Christian mythology similarly imagined a fierce struggle between the beastly powers of unruly passionate flesh and the morally superior, spiritual realm of the soul – a dichotomy that was also projected onto the gender divide as men were associated with soul and reason, and women with passion and flesh. Aristotle (384–332 BC), by contrast, claimed that thought was essential to emotions. He was interested in the ways in which people could be manipulated through the use of rhetorical skills (see Sant Cassia, Chapter 6 in this volume).

Descartes (1596–1650) emphatically separated the functions of body and soul, defining 'passion' as the automatic, passive awareness by the soul of bodily sensations (Lyons 1980: 4). Spinoza (1632–77) asserted that different passions or 'affects' were able to fight and weaken each other (Hirschman 1977: 23). Like Spinoza, Hume (1711–76) reproduced the Cartesian split between body and soul, but argued that perceptions of bodily commotion actively generated behaviour and action. In his view, people were forced by natural instinct to seek good and avoid evil (Lyons 1980). Other eighteenth-century philosophers had less optimistic views, claiming that the passions were mutually strengthening destructive forces. Kant (1724–1804), for example, argued that the 'basic passions' of ambition, lust for power and greed fed on each other, and could be counteracted only by the dictates of reason (Hirschman 1977: 21–3). Various philosophers politicized the argument by insisting on the distinction between harmful and unharmful passions, and claiming that the harmful ones needed to be mastered by reason in order to challenge the existing political status quo. Aiming for the creation of a more just society, they criticized the powerful position taken by the Church and the aristocracy, and attacked the dogmatic traditions that had justified their authority for centuries (Griswald 1999: 11).

The belief in rationality as an emancipatory force was formed in the Enlightenment in the context of rising capitalism. Montesquieu (1689–1755) optimistically argued that the new economic system helped to tame the negative passions, a process that would have a liberalizing effect on society (Hirschman 1977: 107). By contrast, Rousseau (1712–78) created an opposition between the natural feelings of the uncivilized, and the false sentiments of those who had been affected by the moral and political forces of civilization. In his view, natural feelings were a fundamental aspect of knowing, and should be nourished to create a better society (Berlin 1981; Levy 1984: 234; Lutz 1988: 53; Blackburn 1994: 332–4) Also creating an opposition between positive and negative emotions, Adam Smith (1723–90) classified 'self-interest' and the rationally conducted appropriation of wealth as 'calm passions' that would eventually weaken the unsocial, destructive sentiments of hatred, anger and resentment (Hirschman 1977: 66; Griswald 1999: 117–19,). Obviously, his view did not promote equality, but advocated individualism and competition. His paradigm strongly influenced liberal economists and politicians who claimed that progressive humans should be primarily motivated by the pursuit of rational self-interest.

Rationalist perspectives were dominant at the time when anthropology was established as an academic discipline, and it is therefore not surprising that many influential early anthropologists were strongly influenced by the belief in the power of reason. At the same time, their ideas were shaped by ethnocentric evolutionist theories of racial progression (Bock 1980: 17–18; Shweder 1984: 31). Tylor (1913 [1881]: 341), for example, called the primitive reasoning of savages '[l]oose and illogical', and argued that evolution had liberated civilized man from the oppressive laws of natural instincts, allowing 'the superior intellect of the progressive races [to] raise their nations to the heights of culture' (Tylor (1913 [1881]: 75). In a similar vein, Spencer argued that the inferior human races lacked both 'intellectual persistence' and 'emotional persistence', and claimed that savages were 'impulsive' and expressed 'unenduring emotions ... which sway the conduct now this way and now that, without any consistency' (Spencer 1975 [1876]: 193–4). In his view, the 'gusts of feeling which men of inferior types display' could cause serious social unrest and physical infliction (Spencer 1975 [1876]: 194).

Tylor's theory of language claimed that the linguistic skills of savages could be compared to those of civilized children, and that the frequent use of 'direct emotional utterances' by children and savages demonstrated a similar low level of emotional development. Their utterances belonged to the domain of *instinctual* behaviour, and were radically different from the civilized, mentally processed 'emotional interjections' that expressed 'some passion or emotion *of the mind*' (Tylor 1958 [1871]: 176, my italics).[1] Tylor only partly accepted Darwin's thesis which stipulated that certain emotions were shared by humans and animals. As argued by Peter J. Bowler in his contribution (Chapter 2), it is rather telling that the latter's theory of emotions was not widely accepted by his contemporaries, as most of them argued that the minds of the more progressed humans had transcended their animal origins.

It is important to note that, within the context of European imperialism, the discourse of scientific rationality was politically highly significant. The development of academic anthropology took place in the context of intensifying colonialism and increasing missionary activity, and since rational behaviour was regarded as a force necessary to tame the wild passions, the political and religious domestication of the wild passionate savages was fully justified. From this perspective, civilized humans even had the *moral obligation* to conquer and convert the natives. Reproducing the belief in the superior rationality of Western civilization, the new discipline of anthropology did little to undermine the colonial project. Instead, the production of knowledge concerning local beliefs and practices was an important strategy in colonial politics, as ethnographic insights and 'facts' helped the colonial powers to map and manipulate the natives.

As will be discussed in more detail at the end of this introduction, the image of the rational scientist who produced objective, factual accounts of reality, ignored the effect of emotional and political subjectivity on ethnographic practice. It also denied the right to the supposedly over-emotional natives to represent themselves, as accounts by the colonized were acceptable only as 'raw material', to be processed by civilized scientific minds.

Diverging Paths: Psychoanalysis and 'Culture and Personality'

During the first decades of the twentieth century, the civilization paradigm was attacked by anthropologists who were unconvinced by the scientific evidence of evolutionary theory. Some were directly influenced by the work of Freud, who looked for universal mechanisms in the human psyche, and developed the method of psychoanalysis. In Britain, Malinowski was interested in Freud's notion of the Oedipus complex, which stipulated that all humans were universally conditioned by unconscious sexual desires for parents of the opposite sex and jealousy of parents of the same sex. Using the Freudian concept of 'emotional ambivalence', Malinowski investigated relationships between parents and children in the Trobriand Islands. He argued, however, against the Freudian idea of psychological universalism, not by pointing at differences in evolution, but by presenting the idea of 'culture' as a differentiating force (see Fortes 1957: 166; Barnouw 1979: 76–88). 'Culture', defined in different ways, became the *key concept* that distinguished anthropology from other disciplinary fields (see Milton, Chapter 1, and Bowler, Chapter 2 in this volume).

Malinowski (1944) claimed that Trobriand culture, regarded as a shared system of beliefs and customs, was strongly shaped by the matrilineal descent system, which, in his view, explained the absence of the desire to kill one's father and marry one's mother. Maintaining the Freudian distinction between *conscious* motives and affections and *unconscious* 'real' wishes and feelings, he focused on the splitting up of the paternal role by fathers and maternal uncles. In systems in which fathers and sons belonged to different matrilineal descent groups, he argued, fathers could express feelings of parental love because they did not need to wield coercive powers over them. By contrast, maternal uncles used their authority to transform their sisters' sons into responsible matrilineal kin who would reproduce the lineage laws. Therefore, he concluded, the Trobriand version of the Oedipus complex consisted of the wish to marry their sisters and kill their maternal uncles.

Directly addressing the issue of emotions, Malinowski developed a theory of needs that defined physiological needs, such as hunger, as 'the driving forces behind instincts, sentiments and emotions'. In his view, however, 'culture' was an important regulating force. While 'individual needs' were biologically determined impulses which demanded universal responsive acts that were necessary for the survival of the individual, 'basic needs' generated particular cultural responses, and 'laid stress on the total conditions necessary to individual and group survival, and not merely on individual impulses' (Piddington 1957: 35; see also Malinowski 1944: 77; Fortes 1957: 170–4). As we shall see, the question of to what extent emotions are universal or culturally specific has continued to dominate the debates in the anthropology of emotions.

After Malinowski and until quite recently (see, for example, Milton Chapter 1, Whitehouse, Chapter 5, and Sant Cassia, Chapter 6 in this volume), hardly any British anthropologist drew inspiration from psychology as emphatically as Malinowski had done. By contrast, British 'social' anthropology began to define

itself as straightforwardly antagonistic to the fields of psychology and psychoanalysis, and as distinct from American 'cultural' anthropology which, as we shall
see, has been strongly influenced by developmental psychology and critical psychoanalysis.[2] Yet numerous leading British scholars who were productive between
the 1920s and the late 1950s implicitly used psychological and psychoanalytical
assumptions in their ethnographic theories and interpretations (Lewis 1977: 15).
In the field of kinship studies in particular, many continued to tackle the problem
of affective behaviour and conflicting loyalties within matrilineal and patrilineal
descent groups, and based their analyses on a commonly shared British perception
which defined feelings as forces independent of, and potentially opposed to,
people's duties and interests (Lewis 1977: 7).[3]

On the other side of the Atlantic, American anthropologists were less concerned
with the social mechanics of kinship. Influenced by developmental psychology,
they were interested in the embeddedness of individuals in culture, and claimed
that personality structures, which partly reflected emotional dispositions, were
strongly shaped by cultural forces. Taking inspiration from Gestalt psychology,
Benedict (1928) argued that cultures formed configurations or patterns that produced specific 'psychological types'.[4] She characterized the pattern of Pueblo
culture, for example, as 'Appolonian', implying that it was strongly shaped by the
avoidance of extreme emotions.[5]

Another influential advocator of the Culture and Personality movement was
Margaret Mead (1949 [1928]), who analysed the behaviour of female adolescents
in Samoa, and found that the Samoan girls did not show the tensions, emotional
conflicts and acts of rebellion that characterized American girls. She concluded,
like Benedict (1928), that culture had an important influence on the formation of
personality.

Other scholars combined the perspective of culture as 'integrating force' with a
psychoanalytical understanding of personal development. Kardiner (1939, 1945),
for example, who rejected the rather static, mechanistic British functionalist view
of institutional integration, introduced the concept of 'basic personality structure'
to explain how individuals were formed by early life experiences and integrated in
society. In his view, culturally specific basic personality structures reflected particular anxieties, defences and neuroses, and these intrapsychic conflicts shaped
the 'secondary institutions' of religion, mythology and folklore (Barnouw 1979:
389; Bock 1980: 86–9). The 'basic personality' theorists used research methods,
such as projective tests, that had been developed in psychology.

Du Bois (1961 [1944]), who examined a mountain community on the island of
Alor in the Dutch Indies, rejected the basic personality thesis for its crude over-
generalization. Instead, she used the notion of 'modal personality' to describe the
most frequent character traits in limited samples of informants. Even though she
maintained that culture, as an integrating force, strongly influenced the emotional

make-up of people, her critique expressed a concern for the idiosyncrasy of individuals within cultures. As we shall see, this is a theme that has continued to interest contemporary scholars, in particular those who have developed theories of orality (see, for example, Tonkin 1992), and scholars who, as will be discussed later in this introduction, have been influenced by recent developments in critical psychoanalysis.

In this volume, Milton (Chapter 1 and Afterword) and Josephides (Chapter 4) emphasize that 'the individual' should be an important focus for analysis, and Gay y Blasco (Chapter 9), Heatherington (Chapter 8), Sant Cassia (Chapter 6), Tonkin (Chapter 3) and myself (Chapter 11) examine the embeddedness of individual bodies and minds in sociality and intersubjectivity. Gay y Blasco (Chapter 9), for example, uses Overing and Passes' (2000) concept of 'conviviality' to examine how Gitano individuals are linked through love and grief for kin, and Casey's (1987) notion of 'internalized presence' proves to be helpful in analyzing the dialectics of individuality and sociality among Sudeten German expellees (Chapter 11).

In the post-Second World War period, some Culture and Personality theorists looked, by contrast, for dominant emotional inclinations of whole nations. Several scholars tried to understand Hitler's popularity among the Germans (Erikson 1963 [1950]) and, in the context of the Cold War, others tried to pin down the national character of 'the Russians'. The British anthropologist Geoffrey Gorer, for example, developed the 'swaddling hypothesis' according to which the tradition of tightly swaddling young infants socialized young Russians into a political system of strong external authority (Wallace 1970: 151; Bock 1980: 115). Kluckhohn's (1962) psychoanalytically oriented study of character building distinguished a conflict between the 'oral-expressive', warm and trusting traditional Russian personality, and the 'anal-compulsive', formal, 'conspirational' ideal Soviet personality type (Bock 1980: 119).

From the late 1940s onwards, the various brands of Culture and Personality theory were increasingly accused of invalid theoretical assumptions. Critical scholars attacked the idea of adult personality being fully determined by childhood experiences, and disagreed with the projection of psychoanalytic concepts on other cultures. They also criticized the assumption that individuals within distinct cultures had uniform personalities, and argued against the circular argument that theorized 'personality' as a result from the internalization of culture, and 'culture' as the outcome of the projection of personality. Finally, the naïve reliance on projective tests and doubtful statistical evidence was condemned (Lindesmith and Strauss 1950; Barnouw 1979: 398–9; Bock 1980: 131–8).

Theorizing 'Emotions'

'Inner' and 'Outer' Aspects of Emotions

During the 1970s, some anthropologists began to focus more directly on the study of emotions, and questioned the extent to which emotional dynamics were influenced by social structure and cultural rules. Scholars like Hildred Geertz (1974) and Fred Myers (1973) were influenced by orthodox psychological research, arguing that while 'the range and quality of emotional experience is potentially the same for all human beings … socialization selects, elaborates, and emphasizes certain qualitative aspects from this range' (Myers 1973: 343). They thus regarded 'emotions' as a pan-human, inner potential that was moulded by the outer forces of social life, a view that reproduced the dichotomy of 'nature' as a universal, inner reality versus 'culture' as a particular, public outcome.

In a study of emotions and constructions of self among Australian Pintupi Aborigines, Myers (1973) demonstrated that related kin were expected to show a particular repertoire of morally correct emotions towards each other. Local concepts of happiness, compassion, grief, melancholy and shame formed a culturally specific ideology that constituted a moral system, and helped to maintain order in society. With regard to the Pintupi notion of *pukulpa* (happiness), Myers (1973: 353) argued that '[w]hile feeling happy is an endopsychic matter – a "rising of the spirit" – Pintupi seem to think that an individual experiences such states largely as the result of smoothly-running relations between the individual and those he or she considers *walytja* [meaning "kin" or "those who share camp"]'. Myers maintained, in contrast to Pintupi understanding, that emotions were basically inner states. As we shall see, the cultural constructionists would later argue that scholars like Myers had been biased by Western universalist assumptions which – reflecting the much earlier notion of emotions as 'instincts' or 'passions' – located emotions inside the human body. In their view, the Pintupi notion of emotions had to be taken more seriously.

Dealing with the problem of inner versus outer aspects of emotional dynamics, Schieffelin (1983) tried to create conceptual clarity by defining 'emotion' as the inward, experiential side of feeling, and 'affect' as its more behaviourally manifested expression. In a study of emotions among the Kaluli in Papua New Guinea, he emphasized that, in order to understand Kaluli emotions, a focus on social dynamics was vital: 'Kaluli emotions, however privately experienced … are socially located and have a social aim. To this degree they are located not only in the person, but in the social situation and interaction which, indeed, they help construct' (Schieffelin 1983: 190–1).[6]

From Inner States to Discourse and Power

The idea of emotions as biologically based, universal inner states was strongly attacked in the 1980s by scholars who defined emotions as cultural constructions.

Lutz (1988: 67) argued that the universalist perspective regarded '[c]ulture or civ-ilization ... predominantly as a conscious, cognitive process; emotion then takes its place as the natural complement to cultural processing – as material which culture may operate upon, but which is not culture'. Defining emotions as cultural artefacts and moral acts that negotiate aspects of social reality, she claimed that 'emotional meaning is fundamentally structured by particular cultural systems and particular social and material environments ... emotional experience is not precul-tural but pre*eminently* cultural' (Lutz 1988: 5, original italics). In a similar vein, inspired by Wittgenstein's theory of language games, Michelle Rosaldo (1980) noted that the meaning of emotion words did not necessarily lie in pre-cultural emotional experience, but derived from the pragmatics of social life. Even though she acknowledged that emotional experience had a physical component and defined emotions as 'embodied thoughts', she mainly saw them as cognitive judge-ments (M. Z. Rosaldo 1984: 143).

Lutz's study of the emotional life of the Ifaluk, a community of about four hundred people who live on a small coral atoll in the Pacific, examined several Ifaluk emotion concepts, including *fago* (compassion/love/sadness), *song* (justifi-able anger) and *metagu* (fear/anxiety). Claims to these particular emotions helped individuals both to reproduce and to contest social structure and cultural values, clearly demonstrating that emotions were used in a context of power struggle. The cultural constructionists followed the French philosopher Foucault in his interest in 'knowledge regimes', or 'the way in which knowledge circulates and functions, its relations to power' (Foucault 1982: 212; see also Foucault 1972, 1980). Foucault conceptualized the relationship between knowledge and power as 'dis-cursive practice', or as the formation of 'group[s] of statements which provide a language for talking about – a way of representing knowledge about – a particular topic at a particular historical moment' (Hall 1997: 44). Emphasizing that dis-courses actively produce knowledge, Foucault (1988) stressed that it is necessary to analyse the existence and functioning of discursive practices and to recognize that discursive formations can be articulated on a whole range of institutions, eco-nomic processes and social relations. Inspired by this theoretical perspective, the cultural constructionists claimed that discourses of emotions actively constructed knowledge about self and society that were 'implicated in the play of power and the operation of a historically changing system of social hierarchy' (Abu-Lughod and Lutz 1990: 15).

Two studies of 'love' in different historical and cultural settings, for example, have demonstrated the strength of discourse analysis. Cancian (1987) examined the changing discourse of love in eighteenth- and nineteenth-century America, and convincingly showed that the changing discourse reinforced gender inequality. She noted that '[p]art of the feminization of love was the belief that women had an enormous need for love and tenderness while men were naturally independent and had much less need for enduring, non-sexual love. This imbalance in emotional dependency bolstered the power of men over women' (Cancian 1987: 26). In another study, Scheper-Hughes (1985, 1990) examined culturally specific discourses of mother love among the poor in Brazil, and attacked the bonding theorists who claimed that a genetically encoded maternal instinct determined motherly feelings. Scheper-Hughes, by contrast, showed that under extreme economic conditions, Brazilian women learned not to attach to infants who seemed weak. The discourse of *doenca de crianca* justified their behaviour of severe neglect, a discourse that interpreted signs of malnourishment as an innate mortal condition that resulted from God's will. As with Cancian's study, Scheper-Hughes' analysis showed that people's emotions were at least in part shaped by cultural forces and power inequality.

Several chapters in this volume demonstrate how culturally specific discourses of emotion have shaped social practices. Gay y Blasco, for example, describes in Chapter 9 how, when close kin die, Spanish Gitanos remove all belongings and images of the deceased after a limited time of public mourning. This is a coping strategy aimed at the avoidance of excessive grief which is thought to be physically and mentally unbearable. 'Forgetting' thus expresses strong love for close kin, and constitutes a culturally specific code that is used by the Gitanos to mark the boundaries between kin and non-kin, and between themselves as 'Gitano' and 'non-Gitano' others.

Knight (Chapter 10) shows how concerns and uncertainties surrounding the nature of contemporary motherhood in Japan are reflected in the kind of attention paid to monkeys in monkey parks. Not only does the behaviour of mother monkeys towards their young attract intense attention from visitors, especially young women, but also particular individual monkeys are sometimes featured in the media, particularly if they have overcome adversity (such as illness, low status or congenital deformity) to bring up their young. Such observations help to fuel an emotionally based public debate about 'proper' and 'natural' maternal emotions, against a background of rapidly changing roles and values.

In his discussion of trauma politics in Cyprus, Sant Cassia (Chapter 6) focuses in particular on the power dimension of discursive practice. Using a psychoanalytical perspective of unresolved mourning, his analysis explores how the Greek authorities have attempted to silence memories of loss as a result of Greek–Turkish violence in an official discourse which has represented those who have disappeared as 'missing persons'. Yet, as he points out, popular painting has served as a powerful counter-discursive medium which has partly resolved the conflict between the official political rhetoric and people's intuitive knowledge that the disappeared are dead and will never return to their families.

From Discourse to Embodiment

Some scholars strongly opposed the culturalist approach to emotions. Leach (1981), who emphatically defined himself as a *social* anthropologist, attacked what he saw as 'the ultimately radical weakness of the basic assumption of cultural anthropology, namely, that not only are cultural systems infinitely variable, but that human individuals are products of their culture rather than of their genetic predisposition' (Leach 1981: 32; quoted by Levy 1984: 217).

More recently, Bowers (1998: 53) argued that scholars like Lutz have largely ignored the role of context and non-verbal elements in communicative interaction, and have taken the role of language in emotional life too seriously. Bowers also accused Lutz of exaggerating the degree of uniformity within cultures, crudely opposing 'Western' to 'Ifaluk' value orientations. The supposed differences in emotional dynamics, he argued, are much smaller when shifting the focus from discourse to practice. Despite Western individualism, he stressed, everyday behaviour shows that Westerners are *social* beings engaged in emotional intersubjectivity. At the same time, the Ifaluk necessarily have a sense of *individual* agency and consciousness because otherwise, they would not be able – as Lutz's own research has shown – to reflect on their own and other people's behaviour.

More fundamentally, Milton (2002, and Chapter 1 in this volume) accuses the cultural constructionists of reducing emotions to cognitions, thereby overemphasizing the social nature of emotional interaction, and ignoring the bodily dimensions of emotions. In Chapter 4, Josephides also attacks the culturalist approach, asserting that, by overstressing the idea of cultural difference, it has lost sight of common human values and dispositions that bind individuals cross-culturally. The idea of cultural specificity is, however, not irrelevant in her analysis as she argues that the feeling of 'resentment' – in her view an emotion common to all people – is a dominant emotion among the Kewa of Papua New Guinea.

From a different theoretical perspective, Whitehouse (Chapter 5, this volume) also aims to move beyond cultural relativism. His theory of ritual frequency distinguishes cognitive, emotional and social mechanisms of cultural transmission that can be found in many different parts of the world. As with Josephides, he does not deny the importance of cultural forces on emotional life, but argues that certain processes, such as the effect of shocking experiences on long-term memory, can be explained by other, more universal factors.

The tension between universalist biological explanations and culturalist views has clearly continued to shape the debate on emotions, and numerous scholars have attempted to find a way out of the opposition. Leavitt (1996: 530) has argued that emotions are especially interesting because they bridge the domain of cultural meanings and bodily feelings. Like Leavitt, the philosopher Nussbaum (2001) has tried to avoid the excesses of extreme cultural relativism and universalist biological determinism. Agreeing with the cultural constructionists that linguistic labelling influences emotional experience, she noted, however, that 'the role of language has often been overestimated, and it is very difficult to estimate it correctly. For example, we should not make the common error of supposing that if there is no single term in a language for an experience, that experience must be lacking' (Nussbaum 2001: 155). She added that '[t]his is just as wrong as the idea that if a word is the same the experience is likely to be the same' (Nussbaum 2001: 155; see also Wierzbicka 2004).

A focus on the English concept of 'fear' may illustrate the latter point. As Darwinian evolutionists and their followers would argue, the emotion of 'fear' is universal, not only in humans but also in many other species, because fear has been crucial in the struggle for survival (see Bowler, Chapter 2 in this volume). Yet even if one would accept the rather specific definition of fear as an 'innate trigger to avoid danger', the suggestion that fear has a universal meaning is problematic when we compare discourses and experiences of fear in distinct settings. In the Northern Irish case, for example, fear of teenage pregnancy differs considerably from fear of interethnic violence. While 'fear of teenage pregnancy' co-produces feelings of shame, and is evoked in the context of kinship dynamics and moral discourse, 'fear of interethnic violence' appears in the context of the political tensions between Nationalists and Loyalists. The latter type of fear is closely associated with distrust and hatred, feelings that have been fuelled by memories of mutual aggression.

As will be discussed in more detail in the next section, it must also be noted that the conceptualization of emotions as 'discourses' largely ignores the fact that emotions are generally experienced in the body. This implies that discourse analysis, even though it is able to isolate and analyse distinct cultural constructions of emotions, potentially misses *experiential* differences and similarities of, for example, 'fear'. In her analysis of fear in the streets of Belfast in Chapter 7, Lysaght clearly shows that the bodily dimension of anxiety cannot be ignored because people's perceptions of danger, which inform their spatial behaviour, are strongly embedded in and shaped by embodied experience.

The return of 'the body' as a focus in anthropological theory of emotions (not locating emotions as 'bodily passions' outside the realm of the mind, but regarding bodily experience as an inherent factor in emotional processes) has mainly been pushed by French and American social scientists (Jackson 1983; de Certau 1984, 1989; Lock 1993; Lyon and Barbalet 1994; Lyon 1995). Inspired by Mauss' (1950) work on the socialization of body techniques, Bourdieu (1977: 90) introduced the concept of 'body hexis', a set of learned bodily habits that reflect deeply ingrained dispositions and reproduce dynamic but structured 'fields' of social relations. In this perspective, bodily behaviour is part and parcel of 'habitus' – a system of self-constitution in which the individual is neither a fully autonomous self, nor a self that is fully determined by society. Field theory thus theorizes the relationship between self and society as a dialectical one, a relationship that is maintained through situationally specific practices and representations. From this perspective, emotional acts are simultaneously bodily movements, symbolic vehicles that reproduce and affect social relations, and practices that reveal the effects of power (Abu-Lughod and Lutz 1990: 12). As Leavitt (1996: 524) put it, Bourdieu conceptualized 'a lived body that is as social in nature as it is biological, a body for which there would be nothing problematic about experiences centrally involving both meaning and feeling'.

One of the scholars who has been strongly influenced by Bourdieu's work is Csordas (1990, 1994a, 1994b) who, also drawing on the phenomenological insights of Merleau-Ponty, argued that the social self is constantly reconstituted through perceptual experience. In his view, perceptual experiences start in the body, and 'cultural objects (including selves) are constituted or objectified, not in the processes of ontogenesis and child socialization, but in the ongoing indeterminacy and flux of adult cultural life' (Csordas 1990: 40). In Csordas' theoretical framework, bodies are an integral part of the perceiving subject, and become objectified through reflection and engagement with the world. Perception, inherent in the experience of being-in-the-world, is then a process that cannot be understood in terms of nature–culture or mind–body oppositions. In Csordas' terminology, there is no biologically based, pre-cultural realm that is subsequently moulded by cognition. Instead, he introduced the concept of 'embodiment' to explain existential dynamics, defining it as a process in which pre-objective (instead of pre-cultural) multisensory experiences are experienced and objectified. In this view, embodiment is the existential ground of culture and self (Csordas 1994a: 6).[7]

It is important to note that the perspective of embodiment criticizes, but does not fully undermine discursive approaches to emotions: '[t]he point of elaborating a paradigm of embodiment is ... not to supplant textuality but to offer it a dialectical partner' (Csordas 1994a: 12). In line with this view, two chapters in this volume combine the perspectives of embodiment theory and discourse analysis, and examine the ways in which emotional processes have shaped and have been shaped by local, national and transnational politics. Heatherington explores in Chapter 8 how local Sardinians have objectified and transmuted embodied experiences of the common lands as a form of political action against regional and national authorities who have planned to designate the lands as a nature park. My own ethnographic chapter examines Sudeten German experiences and narratives of trauma, and shows how expellee suffering has been politicized in the context of social and ritual life. The analysis points out that rather particular discourses and partly orchestrated embodied experiences of collective suffering have been central to the politics of expellee co-victimhood.

Naturalistic Approaches Revisited

The discussion so far has shown that the more narrow definitions of emotions as 'either springing from the depths of the body or being laid over individuals as a pervasive cultural grid' have proven to be highly limiting (Leavitt 1996: 524–5). A small number of anthropologists (such as Sperber 1985; Guthrie 1993; Boyer 1994), who have leaned towards universalist explanations, have recently shown an interest in developments in the 'hard', naturalist sciences. Open to interdisciplinary debate and cooperation, they have incorporated findings by neuroscientists, evolutionary psychologists and cognitive scientists in their theoretical approaches.

Whitehouse (2002) has propagated a more systematic, 'scientific' approach to the study of emotions which does not shy away from lab-based experiments and large-scale comparisons. In Chapter 5 of this volume, he examines the interaction of emotional and mnemonic dynamics in ritual settings, and critically compares his own ritual frequency hypothesis with McCauley and Lawson's ritual form hypothesis.

Milton (Chapter 1, this volume) has been inspired by the neuroscientist Damasio (2000) who has defined 'emotions' as empirically observable bodily changes that are induced outside consciousness, and 'feelings' as the subjective experience of these changes. In Milton's 'ecological' perspective, this process of awareness can be regarded as a learning mechanism in which individuals form emotional attachments with their social and natural environments (see also Tonkin, Chapter 3, for a critical discussion of Damasio's work).

Fieldwork and Emotional Intersubjectivity

As noted at the beginning of this introduction, 'emotions' have not only served as an object of anthropological study, but also affected and shaped fieldwork itself, a fact that is nowadays acknowledged in key texts on ethnographic methods (see, for example, Sarsby 1984; Hammersley and Atkinson 1991: 101–15; Kulick and Wilson 1995). The posthumous publication of Malinowski's diaries in 1967 broke the illusion of the emotionally detached, professional scholar, an image that had seemed so convincing in the early history of the discipline. The diary spoke of feelings of confinement, boredom, frustration, irritation, anger and indifference.[8] The confessions of sexual feelings for certain native females, in particular, produced a shockwave in the professional community.[9] The diary unveiled what had previously been unacknowledged or consciously denied: the influence of the anthropologist's own emotional agency on his or her work.

From the 1960s onwards, Malinowski's confessions inspired numerous anthropologists to reflect more openly on the practical and emotional difficulties of fieldwork. Initially, these issues were discussed in the fictionalized genre of the novel, which meant that the myth of rational objectivity could be upheld within the scientific genre of ethnography (Heald and Deluz 1994).[10] Yet the reflexive turn in anthropology, which became highly influential in the 1980s, considered the role of the fieldworker as an important issue that needed to be addressed, both theoretically and in terms of ethnographic writing. Influential scholars, such as Clifford, Marcus and Fischer, critically commented on the representational practices that produced ethnographers as objective observers. Such authoritative ethnographic accounts often began 'with a tumultuous or difficult arrival scene ... and/or a claim to fluency in a local language', after which the ethnographers 'vanished from their texts' (Kulick 1995: 3; see Clifford and Marcus 1986; Marcus and Fischer 1986).

From the 1980s onwards, various scholars decided to examine the emotional intersubjectivity of fieldworkers and informants, sometimes making it one of the major themes in their ethnographies. In a book resulting from research into Moroccan religious brotherhoods and spirit possession, Crapanzano (1980) discussed his relationship with his main informant Tuhami. He argued that 'desire' had been an important emotional force which had structured their interaction, and this explained why certain themes had been recurrent during their encounters. His own motivation to endlessly discuss Tuhami's relationship with the she-demon 'A'isha Qandisha was caused by the 'desire' to constitute himself as an anthropologist who (as is commonly expected) produced knowledge about an 'exotic' theme. To understand Tuhami's response, he further argued, 'it would be necessary to understand his desire for recognition both by me, the concrete but symbolically typified individual whom he is directly addressing, and by a more abstract, less transient Other who is for the moment more or less embodied in me, and from whom he derives that sense of continuity that we call personal identity' (Crapanzano 1980: 10). The concept of 'desire' clearly acknowledged an emotional component of what has often been called 'professional interest'.

Numerous anthropologists who have examined emotional intersubjectivity during fieldwork have turned to psychoanalysis as a source of inspiration (see, for example, Briggs 1987; Ewing 1987; Kracke 1987). In this context is important to note that, since the mid-1980s, psychoanalysis has changed in ways similar to anthropology, as both have acknowledged the active role of the analyst in the construction of the object of study.[11] In a comparative analysis of counselling and ethnographic fieldwork, Ewing (1987) demonstrated that, in dialogues between psychoanalysts and patients *and* between fieldworkers and informants, the speakers constructed shifting, inconsistent notions of 'self' and 'other' which directly shaped their relationships. In Ewing's view, sensitivity to the ways in which the speakers used subtle socio-emotional dynamics was vital for the analysis of the multiple layers of significance that shaped the interaction. In her own words, '[o]ne of the most valuable lessons that the psychoanalyst has to teach the interviewer is how to be constantly attuned to the significance of what the patient or informant is saying for the immediate, ongoing interaction' (Ewing 1987: 36).

Yet as Crapanzano argued, one has to be cautious when using insights from psychoanalysis. As he found out during his fieldwork in Morocco, the psychoanalytical concept of 'projection' was unsuitable to explain spirit possession because it is 'based on a particular idiomatically determined conception of man and his motivations' (Crapanzano 1980: 15). While first trying to understand the she-demon 'A'isha Qandisha as a 'collectively sanctioned projection of some endopsychic disposition or conflict' (Crapanzano 1980: 15), he later recognized that Moroccans rather conceptualized possession as an outside force that directly influenced their health and well-being.

As Tonkin notes in Chapter 3, intersubjectivity or 'co-presence' during fieldwork has become an obvious fact that can no longer be ignored by ethnographers. Her humorous examples of emotional interactions between herself, as a fieldworker, and her Liberian informants, clearly demonstrate how culturally specific emotional dispositions may create anger and confusion which partly shape the unfolding encounter. According to Tonkin, the social dynamics of emotions cannot be simply explained through an interactionist model which focuses on social roles and identities. Her own model of co-presence provides a more complex picture that emphasizes the importance of memory and imagination. Tonkin also stresses that assumptions of shared feeling can be illusory because of cultural or personal idiosyncrasies, and notes that the concept of 'empathy' is therefore rather problematic.

In Chapter 4, Josephides, by contrast, argues that despite obvious cultural differences, anthropologists can gain a good understanding of their informants' preoccupations through mutual embeddedness in what she calls 'emotional maelstrom'. Influenced by Kantian philosophy, she pleads for an ethnographic genre that demonstrates and produces cross-cultural empathy.

Not surprisingly, the possibility or impossibility of empathy has been a hotly debated topic in the anthropology of emotions. Biology-oriented universalists have argued that empathy across cultural boundaries is not just possible, but almost inevitable because of the shared human physiognomy (see, for instance, Ekman 1980a, 1980b). Culture-oriented particularists, by contrast, have argued that cross-cultural empathy is unrealisable because of radical cultural difference. Rejecting both approaches, Leavitt (1996) has argued that fieldworkers should actively 'rework' their own emotions in an attempt to understand their informants in an act of 'sympathy', 'a feeling along with (*sum-patheia*), a realignment of one's own affects to construct a model of what others feel' (Leavitt 1996: 530). Similarly, Wikan (1992: 471) emphasized the importance of 'resonance', 'a willingness to *engage* with another world, life, or idea; an ability to *use* one's experience … to try to grasp, or convey, meanings that reside neither in words, "facts", nor text but are evoked in the meeting of one experiencing subject with another or with a text'

(Wikan 1992: 463, original italics). These ideas accord with Renato Rosaldo's (1984: 192, 193) view that '[t]he ethnographer, as a positioned subject, can grasp certain ethnographic phenomena better than others', and that 'one's own lived experience both enables and inhibits particular kinds of insight'.[12] They also correspond to Heatherington's observation in Chapter 8 that her informants did not expect her to *automatically* comprehend their intimate connection to the Sardinian landscape, but thought it to be of vital importance that she would gain an understanding of their feelings through her own embodied experience.

These particular chapters show emphatically that 'emotions' are central to the production of ethnography, and vital to the functioning of social life in general. In view of this, and as all the chapters in this volume will demonstrate, the study of emotional processes is of major importance to anthropology, and provides essential insights into the human condition. This also implies that the 'anthropology of emotions' deserves to be an important element in all anthropology courses, and – as one of my students remarked recently – even as a compulsory part of the curriculum.

Acknowledgements

I would like to thank Kay Milton for comments on an earlier version of this Introduction.

Notes

1. The following quote clearly demonstrates his perspective: 'When the African Negro cries out in fear or wonder *mámá! mámá* he might be thought to be uttering a real interjection … but in fact he is simply calling, grown-up baby as he is, for his mother' (Tylor 1958 [1871]: 176).

2. In 1974, the organizers of the conference Symbols and Sentiments attempted to break the antagonism that most of their colleagues felt for psychology and psychoanalysis. Referring to Turner (1964), who had argued that anthropologists should 'explore the nexus which binds together the cognitive and affectual meaning of symbols', Lewis (1977: 2) noted that 'symbols and sentiments feed upon each other and their fruitful interplay lies at the heart of social behaviour'. Over twenty years later, however, Heald and Deluz (1994: 6) noted that 'hostility has remained the keynote in the relationship [between anthropology and psychoanalysis in Britain]'.

3. Radcliffe-Brown, for example, regarded affective behaviour as an important functional aspect of patrilineal descent systems. In his view, the 'cold' relationship between fathers and sons in Nuer society was an important by-product of the patrilineal system which required younger members of patrilineages to respond to lineage authority and take on obligations.

4. Gestalt psychology claimed that '[t]he whole determines its parts, not only their relations but their very nature' (Benedict 1934: 47). Influenced by this approach, Benedict criticized the atomistic approach of anthropologists like Boas, who – himself influenced by Diffusionism – had mapped different cultures according to the absence or presence of material, behavioural and ideological traits. In Benedict's view, cultures were not just random collections of traits, but formed particular configurations.

5. Benedict compared four societies, and characterized them as 'Dionysian', 'Apollonian', 'Paranoid' and 'Megalomaniac'. The 'Apollonian' Pueblo people were 'a civilization whose forms are dictated by the typical choices of the Apollonian, all of whose delight is in formality and whose way of life is the way of measure and sobriety' (Benedict 1934: 129).

6. Schieffelin (1983) argued that anger, grief and shame were of central importance in the Kaluli cultural system, reinforcing important notions of egalitarianism, balanced reciprocity and male assertiveness.

7. In his study of embodied imagery in ritual healing among charismatic Christians in North America, Csordas (1990) examined how multisensory imagery was used in healing sessions to free participants from negative emotions, and cast out evil spirits. During the sessions, people experienced bodily changes including vibration of the hands and arms, lightness or heaviness, heat and spontaneous crying and laughter, and objectified these experiences as instances of the 'sacred'. Both the pre-objective experience and the objectification process, he argued, were influenced by a culturally specific obsession with control and loss of control.

8. In a reflection on his fieldwork, Malinowski wrote, for example: '[a]s for ethnology: I see the life of the natives as utterly devoid of interest or importance, something as remote from me as the life of a dog' (1967: 167).

9. In his entry of 22 January 1918, for instance, Malinowski admitted that his '[p]urely fatherly feelings' for two Trobriand girls were 'spoiled', and that he had to 'direct [his] thoughts' at his fiancée 'to shake off *lewdness*' (Malinowski 1967: 192; original italics).

10. See for an early example Bohannan's *Return to Laughter*. Prior to the publication of Malinowski's diary she had published her work under the pseudonym Elenore Bowen (1954).

11. Scholars working from a critical psychoanalytical perspective have argued that one should 'avoid the past tendencies to "pathologize" individuals and cultures, or to unreflectively "put a society on the couch"' (Kracke and Herdt 1987: 4).

12. Several anthropologists have described how their own emotional expressions during fieldwork have functioned as non-intentional means of gaining access to their informants, who, as a result, actively recognized them as co-humans who had feelings similar to their own. See, for example, Feld (1990 [1982]).

References

Abu-Lughod, L. and Lutz, C. A. (1990), 'Introduction: Emotion, Discourse, and the Politics of Everyday Life', in C. A. Lutz and L. Abu-Lughod (eds), *Language and the Politics of Emotion*, Cambridge: Cambridge University Press and Paris: Editions de la Maison des Sciences de l'Homme.

Barnouw, V. (1979), *Culture and Personality*, Homewood, IL: Dorsey Press.

Benedict, R. (1928), 'Psychological Types in the Cultures of the Southwest', *Proceedings of the Twenty-third International Congress of Americanists*, New York.

—— (1934), *Patterns of Culture*, Boston, MA: Houghton Mifflin.

Berlin, I. (1981), *Against the Current: Essays in the History of Ideas*, Oxford: Oxford University Press.

Blackburn, S. (1994), *The Oxford Dictionary of Philosophy*, Oxford: Oxford University Press.

Bock, P. K. (1980), *Continuities in Psychological Anthropology: A Historical Introduction*, San Francisco, CA: W. H. Freeman.

Bourdieu, P. (1977), *Outline of a Theory of Practice*, Cambridge: Cambridge University Press.

Bowen, E. (1954), *Return to Laughter*, London: Gollancz.

Bowers, L. (1998), *The Social Nature of Mental Illness*, London: Routledge.

Boyer, P. (1994), *The Naturalness of Religious Ideas: a Cognitive Theory of Religion*, Berkeley, CA: University of California Press.

Briggs, J. L. (1987), 'In Search of Emotional Meaning', *Ethos* 15 (1): 8–15.

Cancian, F. M. (1987), *Love in America: Gender and Self-Development*, Cambridge: Cambridge University Press.

Casey, E. S. (1987), *Remembering: A Phenomenological Study*, Bloomington, IN: Indiana University Press.

Clifford, J. and Marcus, G. E. (eds) (1986), *Writing Culture: The Poetics and Politics of Ethnography*, Berkeley, CA: University of California Press.

Crapanzano, V. (1980), *Tuhami: Portrait of a Moroccan*, Chicago: University of Chicago Press.

Csordas, T. J. (1990), 'Embodiment as a Paradigm for Anthropology', *Ethos* 18 (1): 5–47.

—— (ed.) (1994a), 'Introduction: The Body as Representation and Being-In-The-World', in T. J. Csordas (ed.), *Embodiment and Experience. The Existential Ground of Culture and Self*, Cambridge: Cambridge University Press.

—— (1994b), 'Words from the Holy People: A Case Study in Cultural Phenomenology', in T. J. Csordas (ed.), *Embodiment and Experience: The Existential Ground of Culture and Self*, Cambridge: Cambridge University Press.

Damasio, A. (2000), *The Feeling of What Happens: Body and Emotion in the Making of Consciousness*, London: William Heinemann.

De Certeau, M. (1984), *The Practice of Everyday Life*, Berkeley, CA: University of California Press.

Du Bois, C. (1961 [1944]), *The People of Alor*, 2 vols, New York: Harper and Row.

Ekman, P. (1980a), 'Biological and Cultural Contributions to Body and Facial Movement in the Expression of Emotions', in A. Rorty (ed.), *Explaining Emotions*, Berkeley, CA: University of California Press.

—— (1980b), *The Face of Man: Expressions of Universal Emotions in a New Guinea Village*, New York: Garland STPM Press.

Erikson, E. H. (1963 [1950]), *Childhood and Society*, New York: Norton.

Ewing, K. (1987), 'Clinical Psychoanalysis as an Ethnographic Tool', *Ethos* 15 (1): 16–40.

Feld, S. (1990 [1982]), *Sound and Sentiment: Birds, Weeping, Poetics, and Song in Kaluli Expression*, Philadelphia, PA: University of Pennsylvania Press.

Fortes, M. (1957), 'Malinowski and the Study of Kinship', in R. Firth (ed.), *Man and Culture: An Evaluation of the Work of Bronislaw Malinowski*, London: Routledge and Kegan Paul.

Foucault, M. (1972), *The Archeology of Knowledge and the Discourse on Language*, New York: Pantheon.

—— (1980), *Power/Knowledge*, C. Gordon (ed.), New York: Pantheon.

—— (1982), 'Afterword: The Subject and the Power', in H. L. Dreyfus and P. Rabinow (eds), *Beyond Structuralism and Hermeneutics*, Chicago: University of Chicago Press.

—— (1988) *Michel Foucault: Politics, Philosophy, Culture. Interviews and Other Writings 1977–1984*, ed. and introd. L. D. Kritzman, New York: Routledge.

Geertz, H. (1974), 'The Vocabulary of Emotions', in R. LeVine (ed.), *Culture and Personality*, Chicago: Aldine.

Griswald, C. L. (1999), *Adam Smith and the Virtues of Enlightenment*, Cambridge: Cambridge University Press.

Guthrie, S. (1993), *Faces in the Clouds: A New Theory of Religion*, Oxford: Oxford University Press.

Hall, S. (ed.) (1997), *Representation: Cultural Representations and Signifying Practices*, London: Sage and The Open University.

Hammersley, M. and Atkinson, P. (1991), *Ethnography: Principles in Practice*, London: Routledge.

Heald, S. and Deluz, A. (1994), *Anthropology and Psychoanalysis: An Encounter through Culture*, London: Routledge.

Hirschman, A. D. (1977), *The Passions and the Interests: Political Arguments for Capitalism Before its Triumph*, Princeton, NJ: Princeton University Press.

Jackson, M. (1983), 'Knowledge of the Body', *Man* (NS) 18 (2): 327–45.

—— (1989), *Paths towards a Clearing: Radical Empiricism and Ethnographic Inquiry*, Bloomington, IN: Indiana University Press.

Kardiner, A. (1939), *The Individual and his Society: The Psychodynamics of Primitive Social Organization*, New York: Columbia University Press.

—— with the collaboration of Linton, R., Du Bois, C. and West, J. (1945), *The Psychological Frontiers of Society*, New York: Columbia University Press.

Kluckhohn, C. (1962), *Culture and Behaviour*, R. Kluckhohn (ed.), New York: Free Press.

Kracke, W. (1987), 'Encounter with Other Cultures: Psychological and Epistemological Aspects', *Ethos* 15 (1): 58–81.

—— and Herdt, G. (1987), 'Introduction: Interpretation in Psychoanalytic Anthropology', *Ethos* 15 (1): 58–81.

Kulick, D. (1995), 'Introduction. The Sexual Life of Anthropologists: Erotic Subjectivity and Ethnographic Work', in D. Kulick and M. Wilson (eds), *Taboo: Sex, Identity, and Erotic Subjectivity in Anthropological Fieldwork*, London: Routledge.

—— and Wilson, M. (eds) (1995), *Taboo: Sex, Identity, and Erotic Subjectivity in Anthropological Fieldwork*, London: Routledge.

Leach, E. (1981), 'A Politics of Power', *New Republic* 184:

Leavitt, J. (1996), 'Meaning and Feeling in the Anthropology of Emotions', *American Ethnologist* 23 (3): 514–39.

Levy, R. I. (1984), 'Emotion, Knowing and Culture', in R. A. Shweder and R. A. LeVine (eds), *Culture Theory: Essays on Mind, Self, and Emotion*, Cambridge: Cambridge University Press.

Lewis, I. (ed.) (1977), *Symbols and Sentiments: Cross-Cultural Studies in Symbolism*, London: Academic Press.

Lindesmith, A. R. and Strauss, A. L. (1950), 'A Critique of Culture-Personality Writings', *American Sociological Review* 15: 587–600.

Lock, M. (1993), 'Cultivating the Body: Anthropology and Epistemologies of Bodily Practice and Knowledge', *Annual Review of Anthropology* 22: 133–55.

Lutz, C. A. (1988), *Unnatural Emotions: Everyday Sentiments on a Micronesian Atoll and their Challenge to Western Theory*, Chicago: University of Chicago Press.

—— and Abu-Lughod, L. (eds) (1990), *Language and the Politics of Emotion*, Cambridge: Cambridge University Press and Paris: Editions de la Maison des Sciences de l'Homme.

—— and White, G. M. (1986), 'The Anthropology of Emotions', *Annual Review of Anthropology* 15: 405–36.

Lyon, M. L. (1995), 'Missing Emotion: The Limitations of Cultural Constructionism in the Study of Emotion', *Cultural Anthropology* 10 (2): 244–63.

—— and Barbalet, J. M. (1994), 'Society's Body: Emotion and the "Somatisation" of Social Theory', in T. J. Csordas (ed.), *Embodiment and Experience: The Existential Ground of Culture and Self*, Cambridge: Cambridge University Press

Lyons, W. (1980), *Emotion*, Cambridge: Cambridge University Press.

Malinowski, B. (1944), *A Scientific Theory of Culture and Other Essays by Bronislaw Malinowski*, Chapel Hill, NC: University of North Carolina Press.

—— (1967), *A Diary in the Strictest Sense of the Term*, London: Routledge and Kegan Paul.

Marcus, E. and Fischer, M. J. (1986), *Anthropology as Cultural Critique: An Experimental Moment in the Human Sciences*, Chicago: University of Chicago Press.

Mauss, M. (1950), *Les Techniques du corps, sociologie et antropologie*, Paris: Presses Universitaires de France.

Mead, M. (1949 [1928]), *Coming of Age in Samoa*, New York: Mentor.

Milton, K. (2002), *Loving Nature: Towards an Ecology of Emotion*, London and New York: Routledge.

Myers, F. R. (1973), 'Emotions and the Self: A Theory of Personhood and Political Order among Pintupi Aborigines', *Ethos* 7 (4): 343–70.

Nussbaum, M. (2001), *Upheavals of Thought: The Intelligence of Emotions*, Cambridge: Cambridge University Press.

Overing, J. and Passes, A. (eds) (2000), *The Anthropology of Love and Anger: The Aesthetics of Conviviality in Native Amazonia*, London and New York: Routledge.

Piddington, R. (1957), 'Malinowski's Theory of Needs', in R. Firth (ed.), *Man and Culture: An Evaluation of the Work of Bronislaw Malinowski*, London: Routledge and Kegan Paul.

Rosaldo, I. R. (1984), 'Grief and a Headhunter's Rage: On the Cultural Force of Emotions', in E. M. Bruner (ed.), *Text, Play, and Story: The Construction and Reconstruction of Self and Society*, Prospect Heights, IL: Waveland Press.

Rosaldo, M. Z. (1980), *Knowledge and Passion: Ilongot Notions of Self and Social Life*, Cambridge: Cambridge University Press.

—— (1984), 'Toward an Anthropology of Self and Feeling', in R. A. Shweder and R. A. LeVine (eds), *Culture Theory: Essays on Mind, Self, and Emotion*, Cambridge: Cambridge University Press.

Sarsby, J. (1984), 'The Fieldwork Experience', in R. Ellen (ed.), *Ethnographic Research: A Guide to General Conduct*, London: Academic Press.

Scheper-Hughes, N. (1985), 'Culture, Scarcity, and Maternal Thinking: Maternal Detachment and Infant Survival in a Brazilian Shantytown', *Ethos* 13 (4): 291–317.

—— (1990), 'Mother Love and Child Death in Northeast Brazil', in J. W. Stigler, R. A. Shweder and G. Hecht (eds), *Cultural Psychology: Essays on*

Comparative Human Development, New York: Cambridge University Press.

Schieffelin, E. L. (1983), 'Anger and Shame in the Tropical Forest: On Affect as a Cultural System in Papua New Guinea', *Ethos* 11 (3): 181–209.

Shweder, R. A. (1984), 'Preview: A Colloquy of Culture Theorists', in R. A. Shweder and R. A. LeVine (eds), *Culture Theory: Essays on Mind, Self, and Emotion*, Cambridge: Cambridge University Press.

Spencer, H. (1975 [1876]), *The Principles of Sociology*, London: Williams and Norgate.

Sperber, D. (1985), 'Anthropology and Psychology: Towards an Epidemiology of Representations', *Man* (NS) 20: 73–89.

Svašek, M. (2002), 'The Politics of Emotions: Emotional Discourses and Displays in Post-Cold War Contexts', *Focaal: European Journal of Anthropology* 39: 193–6.

—— (ed.) (2005), *Postsocialism: Politics and Emotions in Central and Eastern Europe*, Oxford: Berghahn.

Tonkin, E. (1992), *Narrating our Pasts: The Social Construction of Oral History*, Cambridge: Cambridge University Press.

Turner, V. (1964), 'Symbols in Ndembu Ritual', in M. Gluckman (ed.), *Closed Systems and Open Minds*, Edinburgh: Oliver and Boyd.

Tylor, E. B. (1913 [1881]), *Anthropology: An Introduction in the Study of Man and Civilization*, London: Macmillan.

—— (1958 [1871]), *The Origins of Culture*, Harper.

Wallace, A. F. C. (1970), *Culture and Personality*, New York: Random House.

Whitehouse, H. (2002), 'Conjectures, Refutations, and Verification: Towards a Testable Theory of Modes of Religiosity', *Journal of Ritual Studies* 16 (2): 44–59.

Wierzbicka, A. (2004), 'Emotion and Culture: Arguing with Martha Nussbaum', *Ethos* 31 (4): 577–600.

Wikan, U. (1992), 'Beyond the Words: The Power of Resonance', *American Ethnologist* 19 (3): 460–82.

–1–

Meanings, Feelings and Human Ecology

Kay Milton

Introduction

In this chapter I address a problem in the anthropological study of emotions which has been identified by several scholars as a major challenge, the problem of how to develop an approach which will take account of both the biological and the cultural aspects of emotion. There have been several explicit and implicit attempts to do this, and they tend to hang on one central thread – the idea that emotions are essentially social phenomena. I shall suggest an alternative, that emotions are essentially ecological phenomena.

Although the chapter is almost entirely theoretical, my interest in the problem had an ethnographic origin. My research on environmental issues has tried to answer the question of why some people are committed to protecting nature while others are indifferent or hostile towards it. In the course of this research, I became aware of the emotional character of people's connections to the world, and came to the conclusion that emotions are what link us, as individuals, to our surroundings. This conclusion differs, in a significant way, from the view that emotions are essentially social phenomena and, in my view, presents a more effective solution to the problem of how to take both the biological and the cultural aspects of emotion into account.

My argument in this chapter will unfold as follows. First, I shall describe the problem identified above by showing that scholars in several disciplines have observed that emotions are both biological and cultural, and that this has led to two different kinds of approach to the study of emotions which, though not incompatible, are difficult to combine. Second, I shall describe what has often been seen as the solution to this problem, the view that emotions are essentially social, and indicate why I find it unsatisfactory. Third, I shall present an alternative view of emotions as ecological. This involves drawing on the work of psychologists to examine the role of emotions in the creation of knowledge. I shall then show why I think this is a more satisfactory solution to the problem of how to study emotion in both its biological and its cultural aspects. I shall end the chapter by considering briefly why the view that emotions are essentially social has been so popular among social scientists.

The Problem: Emotion as Meaning and Feeling

Scholars in anthropology, sociology and psychology have observed that emotions have a dual character. They are both bodily, in that they consist of physical feelings, and cultural, in that they have meanings. Probably the clearest statement to this effect was made by John Leavitt (1996). He pointed out that Western science has tended to proceed on the assumption that human phenomena are either natural or cultural (see also Bowler, Chapter 2 in this volume). Natural human phenomena are biological and universal and belong to the body (all humans breathe, bleed, digest), while cultural phenomena vary and are produced through action and thought (different worldviews, religious rituals, political institutions and so on). Leavitt pointed out that emotion cannot be neatly assigned to either realm, that we use 'emotion terms and concepts … to refer to experiences that cannot be categorized in this way and that inherently involve both meaning and feeling, mind and body, both culture and biology' (Leavitt 1996: 515).

Other scholars who have written about emotions in ways that suggest this dual character include Michelle Rosaldo (1984), who wrote, 'feeling is forever given shape through thought and … thought is laden with emotional meaning'. 'Emotions are thoughts somehow "felt" in flushes, pulses, "movements" of our livers, minds, hearts, stomachs, skin' (Rosaldo 1984: 143). Wentworth and Yardley (1994: 45) distinguished what they called the 'body/brain' from the 'mind/self' and saw the 'emotional system' as operating between the two. Lupton (1998: 4) wrote, 'emotional states serve to bring together nature and culture in a seamless intermingling in which it is difficult to argue where one ends and the other begins'. Although these statements do not map onto one another precisely, they all seem to be saying more or less the same thing: that emotions are composed of biological (or natural) and cultural elements.

Anthropologists know that the familiar distinctions reflected in these statements about emotion, the distinctions between nature and culture, body and mind, are not present in all cultures; not everyone thinks in these terms, and even for those who do, these distinctions may not be central to their understanding of the world. Anthropological understanding of cultural diversity teaches us that the very model of emotion described above, as a combination of feeling and meaning, is itself a product of a system of language and thought which separates these things in the first place. It is because the cultural traditions of most scholars treat thoughts and feelings as distinct, and because the language such scholars use keeps them distinct, that they can talk about emotions only as a combination of the two.

Two Kinds of Approach

Leavitt (1996) pointed out that, if emotion is both bodily feeling and cultural meaning, it cannot be adequately understood by focusing on just one or the other. But because science has been informed by the nature/culture, body/mind distinctions, most approaches *do* focus either on one or the other. Scientific approaches to emotion have sought to understand it, either on the assumption that it is universal and biological (e.g. Tooby and Cosmides 1990), or on the assumption that it is variable and culture specific (e.g. Lutz 1988). These two kinds of approach are often referred to as 'biological' and 'cultural' respectively, or 'positivist' and 'constructionist' (Lyon 1994: 86–7) or 'organismic' and 'constructionist' (Williams 2001: 39ff.).

These approaches are not divided along disciplinary boundaries. Leavitt pointed out that, within psychology and philosophy, a long period of treating emotions primarily as bodily phenomena was followed by approaches which treated them as cognitions (appraisals or judgements). Within social and cultural anthropology, while the effort has always been to understand emotions in their cultural context, we have seen psychoanalytic approaches (which treat some emotions as universal products of universal experiences) and, more recently, constructionist approaches, through the work of Rosaldo (1980), Abu-Lughod (1986), Lutz (1988; see also Lutz and Abu-Lughod 1990) and others. Constructionist approaches have been even more prominent in sociology, especially through the work of Harré (1986).

The way in which the biological and constructionist approaches differ is important. They are based on different assumptions about emotion, so they produce different understandings of what emotions are, and cannot be used to address each other's concerns. They are not necessarily incompatible. One way of advancing the study of emotions is to suggest that feelings are universal and biological while meanings are constructed and culture specific. This seems to be implied in Elias' 'symbol theory' (1991a, 1991b), in which emotions are presented as having a biological basis to which human beings add the results of social learning (Williams 2001: 51).

Nevertheless, a marriage between biological and constructionist approaches is difficult to bring about, because those who advocate biological explanations of emotions often seek to explain as much as possible in terms of biological evolution, and make generalizations which cultural theorists find unacceptable (for instance, that fear of snakes and spiders has an evolutionary basis; see Ulrich 1993). On the other hand, constructionists often seem to assume that *all* human experience is culturally constructed. Their perspectives do not seem to leave any room for people to experience an unconstructed reality which they then interpret through culture (Ingold 1992). So each type of approach can appear to define out of existence the concerns of the other.

The conceptual distance between the two kinds of approach, and their inability to address each other's concerns, have been commented on several times in the literature. Williams (2001: 54) remarked, 'while organismic theorists neglect or underplay the social dimensions of emotion, constructionists neglect or underplay their explicit "bodilyness"' (2001: 54). Lyon (1998) argued that symbolic anthropology, in which cultures are primarily systems of symbolic representations of the world, finds it impossible to address feeling: 'while one can deal with the cultural representation of emotion in various domains, it becomes impossible to deal directly and explicitly with the human embodiment of emotion – the "guts" of feeling which are a necessary part of its experience' (Lyon 1998: 45). Wentworth and Yardley (1994: 44–5) made a similar point about the constructionist approach.

So the challenge for anthropology and the other social sciences has been to develop an understanding of emotions which takes both their biological and their cultural character into account. As Lyon expresses it for anthropology: 'There is the … question of how the bodily component of emotion can be introduced without treating it primarily as a cultural construct and thus "inside" culture, or as a physical entity "outside" of culture' (Lyon 1998: 47).

The Solution: Emotions are Social

Several scholars have risen to this challenge, and the solution that they most often propose is that emotions are primarily *social phenomena*. This kind of theory of emotion comes in two forms: a general form, which states simply that emotions are generated by and in social relations, and a more specific form which suggests that emotions are ways of communicating. The general form is expressed most strongly in the work of Lyon. In her critique of the constructionist approach, she stated, 'Emotions activate bodies in ways that are attitudinal and physical … The activation occurs always in a social-relational context' (Lyon 1998: 53). She quoted de Rivera (1984) as saying, 'emotional behaviour is always relative to an *other*' (Lyon 1998: 54, original emphasis). For Lyon, the relationship between emotions and social life is dialectical: 'An important implication of a truly social perspective on emotion is to see not only how emotion has social consequences but how social relations themselves generate emotion. Emotion has a social ontology. That is, the experience of emotion, which involves both physical and phenomenal dimensions, has also a social-relational genesis' (Lyon 1998: 55).

Hochschild also treated emotions as social phenomena, stating that, while emotion always has a biological component, such as trembling, weeping or breathing hard, 'it takes a social element … to induce emotion' (Hochschild 1998: 6). And Williams (2001: 132) stated that emotions 'arise or emerge in various socio-relational contexts'. All these statements seem to imply that emotions depend upon social relations, that they arise only in social situations.

Emotions as Ways of Communicating

The more specific form of the 'emotions are social phenomena' theory, that emotions are ways of communicating, was stated particularly strongly by Wentworth and Yardley (1994) and by Parkinson (1995). Wentworth and Yardley (1994: 21) argued that human beings are 'deeply social' in nature, that they have 'the capacity to make emotionally founded, self-to-self relationships' and that the evolution of human society depended on such relationships. Interpersonal relationships depend on communication, and displays of emotion were the mechanisms through which pre-linguistic humans communicated; they remain important today alongside symbolic language. So, '[e]motions may be private, self-feelings, but they are eminently social. They are about the social self that emerged from participation in the social world' (Wentworth and Yardley 1994: 36).

Parkinson, writing from a psychological perspective, argued that emotions find expression in interpersonal encounters, and that 'getting emotional is primarily an interpersonal activity' (Parkinson 1995: 277). He argued that interpersonal encounters, which are moments in evolving social relationships, are generally situations in which people are presenting their own understandings of themselves to an other. What the other conveys in the encounter might confirm or contradict one's own understanding of one's self. Displays of emotion are used to assert one's self-image, or, as Parkinson expressed it, to make 'identity claims'. He gave the example of getting angry with someone in a conversation, not necessarily because their comments are offensive, but because, in the context of the evolving relationship, it is necessary to defend one's own reputation by taking exception to what they say. This is easiest to imagine as part of a contest for dominance, for instance between rivals for political allegiance.

Parkinson (1995) was not suggesting that displays of emotion are always performed in a deliberate and calculating fashion. Anger is provoked, not simulated (though of course it can be simulated). But it is provoked, according to him, by the need to maintain or assert, and therefore communicate, an image of oneself. So his approach to emotion is a functional one; emotions fulfil a function in social life: they 'primarily serve the purpose of conveying identity claims in real interpersonal situations' (Parkinson 1995: 282). Functional explanations necessarily pay more attention to the consequences of something than to its causes, but Parkinson stresses that emotions have social causes as well as social consequences. People get emotional because they are negotiating positions within relationships. Without those relationships, he implies, there would be nothing to get emotional about.

Is this a Solution?

In the context of my argument in this chapter, it is important to ask how these social theories of emotion are understood to meet the challenge of overcoming the division between biological and cultural approaches. How do they provide an alternative both to the idea that emotions are innate and universal, and to the idea that they are constructed and culture specific. Perhaps surprisingly, this is not made very explicit, but I assume that it is for two closely related reasons. The first relates to what is universal about emotions. Social scientists may find it difficult to accept that what they consider to be cultural products might, in fact, be innate and therefore universal, but they can at least agree that social interaction is universal. And social interaction forms the substance of social science; observing social interaction is what social scientists do. So in suggesting that emotions are essentially social, or that they have a 'social ontology' (to use Lyon's term), social scientists are reclaiming the universal component of emotions as their own, and removing it from the control of biologists.

The second reason relates to the physical nature of emotions. Social interaction is a physical as well as a cultural process. It is bodies that interact and, in acknowledging this, social scientists can claim to be admitting the physical, bodily aspects of emotions into their approaches, rather than excluding them as constructionist approaches appear to do. The physical nature of social interaction was made particularly explicit by Lyon: 'what is subject to social relations is not merely the cognitive faculties but living human bodies, for society is also bodies in relation' (Lyon 1998: 55). In fact, in Lyon's formulation, the bodily and the social are combined as one side of emotion's dual character. When describing the dual nature of emotion, she referred to its 'cultural dimensions' on the one hand and to 'social and bodily agency' (Lyon 1998: 43) on the other.

What is Wrong with the 'Emotions are Social' Theory?

I have no difficulty with the assertion that social interaction is a physical or bodily phenomenon; I consider it to be self-evident. But I do have difficulty with the suggestion that to understand emotions as essentially *social* is to offer a genuine alternative to biological and constructionist models. I suggest that it suffers from precisely the same restrictions as cultural constructionism, despite Lyon's argument that it is a way out of those constraints. To explain this point, if emotions are generated in and by social relations, this places them in the same broad category as all other socially produced, that is cultural, phenomena. This is close to what Lyon accused constructionist approaches of doing, when she argued that constructionist understandings of emotion have an ideational bias – they assign emotions to the category of ideas. Behind all constructionist analyses lies the assumption that the mechanisms of cultural construction are at least partly social. Constructionists do not assume that culture is created purely by thought. They assume that it is created and reproduced through a combination of thought and social experience, that we produce our cultural perspectives in the process of interacting with others. So to say that emotions arise in social relations says nothing that would conflict with a constructionist position.

To labour the point a bit further, the implication of the social approach to emotions is that bodies have feelings only because they are in social relationships. This is similar to saying that people have culture only because they are part of a society. The source of emotion becomes the same as the source of all cultural products (knowledge, beliefs, institutions) – society. This is not an alternative to cultural constructionism, it *is* cultural constructionism.

An Alternative Solution: Emotions are Ecological

So, how do we find a way out of this dilemma? Is there a genuine alternative to treating emotions either as biological or as social/cultural? I shall argue that emotions are ecological rather than social phenomena, that they are mechanisms through which an individual human being is connected to and learns from their environment. In arguing this I am not denying that emotions arise in social situations; I am saying that this is only part of the story. The argument I shall make about emotions is related to that which Ingold (1992) made about knowledge, so I shall summarize his argument briefly before focusing on emotions.

Knowledge and Perception

According to the constructionist model, the way we understand the world is assumed to emerge out of the social and cultural environment in which we live. Our knowledge of the world is presented as being entirely socially and culturally produced. Ingold (1992) pointed out that this model sets up a barrier between the 'real' world and our understanding of it, because it implies that nothing can enter our understanding without first being culturally interpreted. The 'real' world is implicitly presented as being beyond direct human understanding; it cannot mean anything to us, it cannot be known, without passing through a cultural filter.

As I understand him, Ingold (1992) was not intending to suggest that no knowledge is produced in this way – it is perfectly obvious that a great deal of what we know is generated and taught to us through social interaction. Because of this, we come to understand the world in very similar ways to those with whom we associate most closely. What Ingold was suggesting is that this cultural construction of knowledge is not the whole story. Indeed, it *cannot* be the whole story, because knowledge and understanding cannot be constructed out of nothing. We have to have some raw material out of which to build our cultural constructs. We have to be able to receive information directly from our environment, independently of our involvement in social interaction. Without being able to do this, how would we learn from social interaction itself? How would we receive information from our fellow human beings if we were unable to receive it from our environment in general? Ingold drew on Gibson's concept of direct perception (Gibson 1979) to describe how humans and other organisms receive information through their direct engagement with their environment, and argued that direct perception, unmediated by cultural construction, is sufficient for us to *know* the world – not to interpret it, or reflect on it, but to know it in some way and to some degree.

This argument is difficult to grasp for obvious reasons. Precisely because we are lifelong participants in societies and cultures and have acquired a huge proportion of our understanding of the world from this participation, it is extremely difficult for us to imagine something outside this context, to imagine that knowledge can be pre-cultural. And trying to do this is almost self-defeating, because in the mental act of trying to identify knowledge which is directly perceived rather than culturally constructed, we immediately start reflecting on what we know, which immediately destroys its directly perceived nature and turns it into a cultural construction. In attempting to describe how direct perception works, we add another layer of difficulty, because we can describe it only through language, a cultural construct.

For these reasons it is difficult to illustrate how knowledge is gained directly through engagement with the environment, but I shall attempt to do so as follows. A man walking through a forest feels tired and sits down on a log to rest. His language might not have words for 'log', 'seat' or 'rest'; he might not even have a language at all. It does not matter. In his act of sitting, his engagement with what English speakers would call a log, the man perceives it directly as something that English speakers would call a seat. I cannot describe the event without using cultural constructs (words, concepts), but the act of perception need not entail cultural constructs. The man did not need to conceptualize his tiredness, or to have an idea of a seat in his mind; he simply felt tired and sat down.

Because it is such a difficult concept to grasp, and even harder to describe, I have doubts about the usefulness of Gibson's model of direct perception as an analytical tool. But I am persuaded by its general implication, made explicit in Ingold's (1992) argument, that we come to know the world through pre-cultural as well as cultural mechanisms. Without being able to receive information directly from our environment, we would not be able to recognize our social relationships or anything else as sources of understanding. In order to learn from something, one must engage with it, and perception is the mode of engagement. A newborn baby cannot come to know its mother as a source of food, warmth or comfort without engaging with her, receiving information from her. Some part of the learning process has to be pre-cultural, or culture itself would never have developed.

An alternative way of expressing this is to say that perception is an ecological process. It is what connects an organism to its environment in such a way that it is able to receive information, to learn from it. The argument I want to make about emotion is that it is part of this process. I shall suggest, as some other scholars have

done, that learning is dependent on emotion. There are two closely related points
in this argument. First, learning does not take place without emotion, and second,
emotions play an important role in memory – they help to determine what we
remember and therefore what we come to know about the world. In order to make
both these points, I need to draw on the work of psychologists.

Emotion, Perception and Memory

Gibson's student Ulrich Neisser developed Gibson's model to show how memory
and thought combine with what Gibson called 'direct' perception in the production
of knowledge. Neisser (1976) envisaged perception as a cyclical process. The per-
ceiver is not simply present in their environment as a passive receiver of information, but is actively exploring that environment and anticipating what they will
find. The information they receive is reflected upon and interpreted on the basis of
what they already know, and their knowledge is modified accordingly and guides
their future explorations. The man in the wood who discovered, through his act of
sitting down, that a log makes a good resting place, will be on the lookout for
another log the next time he feels tired. For Neisser, receiving information direct
from the environment is part of the perceptual cycle, but so, too, are reflection and
interpretation. We assume that reflections and interpretations are, under normal
circumstances, heavily influenced by social and cultural experience. This makes it
fruitless to try to distinguish cultural from pre-cultural knowledge. What Neisser
describes is a process of knowledge creation in which both cultural and pre-cultural mechanisms are involved. For some psychologists, emotion is an essential
part of this process, and, in particular, a specific emotion or range of emotions
which they label 'interest', 'attention', 'expectancy' or (as in Neisser's model)
'anticipation'.

At this point in the argument I have to acknowledge that some theorists might
question whether 'interest' or 'attention' can legitimately be called emotions. This
raises the question of how 'emotion' should be defined, a question which I have
avoided so far in this chapter because, in discussing the work of other scholars, each
of whom has their own understanding of emotion, it would not have been appropriate
to impose a definition. I shall address the question of definition more directly below,
but for the moment I shall adopt, for the sake of argument, the view taken by many
psychologists that the terms 'interest', 'attention', 'expectancy' and 'anticipation' do
indeed describe phenomena that can be called emotions. In 1987, Kemper reviewed
sixteen different lists of what psychologists call 'basic' emotions (assumed to be
shared by all human beings). 'Interest' appears in five lists and 'anticipation' (also
called 'expectancy') appears in two. There is one case in which they both appear and
where they are treated as alternative labels for the same emotion.

If we can accept that 'interest' or 'anticipation', whatever we want to call it, is
an emotion, then it becomes clear that emotion, in this form at least, is part of the

perceptual cycle described by Neisser (1976). Anticipation (or 'interest' or 'expectancy') is the state of body/mind in which we explore our environment. It is a state of readiness to receive information; it thus stimulates or motivates perception, and therefore learning. Izard wrote, 'Interest literally determines the content of our minds and memories, for it plays such a large part in determining what it is we actually perceive, attend to, and remember' (Izard 1991: 92–3).

However, we do not need to accept that 'interest' is an emotion in order to argue that emotions play a role in the process of learning. Izard (1991: 91) argued that interest often operates in combination with other emotions, because our interest in something is heightened by the emotions we feel when we encounter it. So, for instance, if something frightens us, or pleases us, or angers us, we will be particularly on the look out for it in future. The memory of the emotion will guide and motivate our continued exploration of our environment.

Lazarus (1991) also described the role of emotion in the production of knowledge in this way. He argued that we evaluate the situations in which we find ourselves through a relationship between cognition and emotion. What we learn from a situation generates an emotional response, which affects how we think about that and other situations we encounter. And this is not necessarily a conscious, reflective process, according to Lazarus. It can be 'automatic, unreflective, and unconscious or preconscious' (1991: 128). Lazarus was not thinking of 'interest' or 'anticipation' when he described the role of emotion in this process – this does not appear among the emotions he discusses. He was thinking of sadness, joy, anger, fear, love, guilt, and so on – the kinds of things most of us would first think of if asked to produce a list of common emotions. So I interpret him as saying, like Izard (1991), that what we learn from our environment generates these emotions in us and so influences how we approach our environment, which influences what we learn from it, and so on, in a continuous cycle.

Turning more specifically to the role of emotions in memory, it has been suggested many times by psychologists that the presence and intensity of particular emotions affect the ease with which we remember things (see Rolls 1990; Christiansen 1992). For instance, there is evidence (from Bartlett, Burleson and Sandbrock 1982; Nasby and Yando 1982) that heightened enjoyment during a task will increase the chances of it being recalled accurately by children. Whitehouse (1992, 1996) has drawn on the work on so-called 'flashbulb memory' to argue that things are particularly memorable if they are encountered in heightened states of emotion. So, for instance, emotionally challenging rituals are important mechanisms through which some societies transmit central ideas and values from one generation to the next. Initiation rituals, in particular, often involve frightening or surprising experiences (see, for instance, Bloch 1992). The idea of flashbulb memory has entered popular discourse through the common assertion that people can remember what they were doing when they heard of President Kennedy's assassination. The feeling of shock created by the news is supposed to have fixed the moment in their minds, making it easy to recall. Perhaps, years from now, people will talk about events like the death of Princess Diana and September 11 in a similar way.

Emotion as an Ecological Mechanism

To summarise my argument, human beings learn by receiving information from their environment and remembering it. Emotions, it has been suggested, are important in both these processes. If the mechanisms that enable us to learn are pre-cultural, that is, not dependent on social relations, then emotions must also be pre-cultural. It thus makes more sense to say that emotions are ecological than to say that they are social. I agree that they are generated in the context of social interaction, but they are not generated solely or even primarily in this context. They do not have 'a social ontology'. They operate in the encounter between an individual organism and its environment. I can agree with de Rivera (1984), that 'emotional behaviour is ... relative to an other', but this does not have to be a social or human other; it can be anything with which the individual organism engages, for emotion is part of that engagement. For human beings, of course, much of the environment *is* social, and this is one reason why the idea of social interaction as the source of all our understanding is so persuasive. But the mechanisms that connect us with that environment must exist independently of social interaction, otherwise we would not be capable of engaging with our social environment and learning anything from it.

Is this a Genuine Alternative?

Does the argument that emotion is an ecological mechanism present a genuine alternative to biological and constructionist approaches? At first sight it might appear that it does not, for it looks very like a biological approach. It seems to say that emotions are innate, that they are products of biological evolution rather than of cultural processes. It seems to say that, instead of being generated by cultural discourse, emotions are part of our natural apparatus that enables such discourse to take place. It seems to say this, *if* we accept the distinction between biology and culture as our starting point, *if* we assume that human phenomena are either biological or cultural. But we do not have to assume this. If we abandon the assumption that all human phenomena are either products of evolution, and therefore biological, or products of learning, and therefore cultural, we can begin to see how phenomena that appear innate and biological might themselves be modified through the learning process. After all, we know that our bodies are affected, both intentionally and unintentionally, by culturally variable practices (such as diet, scarification, piercing and so on), so why not our emotions?

Here I need to address the question I have so far avoided, of how emotion can usefully be defined. It is helpful to consider a model of emotion originally proposed by William James (1890) and taken up in recent decades by many theorists. James suggested that emotion is composed of two stages. There is the physical response (quickening heartbeat, muscle tension) that takes place when the body encounters a stimulus, and there is the subjective experience of that response – the feeling of fear or excitement which we get when our bodies do these things. In Damasio's (1999) formulation of a similar model, the subjective experience is described as perception. Our bodies react to a stimulus – this happens outside consciousness – then we perceive those reactions in our bodies, making ourselves aware of them. These perceptions are what we recognize as feelings. It has often been pointed out that this model of emotion reverses the commonsense assumption that we cry because we feel sad, that we blush because we feel embarrassed, and so on. In James' model we feel sad because we cry, and we feel embarrassed because we blush – the bodily reaction precedes and causes the feeling (see Laird and Apostoleris 1996).

I have argued that learning is shaped by emotion. James' model enables us to see how emotions might be shaped by learning. First, the initial bodily reaction to a stimulus can be a product of learning. During fieldwork in Africa I learned to fear snakes, as a result of which my leg muscles tightened noticeably whenever I walked through long grass; this effect continued for some months after my return to Ireland, where there are no snakes (see Milton 2002: 155). Through their engagement with different environments, people learn to love, hate, fear, or be disgusted by different things, so their bodies react differently when these things are encountered.

Second, we learn to perceive the same bodily reactions as different kinds of feelings. I suggest that this is an extremely common personal experience. The bodily reactions that take place on encountering a snake, such as quickening heartbeat and tightening stomach muscles, might be the same as those that take place when meeting a lover or anticipating an exam. We learn to perceive these reactions as fear, love or anxiety, depending on the context in which they occur. In some cultures people are moved to tears both at weddings and at funerals, both at partings and at reunions. They do not get confused when their bodies react in this way; they have learned to perceive some tears as joy and some as sorrow, depending on the context in which they are shed.

Third, of course, we learn to express our emotions in different ways, and sometimes to hide what we feel. In some cultures, and in some contexts, tears are shed openly over minor mishaps, in others they might be suppressed except at moments of utter despair. In some cultures and contexts a physical beating is an expression of justifiable anger, in others it is a loss of control.

If emotion shapes learning and learning shapes emotion, in the ways suggested above, then it makes no sense to assign emotion either to nature or to culture. Nor does it make sense to suggest that any particular part or aspect of emotion is either natural or cultural. James' model does not split emotion between nature and culture; it enables us to see how emotional reactions, feelings and expressions arise and develop out of a complex interaction between an individual human being and their environment. Similarly, to return to the models of emotion discussed at the beginning of this chapter, it makes no sense to say that feelings are biological while meanings are cultural, for feelings and meanings both shape and are shaped by an individual's developmental engagement with their environment, an environment which is partly, but not wholly, human, social or cultural. For this reason, I consider the hypothesis that emotions are ecological phenomena that link us to our environments and enable us to learn from them, to be a genuine alternative to both biological and constructionist approaches.

Why do Social Scientists Insist that Emotions are Social?

Finally, I shall return briefly to the question of why the idea that emotions are primarily or essentially social phenomena has been so popular among social scientists, and why the more fundamental ecological dimensions of emotion have been ignored. I would not wish to claim any originality for the idea that emotions are ecological phenomena. Not only has it been explicit in some of the psychological literature I have referred to here, it is also found in the work of neuroscientists (Damasio 1999) and anthropologists and sociologists. For instance, Lyon (1998) cites Scherer (1984) who 'views emotion in terms of a series of aspects or components that function in the relationship of the individual to his or her social and material environment' (Lyon 1998: 53). This clearly implies that the environment was envisaged, at least by Scherer, as extending beyond the social. But when developing her own theory of emotion, Lyon ignores this point and focuses only on the social environment.

Hochschild (1998) seemed to place emotion in the same category as bodily senses: 'Like other senses, hearing, touch and smell, emotion is a means by which we continually learn and relearn about a just-now-changed, back and forth relation between self and world, the world as it means something just now to the self' (Hochschild 1998: 6). This expresses, quite unambiguously in my view, an ecological understanding of emotion, in which it is seen as connecting the self to the world in the same way as hearing, touch, smell (and presumably sight and taste) do. But when she describes the source of emotions, she describes only the social world.

One reason for this tendency among social scientists could be that which I have already mentioned. By claiming emotion as a social phenomenon, they bring it specifically within their sphere of investigation and control, just as biologists do when they claim it is an innate, universal feature produced by biological evolution.

This is part of a larger battle between broadly biological and broadly social or cultural frameworks for understanding humanity. It is part of the struggle to understand 'the kinds of beings we humans are', as Tim Ingold (2000b: 25) put it in a letter to *Anthropology Today* and, it could be suggested, a struggle for power over public understandings of humanity. It has been going on for many years, it has political implications, and those who favour biological understandings of human phenomena seem to have been a lot better at getting their case across than those who favour sociocultural understandings (a point also made by Ingold 2000a), perhaps because biological models seem so much simpler and neater than sociocultural models. The insistence that emotions are social could be seen as part of the social scientists' stand against this onslaught, and part of the broader tendency to explain all human phenomena and humanity itself in social and cultural terms.

As I was preparing this chapter I was reminded of Michael Carrithers' opening passage to *Why Humans have Cultures* (1992). The following comes on the first page:

> The fact that we are social animals is not just an adventitious, accidental feature of our nature, but lies at the very core of what it is to be human. We simply could not live, could not continue our existence as humans, without our sociality. As Maurice Godelier wrote, 'human beings, in contrast to other animals, do not just live in society, they produce society in order to live' (1986: 1). So in an anthropologist's perspective, no enquiry which regards humans merely as individuals could be complete. We cannot know ourselves except by knowing ourselves in relation to others. (Carrithers 1992:1)

There must be countless similar statements by anthropologists. Such statements are claims to intellectual control over what *really* matters about being human, and they also reinforce a perceived discontinuity between human and non-human (as we see explicitly in Godelier's statement quoted above). But what if this emphasis on our sociality obscures rather than enlightens our understanding of ourselves? What if it is no more enlightening than the model it opposes, which emphasizes the biological to the exclusion of sociocultural dimensions of humanity? What I am suggesting, using emotions as a case study, is that we do not have to go down the biological or the sociocultural route, but by focusing on ecological rather than social relations, we might be able to think ourselves out of this opposition.

Acknowledgements

I am grateful to Maruška Svašek, Peter Dwyer, Monica Minnegal and members of the Social Anthropology Seminar at St Andrews University for comments on earlier drafts of this chapter.

References

Abu-Lughod, L. (1986), *Veiled Sentiments: Honor and Poetry in a Bedouin Society*, Berkeley, CA: University of California Press.

Bartlett, J. C., Burleson, G. and Santrock, J. W. (1982), 'Emotional Mood and Memory in Young Children', *Journal of Experimental Child Psychology* 34: 59–76.

Bloch, M. E. F. (1992), *Prey into Hunter: Politics of Religious Experience*, Cambridge: Cambridge University Press.

Carrithers, M. (1992), *Why Humans have Cultures*, Oxford: Oxford University Press.

Christiansen, S. A. (1992), 'Emotional State and Eyewitness Memory: A Critical Review', *Psychological Bulletin* 112: 284–309.

Damasio, A. R. (1999), *The Feeling of What Happens: Body and Emotion in the Making of Consciousness*, London: Heinemann.

de Rivera, J. (1984), 'The Structure of Emotional Relationships', in P. Shaver (ed.), *Review of Personality and Social Psychology: Emotions, Relationships and Health*, Beverly Hills, CA: Sage.

Elias, N. (1991a), 'On Human Beings and their Emotions: A Process Sociological Essay', in M. Featherstone, M. Hepworth and B. S. Turner (eds), *The Body: Social Process and Cultural Theory*, London: Sage.

—— (1991b), *The Symbol Theory*, London: Sage.

Gibson, J. J. (1979), *The Ecological Approach to Visual Perception*, Boston, MA: Houghton Mifflin.

Godelier, M. (1986), *The Mental and the Material*, London: Verso.

Harré, R. (ed.) (1986), *The Social Construction of Emotions*, Oxford: Blackwell.

Hochschild, A. R. (1998), 'The Sociology of Emotion as a Way of Seeing', in G. Bendelow and S. J. Williams (eds), *Emotions in Social Life: Critical Themes and Contemporary Issues*, London and New York: Routledge.

Ingold, T. (1992), 'Culture and the Perception of the Environment', in E. Croll and D. Parkin (eds), *Bush base: forest farm*, London: Routledge.

—— (2000a), 'The Poverty of Selectionism', *Anthropology Today*, 16, 3: 1–2.

—— (2000b), Letter in *Anthropology Today* 16 (4): 25–6.

Izard, C. E. (1991), *The Psychology of Emotions*, New York and London: Plenum Press.

James, W. (1890), *Principles of Psychology*, New York: Holt.

Kemper, T. D. (1987), 'How Many Emotions are there? Wedding the Social and Autonomic Components', *American Journal of Sociology* 93: 263–89.

Laird, J. D. and Apostoleris, N. H. (1996), 'Emotional Self-control and Self-perception: Feelings are the Solution, not the Problem', in R. Harré and W. G. Parrott (eds), *The Emotions: Social, Cultural and Biological Dimensions*, London and Thousand Oaks, CA: Sage.

Lazarus, R. S. (1991), *Emotion and Adaptation*, Oxford: Oxford University Press.

Leavitt, J. (1996), 'Meaning and Feeling in the Anthropology of Emotions', *American Ethnologist* 23 (3): 514–39.

Lupton, D. (1998), *The Emotional Self: A Sociocultural Exploration*, London: Sage.

Lutz, C. A. (1988), *Unnatural Emotions: Everyday Sentiments on a Micronesian Atoll and their Challenge to Western Theory*, Chicago and London: University of Chicago Press.

—— and Abu-Lughod, L. (eds) (1990), *Language and the Politics of Emotion*, Cambridge: Cambridge University Press.

Lyon, M. (1994), 'Emotion as Mediator of Somatic and Social Processes: the Example of Respiration', in W. M. Wentworth and J. Ryan (eds), *Social Perspectives on Emotion*, vol. 2, Greenwich, CT: JAI Press.

—— (1998), 'The Limitations of Cultural Constructionism in the Study of Emotion', in G. Bendelow and S. J. Williams (eds) *Emotions in Social Life: Critical Themes and Contemporary Issues*, London and New York: Routledge.

Milton, K. (2002), *Loving Nature: Towards an Ecology of Emotion*, London and New York: Routledge.

Nasby, W. and Yando, R. (1982), 'Selective Encoding and Retrieval of Affectively Valent Information: Two Cognitive Consequences of Children's Mood States', *Journal of Personality and Social Psychology* 43 (6): 1244–53.

Neisser, U. (1976), *Cognition and Reality: Principles and Implications of Cognitive Psychology*, San Francisco, CA: W. H. Freeman.

Parkinson, B. (1995), *Ideas and Realities of Emotion*, London and New York: Routledge.

Rolls, E. T. (1990), 'A Theory of Emotion, and its Application to Understanding the Neural Basis of Emotion', *Cognition and Emotion* 4: 161–90.

Rosaldo, M. Z. (1980), *Knowledge and Passion: Ilongot Notions of Self and Social Life*, Cambridge: Cambridge University Press.

—— (1984), 'Towards an Anthropology of Self and Feeling', in R. A. Schweder and R. A. LeVine (eds), *Culture Theory*, Cambridge: Cambridge University Press.

Scherer, K. R. (1984), 'On the Nature and Function of Emotion: A Component Process Approach', in K. R. Scherer and P. Ekman (eds), *Approaches to Emotion*, Hillsdale, NJ: Lawrence Erlbaum Associates.

Tooby, J. and Cosmides, L. (1990), 'The Past Explains the Present: Emotional Adaptations and the Structure of Ancestral Environments', *Ethology and Sociobiology* 11: 375–424.

Ulrich, R. S. (1993), 'Biophilia, Biophobia, and Natural Landscapes', in S. R. Kellert and E. O. Wilson (eds), *The Biophilia Hypothesis*, Washington, DC: Island Press.

Wentworth, W. M. and Yardley, D. (1994), 'Deep Sociality: A Bioevolutionary Perspective on the Sociology of Human Emotions', in W. M. Wentworth and J. Ryan (eds), *Social Perspectives on Emotion*, vol. 2, Greenwich, CT: JAI Press.

Whitehouse, H. (1992), 'Memorable Religions: Transmission, Codification and Change in Divergent Melanesian Contexts', *Man* (NS) 27: 777–97.

—— (1996), 'Rites of Terror: Emotion, Metaphor and Memory in Melanesian Initiation Cults', *Journal of the Royal Anthropological Institute* (NS) 2: 703–15.

Williams, S. (2001), *Emotion and Social Theory*, London: Sage.

–2–

Darwin on the Expression of the Emotions: the Eclipse of a Research Programme

Peter J. Bowler

Introduction

Charles Darwin's *The Expression of the Emotions in Man and the Animals* was published in 1872, the year after his comprehensive study of human origins, *The Descent of Man*. The two books were linked in the sense that Darwin had intended to include material on the emotions in the earlier book, but had found the topic too large to include within what was already (in its first edition) a two-volume work. *The Expression of the Emotions* was part of the project on human origins because it presented Darwin's evidence that the way we express emotions, and by implication many of the emotions themselves, are products of our animal ancestry. Darwin was dealing with what Kay Milton in Chapter 1 in this volume calls the 'basic' emotions – fear, anger, etc. – which are by definition more biological in nature. They represent areas of continuity between human and animal behaviour, and were thus prime evidence in Darwin's case that humans do have an ancestry within the animal kingdom. Darwin's efforts to convince his contemporaries that they had evolved from apes was largely successful. Despite initial opposition, from the 1870s onwards scientists and most educated people were reconciled to this position. Yet the research programme comparing animal and human emotional behaviour outlined in Darwin's *Expression of the Emotions* was not taken up by the first generation of evolutionary psychologists who sought to explain the origin of the human mind. Indeed, it was not until the later decades of the twentieth century that serious research in this area began under psychologists such as Paul Ekman. The pioneering efforts of Darwin in this area were acknowledged, and Ekman and others also tried to explain why there had been such a hiatus in the field's development. Various characteristics of Darwin's approach were pointed out as being incompatible with contemporary scientists' preconceptions, and hence identified as the reasons why his efforts to open the subject to investigation were not followed up at the time.

This chapter will assess these explanations and offer a critique based on modern historical studies of the development of Darwinism. I shall argue that Ekman's argument makes perfectly good sense when applied to the question of why early and mid-twentieth-century scientists ignored Darwin's work on the emotions. But it does not work as an explanation of why Darwin's own contemporaries did not take him seriously. To understand why the scientists of the 1870s and 1880s did not follow up his suggestions, we have to look to the prevailing attitudes of those decades. Applying hindsight based on later scientific criteria does not provide a valid basis for a historically informed analysis of the contemporary reaction. My analysis will proceed from the re-evaluation of the 'Darwinian revolution' by modern historians, which suggests that most of the more radical aspects of Darwin's thinking were sidelined, subverted or ignored by his contemporaries. The late nineteenth century was indeed an age dominated by evolutionism, but it was a progressionist, almost teleological evolutionism which presented the human species as the inevitable product of a purposeful trend built into nature's activities. Many of the more disturbing and anti-teleological aspects of Darwin's approach were played down, including his emphasis on divergence and adaptation, and the mechanism of natural selection itself. The late nineteenth century saw an 'eclipse of Darwinism' when non-Darwinian ideas of evolutionism were openly proclaimed. My argument is that Darwin's exploration of emotional expression was ignored along with these other more radical elements of his theory because it too threatened to upset the compromise which had been worked out between the basic idea of evolution and the desire to see the human species as the triumphant product of a progressive trend. This non-Darwinian approach to evolutionism was undermined in the early twentieth century by the developments leading to the modern genetical theory of natural selection. Other aspects of Darwin's theory were also revived, including his idea that the separation of the ape and human families occurred when our ancestors adopted bipedalism. But his work on the emotions did not at first benefit from this more general revival of interest – and this is where explanations based on the preconceptions of twentieth-century psychologists come into their own.

In this chapter I shall argue that the lack of interest in *The Expression of the Emotions* by Darwin's contemporaries makes perfectly good sense once we realize that they were interested in exploring only those aspects of evolutionism which could be interpreted in progressionist terms. In effect, Darwin's work in this area was ignored for reasons which parallel the reaction to Freud at the turn of the century. Where the evolutionists of the late nineteenth century wanted to see humanity as triumphantly rising above its animal ancestry, Darwin and later Freud reminded them all too forcefully that the relics of that ancestry are still driving our everyday behaviour. Freud faced and eventually overcame immense opposition to get his point across. Darwin faced the far more serious threat of being ignored. Yet the later developments could not have taken place had Darwin and his immediate followers not established at least the basic idea of evolution as a foundation for later scientific thought.

Darwin and Modern Psychology

The Expression of the Emotions was an integral part of Darwin's argument that the human species must be understood as the product of an evolutionary ancestry. Darwin needed to minimize the gap between humans and animals in order to convince his contemporaries that evolution could have bridged that gap. His anthropomorphic descriptions of animals experiencing emotions reflected a genuine need to convince his readers that human emotions are not something unique to our species. His insistence that the way we express our emotions makes use of physiological processes which can also be seen at work in the lower animals plays the same rhetorical role. Darwin explicitly criticized the assumptions of the anatomist Charles Bell, who had suggested that the human face has unique muscles designed by the Creator to enable us to communicate our emotions to others. Darwin wanted to argue that all the mechanisms by which emotions are expressed have an animal origin, and he did not believe that these mechanisms always serve the purpose of communication (for detailed analysis of Darwin's work see Barnett 1958; Browne 1985; Richards 1987: 230–4).

Darwin's book begins by outlining three principles which, he believes, govern the ways humans and animals express emotion. The principle of serviceable associated habits links some modes of expression to adaptive behaviour, as when fear is expressed by bodily changes designed to prepare for flight. The principle of antithesis notes that an emotion can be expressed by behaviour which is the exact opposite of that elicited automatically by the opposite behaviour. Thus a dog exhibits affection for its owner through behaviour which is the opposite of that which expresses fear and anger – it lowers its body and its tail, which are instinctively held erect when angry. In cases like this Darwin appealed to the Lamarckian principle of the inheritance of acquired characteristics to explain how a learned habit could become instinctive. The third principle links expression to the direct action of the nervous system, as when fear elicits trembling; such behaviour is an accidental product of the way the nervous system is organized and has no adaptive purpose.

The remainder of Darwin's book is made up of chapters illustrating how the various emotional states are expressed in both animals and humans. In the case of the higher animals, he is anxious to show us how often their mode of expression can be seen to provide an analogue and hence a plausible ancestral state for the equivalent human emotions. In humans, Darwin wants to focus on the biological foundations for the various emotions, which he does by noting the similarities between human and animal emotional behaviour. He also argues for the universality of the basic human modes of expression across the whole range of cultures and races. Darwin's evidence was derived from a variety of sources. He himself had studied human behaviour in many parts of the world while on the voyage of

HMS *Beagle* (1831–6), and had been particularly interested in the natives of Tierra del Fuego. He had made detailed notes on the emotional and psychological development of his own children. He could also report systematic studies by a few other scientists, and his book pioneered the use of photographs to illustrate facial expressions. Much of the evidence was, however, anecdotal, being derived from the reports of zookeepers, hunters, missionaries and colonial administrators. As long as these were seen as 'responsible' people, their reports were thought to offer a reliable source of information.

Because of its obvious human interest, *The Expression of the Emotions* initially sold better than any of Darwin's other books – of the seven thousand printed over five thousand were sold in the first month (F. Darwin 1887, vol. 3: 171–3). Yet writing in a volume published to celebrate its centenary, the psychologist Paul Ekman acknowledged that the book had been a scientific failure, a dead end which had stimulated no active research programmes (Ekman 1973; see also Ekman 1982 and Ekman's introduction to the reprint of Darwin's book, 1999). Only then, in the 1970s, were efforts being made to establish a biologically informed study of emotional expression, allowing Darwin's pioneering work to be recognized. Drawing on the work of the biologist and historian Michael Ghiselin (1969), Ekman noted five reasons why, he believed, Darwin's work had lain unrecognized for so long. Whatever the popular interest, scientists had refused to follow the book's lead for the following reasons:

1. Darwin's anthropomorphism in attributing emotional states to animals was regarded as incompatible with a scientific approach to the study of behaviour.
2. His use of anecdotal evidence derived from untrained witnesses had also been rejected by both psychologists and anthropologists.
3. His assumption that many modes of expression were innate or instinctive was incompatible with the psychologists' and anthropologsts' assumption that all habitual behaviour is learned.
4. His appeal to the inheritance of acquired characteristics linked him to a soon-to-be discredited biological mechanism.
5. His deductive methodology violated the assumptions of scientists conditioned to start their work from pure observation.

There is no doubt that these explanations must have seemed perfectly reasonable to a biologist, psychologist or anthropologist familiar with early and mid-twentieth-century scientific theories and methodologies. But Ghiselin and Ekman were also implying that the same points also sufficed to explain the lack of scientific interest in Darwin's book in the years following its publication in 1872. Here, the modern historian of science has to step in with a caution; attitudes toward the idea of evolution and toward the study of human behaviour changed dramatically from the late nineteenth to the early twentieth century and objections which would have seemed perfectly valid in the 1920s (or 1970s) may not have had any force in the 1870s.

Darwin and his Contemporaries

To evaluate whether any of the five points listed above may be applied to the contemporary reaction to Darwin's book, we need to discuss them individually.

Darwin's Anthropomorphism

There is little evidence that this would have been an issue with the evolutionary psychologists who were active in the 1870s. Indeed the whole logic of the developmental paradigm within which figures such as Herbert Spencer and George John Romanes (Darwin's closest disciple in this area) approached the study of animal and human behaviour rested on the assumption of a continuity between them (see Richards 1987: 334–53). Romanes (1883) in particular constructed an evolutionary hierarchy defining the order in which he believed the various mental faculties had emerged, in which only the highest faculties such as reasoning power were added at the last, human stage. As a supporter of the recapitulation theory, Romanes drew a direct parallel between evolution through geological time and the development of the human individual through childhood to maturity. Within such a system it was natural to assume that the lower mental powers, including the more basic emotions, were present to some degree among the higher animals. This situation would change dramatically as the century progressed toward its end, as psychology emerged as an experimental science, especially in Germany. But it was only in the 1890s that the evolutionary psychologist Conwy Lloyd Morgan propounded his famous canon forbidding the attribution to animals of any but the lowest mental powers needed to produce their observed behaviour. The school of Behaviourism, which dominated American psychology under J. B. Watson, and which certainly did forbid the attribution of mental states to animals, did not emerge until the early decades of the twentieth century.

Darwin's Use of Anecdotal Evidence

By Darwin's time the role of the untrained observer had been virtually eliminated in biology, but this was by no means the case in anthropology and psychology. The 1870s was the heyday of Victorian cultural anthropology under the leadership of Edward B. Tylor (Stocking 1987). This first generation of anthropologists did not engage in serious fieldwork and routinely used reports from missionaries and other educated westerners as the basis for their evaluations of 'primitive' cultures. Psychologists too used anecdotal evidence about animal and human behaviour. There was no reason why this aspect of Darwin's work should have caused it to be ignored by his contemporaries. Fieldwork among anthropologists, and controlled experiments on animals by psychologists, became commonplace only in the early twentieth century. Since there was no scientific ethology in the 1870s, Darwin's use of untrained observers of animal behaviour would also not have seemed out-of-place.

Darwin's Appeal to Instinct and Innate Behaviour

The evolutionary psychologists referred to in the first point above had no problem with the suggestion that animal and to some extent human behaviour was shaped by inherited instincts. Spencer and Romanes both appealed to Lamarckism to explain how learned habits could become inherited instincts, and Spencer's whole theory of the mind was based on the assumption that its faculties were the products of use and habit by previous generations. The complete rejection of an inherited component of behaviour occurred only among the Behaviourists of the early twentieth century.

Darwin's Use of Lamarckism

The argument developed for the previous point simultaneously disposes of this as a reason for Darwin's work being ignored. Almost everyone in the late nineteenth century, biologists and human scientists alike, accepted a role for the Lamarckian theory of the inheritance of acquired characteristics (named after the French evolutionist J. B. Lamarck). According to this theory, characters acquired by the adult organism (e.g. the weightlifter's bulging muscles) can be transmitted to the offspring. August Weismann began to oppose this theory in the 1880s by arguing that the 'germ plasm' (the material substance which transmitted hereditable characters from parent to offspring) could not be affected by the body which carries it. This position is now seen as a foundation stone for modern theories of heredity, but it was highly controversial at the time. Even within biology there were prominent schools of neo-Lamarckism which remained active into the early twentieth century (Bowler 1983). Only then did the emergence of Mendelian genetics begin to whittle away at the scientific support for the Lamarckian theory, especially in Britain and North America. The concept of the gene, elaborated from Gregor Mendel's earlier experiments on the inheritance of clearly defined characters, did not allow for gradual modification of the units of heredity.

Darwin's Use of a Deductive Method

Although his use of hypothesis as a guide to research was attacked by some conservative biologists in the 1860s, I see little evidence that the following generation which accommodated itself to evolutionism displayed any reluctance to allow its empirical investigations to be guided by its theoretical preconceptions. To be frank, I do not see any evidence for this point holding good even for the twentieth century – Ghiselin (1969: 212) cites Konrad Lorenz as an ethologist who adopted a purely empiricist methodology, but in fact Lorenz used a pre-Darwinian approach analogous to that of the comparative anatomists (Burkhardt 1985).

The Ideology of Development

If the above arguments are accepted, none of these characteristics allow Darwin's study of emotions to be seen as controverting the accepted ideas and methods of his own time, whatever the opinions of later generations of psychologists, anthropologists and biologists. Which leaves us with the interesting question: why did his work fail to spark any response among the scientists of the time? Ekman points out that Darwin was already famous by 1872, apparently under the impression that his every word must therefore have commanded the respect of his contemporaries. But the answer to our question must be sought in historians' re-evaluations of the Darwinian revolution, which have shown that the Victorians based their evolutionism on a very selective reading of Darwin's work. What they took from his theory, with his own partial connivance, was the general idea of evolution adapted to a progressionism which assumed that nature was somehow predetermined to advance life toward the human level (Bowler 1989). Mental evolution was, of course, the defining feature of the hierarchy along which life advanced, and the human species retained, in a modified form, its traditional position as the goal of creation.

The Victorians were much more suspicious of the more radical aspects of Darwin's thought, including the theories of natural and sexual selection, and the implication that evolution has been driven solely by the demands of adaptation to the local environment (physical, organic and social). Late-nineteenth-century biological evolutionism was marked by enthusiasm for Lamarckism, orthogenesis (directed non-adaptive evolution) and the recapitulation theory (Bowler 1988). This was the start of the period which Julian Huxley later called 'the Eclipse of Darwinism' – misleadingly, in the sense that Darwinism as we now understand it had never become popular in the first place. The whole ideology of the time was driven by the image of predetermined progress along a linear hierarchy of developmental stages, best expressed by the recapitulation theory's comparison between global evolution and the development of the human embryo (Bowler 1989). This was the model which dominated the evolutionary psychology of Romanes and the cultural evolutionism of Tylor. Darwin's suggestion in the *Descent of Man*, that the ancestors of the human family had separated from those of the apes when they adopted an upright posture as a means of locomotion on the open plains of Africa, was almost universally ignored in favour of the assumption that it was the expansion of the brain that drove human evolution to advance beyond the apes.

These insights into the nature of late-nineteenth-century evolutionism allow us to identify what it was about *The Expression of the Emotions* that made it unacceptable or uninteresting to the scientists of the 1870s. While developmental evolutionism accepted that humans had evolved from an animal ancestry, its focus was on how we had transcended that ancestry through the addition of the higher mental faculties. The suggestion that the purely animal patterns of behaviour still played a major role in our emotional life was not what Darwin's contemporaries wanted to hear. Thus Romanes' *Mental Evolution in Animals* (1883) devotes only a small part of its last chapter to animal emotions, focusing instead on the development of animal intelligence and the origin of purely adaptive instincts (where evolutionism seemed to have strong explanatory power). Despite constructing a parallel hierarchy of emotional and intellectual development (see Romanes 1883: frontispiece), Romanes virtually ignored the former topic. He also wrote a whole book on the development of animal intelligence (Romanes 1882). The same point holds good for other evolutionists such as Spencer and Lloyd Morgan; their emphasis was on how progressive evolution gave us the capacity to transcend the animal modes of behaviour, not on how relics of that behaviour were still driving our lives today.

One possible objection to this argument is the point noted above that *The Expression of the Emotions* initially sold much better than any of Darwin's other books. Surely a book which sold well to the general public could not have touched such a raw nerve within the culture of the time. But in fact the early sales were misleading – the publisher printed two thousand extra copies at the end of 1872 in anticipation of further sales, but these did not materialize and the book was never issued in a second edition even though Darwin wanted one to accommodate extra information which had come to his attention. The contrast between Darwin's initial euphoria over early sales and his later disappointment is visible in his letters. On 10 January 1872 he told A. R. Wallace that the book 'has sold wonderfully', but writing to Chauncey Wright on 21 September 1874 he lamented the declining sales (see F. Darwin 1903, vol. 2: 98–112). There were some positive reviews of the book, but even potential supporters such as Wallace and the psychologist Alexander Bain found some of Darwin's evidence unconvincing. Wallace and Darwin corresponded over their rival interpretations of the behaviour of kittens, with Darwin finding it hard to believe that Wallace could not see the continuity between their actions when suckling and their later movements when playing with a soft toy (F. Darwin 1903, vol. 2: 110). Bain criticized Darwin for the vagueness of his claims about the direct action of natural selection, and Darwin replied insisting that Bain's notion of 'spontaneity' was equally difficult to apply in practice (F. Darwin 1887, vol. 3: 171–3).

More conservative reviewers were scathing in their dismissal of this latest example of how far Darwin would go to link humans and animals. The *Edinburgh Review* saw the *Expression of the Emotions* as 'another volume of amusing stories and grotesque illustrations', and complained of the *a priori* scheme of interpretation which was now undermining his powers as an observer, leading to 'a marked falling off, both in philosophical tone and scientific interest, in the works produced since Mr. Darwin committed himself to the crude metaphysical conceptions so largely associated with his name' (quoted in F. Darwin, ed., 1887, III, 173). A theological review described the book as his 'most powerful and insidious work' (F. Darwin, ed., 1887: III, 171). The problem highlighted by this remark was that Darwin had explicitly set out to undermine some of the Victorians' most sacred beliefs about human nature. As Janet Browne (1985) notes, even the blush, that external symbol of our ability to feel remorse at wrongdoing, became, in Darwin's hands just a physiological side-effect of self-consciousness under scrutiny.

My suggestion is that *The Expression of the Emotions* did indeed touch a raw nerve even among Darwin's supporters. They welcomed evolution so long as it taught us that we have evolved beyond the apes, but they were uncomfortable with the implication that much of our behaviour might still be dictated by the animal instincts and reactions inherited from the past. Conservatives identified the source of the discomfort in their reviews, and the more radical thinkers who supported Darwin responded by ignoring this potentially difficult area and focusing on those aspects of evolutionary psychology which gave greater comfort to the ideology of progress. Significantly, one psychologist who did eventually make substantial use of Darwin's book was Sigmund Freud, who saw that it provided him with evidence for his own efforts to show that human behaviour is still driven by deeply implanted biological factors (Sulloway 1979: 259). Freud's biology contained a very strong element of Lamarckian recapitulationism, but he subverted the optimistic progressionism of the late nineteenth century by insisting that the more highly evolved functions of the mind cannot control the animal instincts buried in the deeper and hence more ancient layers of the unconscious. Freud, at least, elaborated upon Darwin's insight that our emotions are relics of our animal ancestry. The difference was that, by the time Freud published, others too were beginning to challenge progressionism, so he could not be ignored.

Darwin in the Twentieth Century

In the early decades of the twentieth century, the developmental model of biological, psychological and social evolutionism began to crumble (Cravens 1978). Anthropologists and sociologists rejected cultural evolutionism in favour of a relativism which refused to privilege European society as the goal toward which all others were moving. Psychologists became more experimental and the Behaviourists refused to allow biology any role within their theorizing. Biologists created the new science of Mendelian genetics, which undermined the plausibility of both Lamarckism and the recapitulation model. After a period of initial hostility, this was integrated with the theory of natural selection to give the basis of the so-called modern Darwinian synthesis. Yet paradoxically, these initiatives created new and more effective barriers preventing Darwin's work on the emotions from being appreciated. By the 1920s almost all the factors which Ekman identified were in place. Anthropomorphism and the use of anecdotal evidence were now anathema to psychologists and anthropologists, and biologists had repudiated Lamarckism.

Most of the human sciences thus rejected any input from biology – even Freud vigorously concealed the evolutionary origins of his ideas. Behaviourist psychologists used animals, most notably rats, as models for the learning process, including human learning, but had no interest in the underlying biological dispositions which they exploited as the basis of reinforcement. Curiously, the physiologists now began to take the expression of the emotions seriously – the eminent Harvard physiologist W. B. Cannon published his *Bodily Changes in Pain, Hunger, Fear and Rage* in 1915 (Barnett 1958). But these studies were confined to animals and did not address the more sensitive issues raised by Darwin.

By the 1930s biologists were coming to a greater appreciation of the more radical aspects of Darwin's evolutionary mechanism, but they did not include his pioneering work on the emotions in their studies. Early ethologists such as Konrad Lorenz professed themselves to be evolutionists, but did not really exploit a Darwinian view of how behaviour was modified (Burkhardt 1985). Nor was the work on the emotions the only aspect of Darwin's work whose modern appreciation would be delayed; sexual selection too was ignored until the 1970s when it became central to the new synthesis of sociobiology. It may be no accident that psychologists rediscovered *The Expression of the Emotions* in the same decade that the sociobiologists began to see how their emphasis on reproductive success (the 'selfish gene') might throw light on complex aspects of animal and human behaviour. There was an extensive and acrimonious debate over the human implications of sociobiology (Caplan 1978), but this was driven by the fear that this particular biological approach would revive the ideology of social Darwinism and genetic determinism. Looked at from a wider perspective, the 1970s does seem to have been a decade when the possibility of establishing fruitful interactions between biology and the human sciences began to take on a new lease of life. In this sense, the decision by Ekman and other psychologists to revive interest in Darwin's project may be seen a part of a trend that would play an important role in modern studies and debates.

Conclusion

In conclusion, then, we can see that the delay in scientists' appreciation of Darwin's insights on emotion has to be explained in terms of two consecutive phases driven by different motivations. When Ekman and his colleagues began to take an interest in the 1970s, they naturally sought to explain their predecessors' indifference in terms of their own experience of the previous decades. They thus correctly identified the motivations which had led early and mid-twentieth-century psychologists to ignore Darwin, but incorrectly assumed that the same motivations could be used to explain the initial indifference during the 1870s and 1880s. Modern historical research on the reception of Darwinism shows that there was a quite different set of preconceptions which shaped attitudes to the theory at that time. The failure to follow up Darwin's lead in this area was a consequence of the more general reluctance to explore the more radical aspects of his theory which conservative critics had correctly identified as subversive of traditional values. Darwin's work on emotions was ignored because it threatened the ideology of progress which was built on the assumption that the human mind was intended (by nature or its Creator) to transcend its animal origins. Only when Freud and many others had succeeded in undermining that ideology did it become possible to explore Darwin's pioneering insights – and then only when the newer suspicions about the 'unscientific' aspects of his approach had been overcome.

References

Barnett, S. A. (1958), 'The "Expression of the Emotions"', in S. A. Barnett (ed.), *A Century of Darwin*, London: Heinemann.

Bowler, P. J. (1983), *The Eclipse of Darwinism: Anti-Darwinian Evolution Theories in the Decades around 1900*, Baltimore, MD: Johns Hopkins University Press.

—— (1988), *The Non-Darwinian Revolution: Reinterpreting a Historical Myth*, Baltimore, MD: Johns Hopkins University Press.

—— (1989), *The Invention of Progress: The Victorians and the Past*, Oxford: Basil Blackwell.

Browne, J. (1985), 'Darwin and the Expression of the Emotions', in D. Kohn (ed.), *The Darwinian Heritage*, Princeton, NJ: Princeton University Press.

Burkhardt, R. W. (1985), 'Darwin on Animal Behaviour and Evolution', in D. Kohn (ed.), *The Darwinian Heritage*, Princeton, NJ: Princeton University Press.

Cannon, W. B. (1915), *Bodily Changes in Pain, Hunger, Fear and Rage*, New York: Appleton.

Caplan, A. (ed.) (1978), *The Sociobiology Debate*, New York: Harper and Row.

Cravens, H. (1978), *The Triumph of Evolution: American Scientists and the Heredity–Environment Controversy, 1900–1941*, Philadelphia, PA: University of Pennsylvania Press.

Darwin, C. (1871), *The Descent of Man and Selection in Relation to Sex*, 2 vols, London: John Murray.

—— (1872), *The Expression of the Emotions in Man and the Animals*, London: John Murray.

—— (1999), *The Expression of the Emotions in Man and the Animals*, reprint introd. P. Ekman, London: HarperCollins.

Darwin, F. (ed.) (1887), *The Life and Letters of Charles Darwin*, 3 vols, London: John Murray.

—— (ed.) (1903), *More Letters of Charles Darwin*, 2 vols, New York: Appleton.

Ekman, P. (1973), 'Introduction', in P. Ekman (ed.), *Darwin and Facial Expression: A Century of Research in Review*, New York: Academic Press.

—— (ed.) (1982), *Emotion in the Human Face*, Cambridge: Cambridge University Press.

Ghiselin, M. (1969), *The Triumph of the Darwinian Method*, Berkeley, CA: University of California Press.

Richards, R. J. (1987), *Darwin and the Emergence of Evolutionary Theories of Mind and Behaviour*, Chicago: University of Chicago Press.

Romanes, G. J. (1882), *Animal Intelligence*, 2nd edn, London: Kegan Paul.

—— (1883), *Mental Evolution in Animals*, London: Kegan Paul.

Stocking, G. W. (1987), *Victorian Anthropology*, New York: Free Press.

Sulloway, F. J. (1979), *Freud, Biologist of the Mind: Beyond the Psychoanalytic Legend*, London: Burnet Books.

–3–

Being There: Emotion and Imagination in Anthropologists' Encounters

Elizabeth Tonkin

Introduction: Being There

Anthropologists have often been asked about their methodology. What *are* 'the usual anthropological methods of participant observation' which are often claimed to be constitutive of this discipline? Often, they can be summed up as *being there*, a phrase which is hardly convincing to harder-nosed social scientists, but which, for initiates, attests to the multiplex sensations experienced by fieldworkers and the diversity of knowledge sources that they learn to attend to as they become more immersed in a new world. Being there is a continuing process, a learning process, which pulls together a mass of perceptions into some sort of amalgam with which to gloss and relate the multiple kinds of information that one is simultaneously trying to grasp.[1]

In other words, the complicated process of so-called 'participant observation' is an ordinary, everyday one, which must be undertaken – well or badly – by anyone who enters a new environment. It is also a process that is necessary to think through if one tries to articulate an apparently very familiar environment more systematically, as is increasingly common in fieldwork. Put simply, the work of anthropologists includes interactions between people, one of whom is an anthropologist.

In this chapter, I consider *emotions* and *imagination* as partly constitutive both of 'being there' and of 'writing up'. My focus is on anthropological encounters, but I discuss as well the limits of co-presence for the anthropological enterprise. It is a preliminary, programmatic exploration and I begin with some ethnographic cases. Anthropologists are accustomed to analyse the attitudes of others, but my examples are self-reports. These are largely what anthropologists start with – whether their own or others'– and I shall argue that 'being there' is an activity including interactive encounters with mutual emotional evaluation and response. However, to assume that emotions are straightforwardly produced by face-to-face interaction limits our understanding just as does treating them purely as individual and internal, or 'intrapsychic'.

Negotiating Encounters

A linguist colleague once told me how in South India he went up to a street vendor to ask if he had cigarettes to sell. Faced with a slow shake of the head, Ian felt himself turn away in disappointment even though he knew as a linguistic fact that the shake meant yes. His own bodily gesture responded to the other's immediately and automatically, overriding his learned knowledge of a gestural meaning contrary to his own. Such conventionalized bodily stances are learned very early, in relation to others, and internalized. Even if some postures may have distant origins in acts of submission, flight or fight, they also may be local markers, whether as arbitrary signs in a widely used communication system as here (cf. Farnell 1994), or as individuating practices, as when we recognize a distant figure by his or her movements.

Different walks may be socially and culturally indicative. I was taken aback once when I found that a group of naughty little Liberian boys were marching exaggeratedly behind me. Put out that I might look so military (not a criticism I was used to), I then realized also how a lifetime of wearing shoes radically alters bodily movement. So do the lifetime practices of carrying loads on the head, which make for a typical African female posture that is often striking to Western eyes.

These apparently petty and minor examples reveal a complex confusion between the naturalized and the natural, and, as well, issues of power and uncertain emotional response. I did not like my dignity being mocked; the gleeful little boys may have sensed my discomfiture. Ian felt his need momentarily frustrated; did the vendor feel puzzled at the customer's rejection, or personally criticized in some way? Social interaction is full of misunderstandings and misreadings (as we say) and encounters have cumulative effects, in which remembering too is complicated. I remember the little boys over thirty years later, and now as an anecdotal indicator of cross-cultural style dissonance, but did the incident originally register because of my emotional discomfort?

Through mismatched body stances, some people can believe that 'foreigners are excitable' or that middle-class English people are snooty or cold. Misapprehension may have severe results. Some years ago in Birmingham, where I then worked, it became a commonplace scholarly observation by those discussing racism that teachers often believed Jamaican-origin schoolgirls were aggressive. This was because their body stance did not match English representations of female respect to authority. The teachers' subsequent actions would be coloured by this misrecognition, which triggered quite complex feelings of emotional threat. Pupils' perceptions of teachers' reactions might in turn lead to really aggressive behaviour. Bodily conventions aroused emotional responses in what was an already difficult context of power challenges and racial suspicion.

Fieldwork participation in rural south-east Liberia taught me some of these complexities at the most pragmatic level. The results were not always negative. I had neither land, skill nor time to become a subsistence farmer; I could not live off my own crops. But I found warmth from others when I essayed rice planting. I thereby showed how incompetent I was, and thus how competent the other women were, as well as being someone who would not always stand aside, observing.

Was I a participant? I was trying to persuade the community of my goodwill, even at some level 'to be accepted', though I think that phrase encapsulates impossible and indeed irrelevant dreams. I was acting in more than one sense. As rice planter, I saw myself ruefully and with mockery; I was applying to myself the attitude with which I viewed royalty doing ceremonial tree-planting. So this is also a complicated little example of how we use imagery reflexively – I don't think any watching farmer had ever seen that royal ceremonial!

This incident indicates too the significance of *persuasiveness* in all encounters. Most of us have been nervously aware how easy it is to wrong foot an interview, or even a brief introduction, where to put off another can have important consequences. Of course, too, in a multilateral process, in which interlocutors simultaneously appraise one another, and whose opinions can continue to change, self-interest can be significant. Even humble gatekeepers have power over researchers, who therefore seek their goodwill. Gatekeepers can sometimes also gain from continued involvement with enquirers who have an appropriate status. It is not the anthropologist alone who is engaged both in self-presentation and in trying to suss out the other, while he or she tries hard to learn, to get access, to 'get on' in the research arena. Liking, hostility, boredom and uncertainty arise on both sides.

Cognition, Emotionality, Imagination

An initial look at references to 'emotion' quickly makes clear that the word has culturally specific and changing connotations; it is not a scientific term, even if anglophones agree – roughly – about its meanings. That has not stopped researchers distinguishing cognition from emotional states. In recent years, however, models of brain activity by neuroscientists show that cognition includes what we ('Western' educated readers) regard as emotional responses. Thus, the work of Damasio (2000) is illuminating, even to those who cannot judge – or fully grasp – the science, because he models a consciousness which is very complexly formed through brain activity, and, in the multiple and interconnected 'layers' of sites through which it emerges and operates, what we may recognize as emotion, imagery and memory are interconnected (see also Milton, Chapter 1 in this volume).

The confidence of Damasio and other neurologists that human brains activate what Euro-Americans generally call emotions comes from advances in linking the location and forms of brain damage to kinds of disability that are evinced by patients.[2] There can be effects on emotional reaction as well as on ratiocination and memory. But it is misleading, and probably impossible, to label different brain processes and abilities simply as rational or emotional, since these are variable, lay terms that belong to surface outcomes, rather than manifold and interconnected neural processes.

Damasio wishes to model the sequencing 'from wakefulness to consciousness' (see e.g. Damasio 2000: 310). For him, a model for the brain should account for all mental activities, including feelings and senses of personal identity. This means that he needs at the least to explain behaviours of brain-damaged people for which narrow definitions of cognition as rationality cannot cope, and thus he is also anxious to shift his discipline's long recoil from emotion so as to make it part of its subject matter.

Neuroscientists have not been alone in recoiling. We live in a world committed to an ideology of scientific validation, for which emotions are often rejected as inimical. Likewise, the word 'imaginative' can imply criticism as well as praise. In the production of anthropology, multiple discussions of narrative strategy and discourse construction have not dissolved all the disputes over the differences between ethnography and fiction, although the point that cognitive work *implies* imagery was firmly made in social science contexts through studies of metaphor (see e.g. Schon 1969; Sapir and Crocker 1977; Lakoff and Johnson 1980; see also the magisterial arguments of Ricoeur 1978).

I have followed the poet Samuel Taylor Coleridge's model of imagination, produced some two hundred years ago, which centralizes creativity in ways that sit well with contemporary scientific findings. Coleridge defined primary and secondary imagination so as to show (using my words) '(1) the central necessity of imagination, (2) that it is a fundamentally *creative* power, it makes *real*, (3) the means which create what are so-called "works of imagination" are not specific to them, but part of universal mental equipment' (Tonkin 1979: 237–8). What we often designate as 'imaginative' is what Coleridge defined as the secondary imagination, 'differing only in degree and the *mode* of its operation' from the primary kind (in Tonkin 1979: 237–8).

Coleridge had no neuroscientific backing available, but he argued that such means were necessary for conceptualizing and indeed for generating thought. I return below to some practical implications for anthropological encounters, since as human beings, we all use the symbolic system of language,[3] we live in a symbolically marked world, we know how to lie, and we can envisage places and people not presently visible to us. Neuroscientists do not emphasize the interactive aspects of communication, though of course these are fundamental to research that depends on systematized recognition of damaged response. There is therefore no developed neuroscientific theory of emotionality and imagination in interaction, but that need not stop us from at least bringing some of the issues to view.

Emotions: Three Aspects of Distrust

First, though, I ask why so little attention has been paid to the emotions involved in fieldwork/'participant observation', given that in recent years, relative status, gender, and the importance of reflexivity have been written about so much. I believe that accounts of fieldwork that emphasize emotional components still arouse distrust, which I take it derives from presumptions operating in earlier theory. I note them here, very briefly.

Positivism and the Personal

As we know, social science has had a long positivist tradition in so far as it has claimed to be scientific; thus the work of the investigator was subsumed into the conclusions which were produced as research findings. I discovered when I wrote (critically) on 'participant observation' for the Association of Social Anthropologists' *Ethnographic Research: A Guide to General Conduct* (Ellen ed. 1984) that there was virtually no methodological literature to review, although the term seemed to have been first used for anthropology by Frankenberg in 1963, and had initially been a sociological command to be a 'fly on the wall'. Anthropological production of knowledge gained by direct relationships with individuals inverted the methodological tenets of quantitative research, and this was one reason why anthropologists claimed that their 'methods' led to robust findings, because these were analytical abstractions, generalized out of untidy experience (see e.g. Nadel 1951: 92). Thus their status was properly comparable to statistical or experimental research.

The really very mixed and complex processes, through which these 'action patterns', 'structures', 'norms', ' roles' and the like were identified, were largely ignored, as was the observer's interposition, and so the work of participant observation, although illustrated through telling examples (just as in reports of quantitative, statistically based sociological findings), became *evidence* that was effectively undifferentiated and unmediated. For a considerable time, then, there was a paradoxical combination of a strong assertion that participant observation is the defining method of anthropology and an absence of commentary on how it operates – even a reluctance to produce such a commentary.

As we know, this gap was identified, often through feminist perspectives, and very considerable theoretical discussions resulted which have been largely about the status of anthropological statements from interpretivist points of view. Nevertheless, while the character of particular relationships has been described in some detail (see e.g. Spindler ed. 1970 for early examples), there has been less analysis of the mind–body process through which the anthropologist came to experience and understand – or misunderstand – the relationship. Reasons for this lack include extreme difficulties of analysis, particularly in the short time available when it was required to concentrate on the ethnographic information that had to result from the encounters. For their methodological implications to be explored, these modalities of interaction have to be treated analytically as a dynamic process in which intellectual, emotional and imaginative apprehensions may fuse (see Jackson 1983, 1998).

Professional and Cultural Inhibition

That 'the personal should be distinguished from the professional' has been more than a simple professional rule, since the distinction is often maintained even where there is an ideology of openness, suggesting deeper cultural controls on emotional expressivity (cf. Reddy 2001). Indeed, personal as well as authorial authority depends on convincing others that your account is dependable (see e.g. Tonkin 1992: Chapter 2), and that means they should not infer from it that you are 'easily swayed', that is emotional. We see here cultural underpinnings to the positivist ideal, which has been so much reported and discussed as a Western, post-Enlightenment worship of rationality.

Division between Psychology and Anthropology (and, until recently, Sociology)

The first two reasons for ignoring emotionality are interconnected, as they are also with a third major reason which has partly to do with the maintenance of academic fiefs and traditions. The disciplines of psychology and social anthropology have a long history of separation and, given the character of financing and university composition, that has of course been supported by strong boundary maintenance. The positivist stance of psychology remains strong too, with a powerful commitment to experimental method. Social anthropologists used to detach themselves from what they said was psychology's realm, and in my more recent experience, encounters with social psychologists could be characterized as mutually wary, with frequent talking past one another.

Psychologists claimed to study emotions, but their emphasis on 'the individual' meant that they seemed to work in a different theoretical plane from those examining 'society'.[4] Parkinson (1995) testifies to a determined concentration on the 'intrapsychic' which has meant that psychological research into emotions that considers social interaction has been very limited and relatively recent. I was struck on reading his book recently to find how little attitudes had changed over the twenty-odd years since I had consulted the literature for an article on socialization (Tonkin 1982b). Furthermore, as then, 'the individual seems to be the focus of classical psychology as an instance of the species; that is why variations in the behaviour of a small number of university students may be held to instantiate variations at large in the world' (Tonkin 1982b: 245).

Psychology and anthropology (or sociology) have therefore not 'covered for' one another, in the sense that one might be able to use findings from the other discipline so as to fill a gap in one's own. That is because they proceed from different kinds of premise. Methodologically, they may proceed comparably in that they edit out what is perceived as irrelevant. By randomizing, psychologists edited out characteristics perceived as social, while to social anthropologists, 'non-criterial features are … idiosyncratic, individual and *psychological*' (Tonkin 1982b: 245, original emphasis). It is hoped that we have moved on somewhat since I wrote that, for, as some social psychologists have also realized, we cannot learn what is 'individual' – or, better, what an individual is – if we separate humans' experiences from their social relationships.

Forward Directions: Towards Conceptual Integration?

In complete contrast to earlier psychological perspectives on emotions, Parkinson (1995) urges one of *intersubjectivity*. 'My conclusion will be that emotions typically arise as a function of interpersonal interactions rather than encounters between a single individual and an independent reality, and the ongoing negotiation of emotional experiences is fundamental to the phenomenon' (Parkinson 1995: 24).

Before discussing his claim (which is put forward as a research agenda, not a summary of findings) I note an absence of relevant entries in Parkinson's index to neuroscience, as also for gender or class, while the consciously wide-ranging and humanistic Antonio Damasio (2000) does not take up psychologists' writings; for him, the significant cross-disciplinary connection is with philosophy.

Cosmides, Tooby and Barkow (1992), introducing a volume which sought to discuss 'the complex, evolved, psychological mechanisms that generate human behavior and culture' (Barkow, Cosmides and Tooby 1992: 3), stressed the lack of 'conceptual integration', 'the principle that the various disciplines within the behavioral and social sciences should make themselves mutually consistent, and consistent with what is known in the natural sciences as well' (Barkow et al. 1992: 4). Clearly, research on the emotions seems to lack such integration, but the level of knowledge developed in each relevant discipline means that it is a formidable or indeed impossible task to master it all in addition to one's own specialism. Should we then give up? This is an old question, once addressed by anthropologists as a question of 'the limits of naivety' (Gluckman 1964).

An absence of apparently appropriate knowledge from another discipline may be due to its perceived irrelevance. To imagine an example, anthropological discussion of commensality – rules about who eats with whom – might be enhanced by sophisticated physiological knowledge, but very possibly can do without it, if the analysis is of social hierarchy or different kinds of sharing. It is also possible that the 'affective' (emotional) aspects of commensality have deep and significant biological roots which anthropologists should not ignore; that is the promise, and the threat, held out by advances in neuroscience.

The price of working from carefully delimited premises is the exclusion of points that may be relevant but are apparently not salient according to those premises. This is not just a problem of disciplinary distinction; it can occur from the application of any theory or model (Thoden van Velzen 1973). In fact, to build up an integrated approach to a particular topic requires modelling or indeed theorizing afresh.

I propose that we need to attempt a cautious *consonance* which I hope does not evade the challenge of conceptual integration but which accepts there may be limits to total consistency. The requirement of consonance does not include the necessity for anthropologists to assess the detail of Damasio's model as against other neuroscientific ones, for instance, but it allows us to treat the many descriptions and definitions of emotion offered in psychological and ordinary language accounts just as that, 'surface' or commonsense accounts, which in fact are what Damasio uses, self-reports which he accepts as relevant in particular theoretical contexts.

We can start from the scientific propositions that 'emotions' do not necessarily form a separable psychological unity and that ordinary perception and communication require an extraordinary range of abilities complexly linked (cf. Leavitt 1996). I propose merely to accept that these have multi-site sources in the brain and different sequences or levels activating cognitive abilities, language production and reception, modes of feeling, and so on. These are activated in social interaction and may be accepted or challenged according to how they are perceived or understood.

The Limits of Intersubjectivity

We can learn much about social interaction from critical social constructionists such as Rom Harré (Harré 1983, 1986 are just two examples), but as an anthropologist who is not a fully paid-up interactionist, I stress, against Parkinson, that interactions are not the sole generators of emotion. We must pay attention to the contexts that often structure interactions; they cannot explain themselves. Barth (1992) expresses this point forcefully, while reminding us that 'social' is not a simple adjective of the noun 'society' if that is taken to mean a bounded unit. Therefore, the emotional implications of encounters cannot be captured in models which oppose atomistic 'individuals' and a holistic 'society'.[5]

Parkinson's understanding that intersubjectivity is constituted by 'interpersonal interactions' still contains this psychologistic bias (cf. Jackson 1998 for richer perspectives). My example of teacher–pupil relations in Birmingham supports his claim that emotions develop through interaction, yet these relations cannot be interpreted anthropologically without grasping the participants' presuppositions about race, gender and authority.

Any analysis of verbal interaction (on which anthropologists rely) shows the complexity of presupposition. Meanings are not purely semantic, nor does defining other components simply as expressive or emotional capture non-semantic meaning (Tonkin 1982a). People mean, and meanings are signalled, in ways that differ cross-culturally and subculturally as I have instantiated, and poor translations may arise from mismatches of salient components of linguistic and paralinguistic communication. Consider intonation as one example. In tonal languages, semantic or grammatical meaning can be carried by contrastive tone. British English speakers often find it hard to recognize tonal meanings since their speech system is not tonal but intonational, and meanings such as surprise or doubt as well as straightforward information-giving can be conveyed by intonation. The non-tonal speaker hears another speak emphatically or excitedly (tone interpreted as pitch); the tone-user tries to grapple with the other's apparently muddled or even obscene utterances.

One conclusion is very obvious: anthropological encounters may be exceptionally subject to misrecognition on both sides. Often the mistakes derive from differences in simple cues. Languages everywhere use acoustic and conceptual means for sign formation, but different components of each system are selected for different ends. Paralinguistic means – gesture, bodily orientation – are similarly conventional, but perhaps more deeply naturalized. Minimal linguistic distinctions can maintain difference within a street or two of one another. Milroy (1987) showed how in Belfast such differences mark politico-social identifications, within as much as without. They provide stable cues, comforting to insiders but watched for warily as indicators of otherness. Ignorant outsiders can be unaware of these effects and thus miss both social information and emotional connotations.

Memory, Imagination and Inter-subjectivity

Another striking absence from Parkinson's model of intersubjectivity is *memory*, a crucial component of cognition. Here, I cannot consider the substantial, fast growing and multidisciplinary literature on memory, and simply note that it is constitutive of both identity and consciousness (see Tonkin 1992). I stress, however, that we have to take into account the temporal context of encounters, the dynamism of agents and social relationships. Encounters are accumulative – thus affecting presuppositions – while anthropologists and their 'subjects' respond to one another and decide, among many other reactions, how far to continue. References in publications to 'key informants' imply longstanding, developed relationships, and consciously felt attitudes to one another, though these have been rarely analysed with the painful candour of Michael Jackson's retrospective attempt to grasp the mismatches of apprehension between him and his research assistant Noah Marah (see e.g. Jackson 1998: 98–113).

Attentiveness to the triad of memory, imagination and emotion, then, enables us at least to look more clearly at the significance of anthropologists' 'field' relationships. Of course, the collocation of self-reports will still be insufficient to account for the dynamics of interaction, even with evidence of others' responses. We have evolved as social beings who must connect with others to survive, and some of the ways to do so are below the thresholds of consciousness. 'Intersubjectivity' rightly points to an emotional climate that is not reducible to articulable, separate participant perceptions only.

Do the Difficulties Matter?

To demonstrate the potential for emotional complexity in encounters, I have briefly described some limited situations in which emotionality can be unintended. Given all the causes of confusion, it may seem surprising that anthropology can work! How has our ethnographic learning come about, even at the price of communicative – and emotional – costs?

I do not consider the answer to be *empathy*, though I suspect most fieldworkers at times presume this, because the examples I have given show how misleading assumptions of shared feeling can be. Nor is it the case that useful reports depend on empathy, or on interactions which generate sympathetic emotion. The Society of African Missions kindly lent me missionary diaries by Catholic priests working in my field area before 1920, where I found that the one who was often angry and unhappy with his situation was often much more informative than another, who was rather enjoying himself (and thus presumably felt no need to work off his feelings in a diary).

A better term than empathy, perhaps, is Evans-Pritchard's stress on 'trust'. Notorious among his former students for his lack of field advice or help with thesis writing (and see Gilsenan 2000: 605–7), 'E-P' did write some advisory reminiscence, in which he responded to criticisms that anthropologists had no way to check if they were told lies. He said that some degree of trust was essential to ordinary social relationship, and without some kind of relationship with the people the anthropologists lived among, 'disorientated craziness' would result (Evans-Pritchard 1973: 4).

Evans-Pritchard's brief comments suggest that 'being there' also includes the human need to interact as a social being, to recognize others as human (and therefore to be able to judge their weaknesses or evil), in short to act as we have evolved, as a species that operates in relation to others. This also suggests that anthropological findings result inevitably from social, interactive and emotional encounters that involve deep, largely non-conscious cognitive and bodily intuitions working together, however limited the interaction may be.

One important reason for anthropological success is communicative redundancy. Languages themselves have many redundant features, so what is unclear in content may often be picked up by context or gesture. Anthropologists build up accounts circumstantially, and accumulate understanding through inference, comparing different encounters, deploying information gained from colleagues, articles and books, guided by theory. Redundancy occurs again and is not encompassed by 'being there'.

The Limits of Co-presence: Imagination and Emotion in Persuasive Anthropological Narrations

Fieldwork indeed demands the application and relating of a very mixed array of sources, which is one reason why it is not merely impressionistic, as researchers using statistical methods often presume (see Tonkin 1984). It is a temporal process and 'the decisive battle is not fought in the field but in the study afterwards' (Evans-Pritchard 1973: 3). 'Being there' is only part of the story, and as this comment suggests, emotionality, memory and imagination operate just as much when 'writing up'.

Indeed, 'being there' and 'co-presence' are actually complex activities, difficult notions that deserve a paper to themselves (which I hope to write elsewhere). As anthropologists, we have to be sensitive to the implications ('rational' and 'emotional') of eyewitness and orality. Yet our findings are never limited to direct interaction with those we describe. The views of other people – friends, mentors, theorists and evidence from local media – are important, and do not always involve co-present encounters. A huge amount of anthropological evidence has always been derived from hearsay – from others' accounts and explanations, sometimes at more than one remove from any participant encounter – but this too has emotional dimensions (Tonkin 2004). New feelings develop in the subsequent 'battle' to write the anthropological account.

Imagining and evoking past scenes are crucial to report and presentation. Crossovers between orality and literacy, co-presence and memory are commonplace for anthropologists, whose academic status largely depends on their publications, but who spend much time on lectures and presentations which involve co-presence, and often audio-visual technologies. All this means that imagery and memory are constantly in play for us all. Representations must be developed, articulated and skilfully deployed by anthropologists, who first struggle to enter others' worlds, emotionally and imaginatively, and then to re-present them persuasively so that new others may imagine them in turn, using their own emotional abilities and memories to do so.

We have both to communicate the emotionality of others and to evoke appropriate emotions in others if we are to persuade readers, students and colleagues of our work's significance. Emphasis on objectivity and rationality has – yet again – disfavoured proper thought about the nature of emotion in persuasion, which generally continues to have a bad press. In the classical Greek and Roman world the arts of persuasion were studied and taught as rules of rhetoric, a practical skill indicating how serious was pre-scientific attention to affective implications of co-presence, even when literate media were used.[6]

Conclusion

Working as we must at the surface, it is still possible to look for the immediate grounds on which communicative interaction proceeds. The anthropologist should assume that emotions will be felt on both sides, but it is important to realize that they need not be mutually constructed, or agreed. Emotional attitudes may be givens for one interlocutor but absent for another. Interactions in social relationships mediate in very complex ways tacit knowledge, learned perceptions and many considerations of power and duty; they help to create, maintain and destroy social rules and cultural forms.

By using a perspective that notes the constitutive work of emotion, memory and imagination along with agency, and recognizes the complex interactions of brains and bodies needed to produce them, we can also start to work anew with older terms like observation, symbolization and rationality. These name abilities which all of us have to employ, but which we must try to raise to conscious attention if we are to understand the fundamental, empirical interactions which are the source of so much anthropological knowledge.

Notes

1. Watson and his contributors (Watson 1999) vividly evoke the complexity of 'being there'. They emphasize the processual nature of fieldwork and its many inputs over time, including those which contribute to a publication, delineating well their own emotional feelings and the difficulties of incorporating them into anthropological accounts.

2. These ideas were also presented 'popularly' in a radio series as the 2003 BBC Reith Lectures by V. S. Ramachandran.

3. Psychological emphasis on individuals may also testify to an ideological centring of Me. Thus Nancy Chodorow (1999) criticizes psychoanalysis from within, but from a background training in anthropology which leads her to stress the ubiquity of 'transference', such that her preferred 'psychoanalytic theorists argue that emotion is always interwined with cognition, perception, language, interaction and

the experience of physical, and cultural reality, at least on those areas of our lives that matter to us' (Chodorow 1999: 27). Yet, despite this perception of constitutive sociality, Chodorow does not discuss a *social* theory and somehow detaches 'personal meaning', which is an individual analysand's, from culture and indeed gender. 'Psychoanalysis is a theory about how we create personal meaning, our unconscious psychic reality, through what I am calling the power of feelings' (Chodorow 1999: 13–14).

In contrast, Mikhail Bakhtin writes of 'sympathetic co-experiencing', a concept intended as a contribution to aesthetics and a counter-proposition to 'expressive theory', with 'everywhere the same *closed* circle of a *single* consciousness, of *self*-experience, and of a relationship to *oneself*' (Bakhtin 1990: 80, cited in Wardle 2000, original italics). This is consonant with his view of language as always existing through interactions and carrying meanings for interlocutors that have aggregated and altered out of previous interactions. Though Bakhtin did not develop his view of interaction sociologically (any more than the rather similar George Henry Mead), it is both insightful and potentially fruitful for considering anthropologists' encounters.

4. Edmund Leach, analysing Michelangelo's paintings in the Sistine Chapel in his structuralist mode, described imagination as a (non-linguistic) 'process' which 'is the outcome of some deeper level mental process, a kind of meta-thinking which does not, of itself, generate conscious thoughts but makes creative originality possible in that it consists of the establishment of relations between relations' (Leach 1985: 5, noted by Tambiah 2002: 245ff.). Leach was a mathematically trained engineer as well as an anthropologist.

5. My emphasis is obviously on movements in *social* anthropology, but *culture* as often hypostatized is equally incapable of modelling intersubjectivity.

6. We have to rely on written texts for our knowledge of classical rhetorical training, which means missing its elements of practical, co-present method. The rules of classical rhetoric as they came to be transmitted textually in the medieval world, with their ornately named tropes, nevertheless bridge the communication worlds of speech and writing. The contributors' choice in Lutz and Abu-Lughod (eds 1990) to focus on emotional language turns out to privilege its non-oral aspects, and seems to be a kind of regression to behaviourism, by assuming it is appropriate only to study transcribed representations of inaccessible interior states. The contributors therefore do not really tackle the interactions in which the emotions that they discuss are presumed to arise.

References

Bakhtin, M. (1990), 'Author and Hero in Aesthetic Activity', in M. Holmquist and
V. Liapunov (eds), *Art and Answerability: Early Aesthetic Essays by M. M.*

Bakhtin, Austin, TX: University of Texas.

Barkow, J., Cosmides, L. and Tooby, J. (eds) (1995), *The Adapted Mind: Evolutionary Psychology and the Generation of Culture*, New York, Oxford: Oxford University Press.

Barth, F. (1992), 'Towards Greater Naturalism in Conceptualising Societies', in A. Kuper (ed.) *Conceptualising Society*, London and New York: Routledge.

Chodorow, N. (1999), *The Power of Feelings: Personal Meaning in Psychoanalysis, Gender and Culture*, New Haven, CT and London: Yale University Press.

Cosmides, L., Tooby, J. and Barkow, J. (1995), 'Introduction: Evolutionary Psychology and Conceptual Integration', in J. Barkow, L. Cosmides and J. Tooby (eds), *The Adapted Mind: Evolutionary Psychology and the Generation of Culture*, New York and Oxford: Oxford University Press.

Damasio, A. (2000), *The Feeling of What Happens: Body and Emotion in the Making of Consciousness*, London: William Heinemann.

Ellen, R. (ed.) (1984), *Ethnographic Research: A Guide to General Conduct*, London: Academic Press.

Evans-Pritchard, E. E. (1973), 'Some Reminiscences and Reflections on Fieldwork', *Journal of the Anthropological Society of Oxford* 4: 1–12.

Farnell, B. (1994), 'Ethno-graphics and the Moving Body', *Man* (NS) 29: 929–74.

Frankenberg, R. (1963), 'Participant Observers', *New Society* 1: 22–3.

Gilsenan, M. (2000), 'Signs of Truth: Enchantment, Modernity and the Dreams of Peasant Women', *Journal of the Royal Anthropological Institute* (NS) 6: 597–615.

Gluckman, M. (ed.) (1964), *Closed Systems and Open Minds: The Limits of Naivety*, Chicago: Aldine.

Harré, R. (1983), *Personal Being*, Oxford: Basil Blackwell.

—— (ed.) (1986), *The Social Construction of Emotions*, Oxford: Basil Blackwell.

Jackson, M. (1983), 'Knowledge of the Body', *Man* (NS) 18: 327–45.

—— (1998), *Minima Ethnographica*, Chicago and London: University of Chicago Press.

Lakoff, G. and Johnson, M. (1980), *Metaphors We Live By*, Chicago and London: University of Chicago Press.

Leach, E. (1985), 'Michelangelo's Genesis: A Structuralist Interpretation of the Central Panels of the Sistine Chapel Ceiling', *Semiotica* 56: 1–30.

Leavitt, J. (1996), 'Meaning and Feeling in the Anthropology of Emotions', *American Ethnologist* 23: 514–39.

Lutz, C. and Abu-Lughod, L. (eds) (1990), *Language and the Politics of Emotion*, Cambridge: Cambridge University Press.

Milroy, L. (1987), *Language and Social Networks*, 2nd edn, Oxford: Basil Blackwell.

Nadel, S. (1951), *The Foundations of Social Anthropology*, London: Cohen and West.

Parkinson, B. (1995), *Ideas and Realities of Emotion*, London and New York: Routledge.

Reddy, W. (2001), *The Navigation of Feeling: A Framework for the History of the Emotions*, Cambridge: Cambridge University Press.

Ricoeur, P. (1978), *The Rule of Metaphor: Multi-disciplinary Studies of the Creation of Meaning in Language*, London: Routledge and Kegan Paul.

Sapir, D. and Crocker, C. (eds) (1977), *The Social Use of Metaphor: Essays on the Anthropology of Rhetoric*, Philadelphia, PA: University of Pennsylvania Press.

Schon, D. (1969), *Invention and the Evolution of Ideas,* London: Tavistock.

Spindler, G. (ed.) (1970), *Being an Anthropologist: Fieldwork in Eleven Cultures*, New York: Holt, Rinehart and Winston.

Tambiah, S. (2001), *Edmund Leach: An Anthropological Life*, Cambridge: Cambridge University Press.

Thoden van Velzen, H. (1973), 'Robinson Crusoe and Friday: Strength and Weakness of the Big Man Paradigm', *Man* (NS) 8: 592–612.

Tonkin, E. (1979), 'Masks and Powers', *Man* (NS) 14: 237–48.

—— (1982a), 'Language vs. the World: Notes on Meaning for Anthropologists', in D. Parkin (ed.), *Semantic Anthropology*, London: Academic Press.

—— (1982b), 'Rethinking Socialization', *Journal of the Anthropological Society of Oxford* 13: 243–56.

—— (1984), 'Participant Observation', in R. Ellen (ed.), *Ethnographic Research: A Guide to General Conduct*, London: Academic Press.

—— (1992), *Narrating our Pasts: The Social Construction of Oral History*, Cambridge: Cambridge University Press.

—— (2004) 'Consulting Ku Jlople: Some Histories of Oracles in West Africa', *Journal of the Royal Anthropological Institute* (NS) 10 (3): 539–60.

Wardle, H. (2000), 'Subjectivity and Aesthetics in the Jamaican Nine Night', *Social Anthropology* 8: 247–62.

Watson, C. W. (ed.) (1999), *Being There: Fieldwork in Anthropology*, London: Pluto Press.

–4–

Resentment as a Sense of Self

Lisette Josephides

Introduction

This chapter has a dual character: it discusses the role of emotions in the local production of cultural knowledge, and shows how ethnographic knowledge is generated by an understanding of emotions in everyday social dynamics. Drawing on long-term fieldwork in the Papua New Guinea Highlands, I begin by chronicling the hubbub of daily emotions that animate the small-scale interactions through which life is lived and culture is produced. They create a vibrant, living community, its moods and tempo. They are felt within a group, not necessarily experienced in a phenomenological, intersubjective way, but palpably, as forces, moods, omens, pacifiers, sources of anxiety and morbid interest, magnetic fields outside the individual. They create a maelstrom of human passions, where resentment blows about with complacency, apprehension and fear darken a brighter mood, greed collides with jealousy, scorn circles around frustration, generosity becomes tainted with hubris and runs into suspicion and wariness. All the while humour hovers above everything, not entirely benignly but maintaining an alertness, mediating a sort of understanding. It was in this maelstrom that I began to gain an understanding of the Kewa.

I call this maelstrom 'empathy'. Out of the sense-data that assaulted me in the field, an impressionistic ethnographic picture took shape. Slowly the sense-data acquired meaning, as the ethnographic vignettes turned into longer, coherent accounts. They showed people as acting and then as strategizing agents, whose actions and statements constantly elicited the responses of others. Of course, resentment, apprehension, greed and generosity are not sense-data. Elsewhere (Josephides 2003a) I discuss them as my interpretations of people's expressed emotions, which in turn exerted a profound influence on my own emotions. My strong feeling that I had arrived at an understanding of the Kewa in the emotional maelstrom I call empathy locked me into a chain of further implications: that emotions link people in understanding (they enabled me to understand Kewa people, despite cultural differences); that there is a quality of being human that all humans share; that emotions form judgements about what it is to be human; and hence that emotions act as moral judgements (on Kantian forms of judgement, see Solomon 1984). The corollary of this was that empathy, an emotional response, became a moral quality (see Josephides 2003a).

My early work on the Kewa (e.g. Josephides 1985) had a different focus. It stressed the politically strategizing aspects of people's actions, depicting them as pragmatic Highlanders in the interactionist mode of 1970s theorizations. This slant coated all talk and action with the veneer of calculation. On reviewing my field-notes years later, I became acutely aware of the seething emotions that kept all interactions at boiling point. I had documented how individual actions (and talk) could be seen as motivated by strategies of self-fulfilment; now I must demonstrate how they also spring from a personally felt emotion, a desire or need to express oneself, to map out an area and construct a claim for oneself as a worthy person. The strongest motivator of emotional expression which emerges from the ethno-graphic vignettes is the feeling of resentment, which impinges on the actor's sense of personal worth. Resentment is experienced as an arrow to the heart, and draws immediate and often violent response. This chapter shows how this insight into emotional experience and motivation can add ethnographic depth, and thus revise earlier, interactionist accounts of social and political action in the Papua New Guinea Highlands.

Knowing the Kewa[1]

Whenever I think of the Kewa village in which I lived for varying periods over thir-teen years, I become physically transported there. Dusk is falling as I sit in my thin-walled house, listening to the breeze carrying the gossip of the village in and out of surrounding houses, through bamboo walls and onto open porches. The ebb and flow of the low murmuring is part of the rhythm of life. It lulls children to sleep, but suddenly turns violent and wakes them to the volatility of social life. The talk is the constant input from community members: of knowledge of outside events, of changing trends, new technologies, tentative revisions and redefinitions; of attitudes and perceptions, interests and feelings, complaints and demands; it throws out hints, sows doubts, foreshadows claims or troubles ahead, makes public, initiates strategies and negotiations, redresses the balance of discourse; it expresses aesthetic pleasure, frustrated desire, sorrow and joy, sharp criticism and deep resentment. The talk is not put in a basket in the middle of the open ground for all to partake, but gets passed round, elaborated upon, internalized and trans-formed. Meanings are negotiated and appropriated, softening the contours of con-flict and muffling up the malingering whines. But as the night deepens the talk that lingers blends with the child's dry cough, thickening the air with portents of doom.

My earliest impression of the Kewa village was how mercurial and contagious moods can be. One moment the settlement was swaying to the rhythm of the saddest threnodies, the next moment the chief mourners stepped back and engaged in mirthful conversations. Older, more 'traditional' men's bodies easily assumed a fighting posture, head cocked and face set in a ferocious frown. But just as suddenly the frown crumbled into a wide smile, or succumbed entirely to helpless laughter.

In the early days of fieldwork my note-taking practices reflected an unexamined dichotomy. 'Culturally salient' talk, whose analysis would provide support structures for my arguments and bridges for my understanding, was to be recorded in my fieldnotes. My diaries were the repositories of other talk, events and observations that conditioned my senses and emotions. I noted the companionable cosiness of sitting on the ground together and performing one task, such as peeling vegetables or husking coffee, stripping and flattening the cane that would be woven into house walls, or preparing food around the fire. I considered these 'enablements' as facilitating fieldwork, not as the object of it.

In their daily exchanges people bicker, banter, bait each other and stake out their claims. A woman and her brother-in-law argue over rights to a banana tree, which he claims to have tended. Another woman delivers a homily to her sister-in-law, who hangs her head in silent resignation; her chickens have taken the thatch off her sister-in-law's roof, so she 'has no talk'. A husband and wife argue about everything: housecleaning, child care, pig care and distributions, coffee garden care and the sharing of proceeds from coffee sales. A recently widowed woman and her daughter-in-law fight over the distribution of the deceased's things. A father berates his sons for not building him a new house, threatening to move back to the abandoned ancestral settlement, where, he implies, only death awaits. One brother complains to another that he never thought to compensate him for his work on the coffee garden whose proceeds he enjoys as the nominal owner. A daughter-in-law gets into a shouting match with her husband's stepmother, and her husband's father's brother's widow comes to berate her: she always quarrelled with her husband's father's brother while he was alive, and no sooner does he die than she starts on another affine (relative by marriage). The older woman storms off flanked by her daughters, and the younger woman follows, weeping and protesting. The implied charges and threats are grave: that her husband's stepmother will die as the husband's father's brother died, and she will be held responsible.

Sexual bantering abounds. One young married woman sat in the middle of the settlement, complaining for hours on end about her husband's habit of sleeping at other people's houses. 'Why won't he sleep with me, what's wrong with me, am I dirty or something?' she asked of no one in particular. People began to bait her, but in between peals of laughter they also advised her to pull herself together and stop sulking. (Sixteen months later the woman ran away and the husband had to propitiate her to return.) *good for her!*

Late one afternoon Kiru returned from the bush carrying a possum he had killed. In the night his wife Liame, woken by the dog, saw the possum hanging outside and took it into her room. Kiru was furious when he saw what she had done; the possum, he told her, was for his clan brother's wife. Liame went into a screaming rage that roused the whole settlement. At first light she packed the dog in her netbag and took off for the bush, determined to kill her own game. She returned in a complacent mood late in the night, having killed and eaten some bush rats.

Anyone can put anyone else in his or her place and cut down to size an inflated ego. On the occasion of a bridewealth exchange many pigs were tied to stakes while transactions took place. In the midst of this Kumi, a local big man's younger brother, appeared on the scene and began to scold: 'Look at the pigs fainting away in the scorching sun while you chatter on! The poor pigs will die!' 'Oh, Kinyoko has come,' the cry went up. This was an allusion to an occasion when they had been invited to sing in a fairly distant village and were made to wait in the scorching sun for the local big man to show up. 'When will Kinyoko come?' they kept asking. Finally the cry went up: 'Kinyoko has come!' But when they turned to see the big man what they saw was a 'half man', a rubbish man. This humorous allusion to an occasion when they themselves were roasting in the sun like pigs was intended to put Kumi in his place: he could not treat them like pigs who needed a 'rubbish man' to point out the obvious.

Anger is not good. A person who feels another person's unspoken anger will become sick. Roga was made ill by the resentment of Mapi's lineage, Yadi took sick when he smoked a cigarette given to him by a brother who bore him a grudge. Rimbu resentfully avoided me but sent messages that he was not angry, protestations that always signal the opposite. He could not admit that he was angry because his attempts to control my exchange networks were thwarted, but nor could he allow his anger to make me ill. His *siapi* (veiled speech) revealed his anger by pretending to hide it.

Most grudges are nursed and fights break out afresh. Rero resented Yadi for crashing the clan truck, following which clan members had to contribute to compensation payments. His anger exploded when Yadi styled himself the 'father' of the longhouse built in preparation for the pig kill. He snatched a log from the fire and dealt Yadi a blow on the side of the head. 'Yadi is always pouring scorn on Rero,' Rimbu told me, 'calling him a rubbish man and challenging him to show his wealth and his mettle. But Rero says, "What can I do, when you yourself brought about the ruin of the clan with your bad driving?"'

One night Komalo, Rimbu's younger brother, returned from plantation labour bringing a woman he proposed to marry. On the advice of the village magistrate Komalo left the woman with Rimbu and went back to the plantation to fetch his savings. (It was said that the woman's brothers wanted seven hundred kina in brideprice.) To Rimbu's barely disguised displeasure, the woman (Wata), her baby daughter from a previous marriage, her mother and her sister's son were all installed in Rimbu's house.

In the midst of these events Wapa, the father of Rimbu and Komalo, died. Wata's brothers sent word that they would not press for brideprice payment before funeral expenses were absorbed. Rimbu welcomed this gesture, but he could not abide Wata's mother's constant references to the brideprice. Eventually he asked her to leave. Mother and daughter mournfully collected their belongings and began to make their doleful way. At the entrance of the settlement Wata broke down by Wapa's grave and wailed aloud. The trigger worked: Rimbu remembered the *temali* (threnody) Wata had sung for Wapa and was softened. He called out to her: 'You've been with us for so long and you cry for us so much, come back.' Later Rimbu told me he had also been concerned about the baby's welfare, as Wata's brothers would hold him responsible if she came to harm on the road. (At the time I thought this reason cancelled out Rimbu's emotional response, simply because it concerned a material and political economy whose determinant imperatives I was more prepared to recognize.)

The tensions of cohabitation were serious at this time. As Lari put it, 'The more people you have living together, the more they will talk. The more people talk, the more they will disagree and fight.' One day Rimbu returned home to find the house packed with people and filthy with food leavings. He asked Lari to clean up and stormed off to the market. Kamarea, Ragunanu's daughter, rushed off to report the incident to her mother, who accosted Rimbu on his return. She reminded him that he had invited her to stay at his house when her troubles started at home, yet now things were being said behind her back about destroying houses. 'No, no,' Rimbu reassured her, 'you are not the only one responsible.' He made his peace with her by explaining that he was not singling her out for blame.

Emotion and the Sense of Self

As my first jumbled impressions grew into longer observations, a double motivating factor emerged behind people's strategies in daily interactions: the placing of oneself as a person within a value system, and the demand to be acknowledged as such by others. This sense of self was crucial to the dynamics of everyday actions. While persons operated in pre-existing situations with whatever cultural materials were available, they also redefined those materials and their relationship to them.[2]

Rarapalu's case exemplifies these self strategies. She had left her husband, Waliya, for eight months, during which time he took another wife. She returned to contest the divorce in court, arguing that she had left because of disagreement over pork and stayed away because she was sick. In her statement she made her husband responsible for her flight: he had refused to affirm her worth or acknowledge her place in his relations and his affections. He should have treated her flight as an opportunity to acknowledge her status, by propitiating her in the proper manner. Rarapalu moved back into the marital home and a stormy period of *ménage à trois* ensued, as she made desperate efforts to extort from Waliya a sign that he valued her as his wife. He argued that she was too litigious, she retaliated that his dislike of her was responsible for her frequent suits against him. Rarapalu never demanded that the second wife should leave; only that she should not receive preferential treatment. The personhood that Rarapalu was struggling to have acknowledged is enshrined in a range of idioms (or practical beliefs about persons) used in claims and complaints against ill-treatment. They include the following assortment: that each person has certain inalienable rights, equal to other persons; that one person may not presume to speak for another person; that it is grave to single out for blame specific individuals (blame shared with others loses its sting); that a person's grief must be respected and shared. Abnegation of the responsibilities attaching to one's own personhood can also have fatal consequences. This can be seen in the paradigmatic case of the adulterous woman, who died after giving food to her husband and children without confessing her guilt.

Like Rarapalu, Rika felt that he was not treated properly as a person. He accused his older brother, Roga, with breach of promise to their dying father, who had left Rika in his charge. Rika's palpable resentment caused Wapelenu, Roga's wife, to have a nightmare. She dreamt that the parents had come back from the dead to remonstrate with her and Roga, and woke up screaming in the middle of the night: 'Rika's parents are putting me and Roga on trial for neglecting Rika.' Soon after, Roga fell ill. Rika ignored all pleas to come home and pray for his brother, pronouncing the sickness a just retribution. Roga recovered, but the warning did not make him more solicitous of his younger brother. Twelve years later Rika attacked him in a fit of rage, which cost Roga an arm.

The ethnography presented here documented certain types of recurring interactions that dominate Kewa daily life. My intention was not to explain them by reference to a set of norms derived from an uncovered structure, but rather to explore what had motivated them from the perspective of the actor. The major motivation to emerge was the desire for the acknowledgment of the social self. From my observations, people did not merely respond to situations; they responded to their implications for the perception of the self (Josephides 1998). Following a brief overview of anthropological and philosophical approaches to emotion, the rest of the chapter will use these ethnographic vignettes to ask where the deepest sense of Kewa self is located.

Theories of Emotions

From Philosophy

The heightened interest in theorizing and understanding emotions since the early 1980s has led to a cross-pollination which is shaping the field in a decidedly interdisciplinary way. While earlier anthropological theorists turned to psychology for their models, philosophers working on the emotions are increasingly dipping into a rich ethnographic pool for a heterogeneous sample of the experience and cultural meaning of emotions. Neuroscientists have also joined the fray. Summing up the field for philosophy, Prinz (2003: 69) writes that there are two kinds of emotion theorists, those who argue emotions are essentially cognitive states and those who argue they are non-cognitive. Prinz suggests that the latter should acknowledge that emotions are meaningful and the former realize that 'being meaningful does not require being cognitive' (Prinz 2003: 78); but the real subject of his critique is the poverty of non-cognitive theories. Philosophers who concern themselves with emotions undoubtedly find a cognitive approach more fruitful than a non-cognitive one. Solomon, the champion of emotions as interpretations, is most uncompromising in rejecting the relevance of biology to the understanding of emotion: 'An emotion is a system of concepts, beliefs, attitudes, and desires, virtually all of which are context-bound, historically developed, and culture specific (which is not to foreclose the possibility that some emotions may be specific to *all* cultures)' (Solomon 1984: 249). His target is William James, but it might easily have been the neuroscientist Damasio, whose work accommodates James' insights. Damasio's account of emotions begins with chemical and neural signals and ends with changes to cognitive states, when emotions are experienced as feelings. Both emotions and feelings are survival mechanisms. Emotions are 'regulatory mechanisms with a homeostatic function', 'coordinated and largely automated physiological reactions required to maintain steady internal states in a living organism' (Damasio 1999: 39). Feelings, on the other hand, allow us to plan, and having them is thus 'of extraordinary value in the orchestration of survival' (Damasio 1999: 284).

The relationship between feelings and rationality, which Damasio develops in an earlier work (Damasio 1994), allows Nussbaum to describe emotions as 'forms of intelligent awareness', quoting Damasio to the effect that they are 'just as cognitive as other percepts' (Nussbaum 2001: 115). This accords with Nussbaum's own analysis of emotions as appraisals or value judgements. Three salient ideas comprise Nussbaum's view of emotions: they are cognitive appraisals or evaluations, they focus on *my* goals, and they incorporate external objects in the scheme of my goals (Nussbaum 2001: 4). Emotions are evaluative judgements because, as Prinz paraphrases Nussbaum, 'If I feel sad, it is not just that I recognize a loss; I also judge that my sense of loss is warranted' (Prinz 2003: 72). Nussbaum rejects the critique, made by Wollheim (1999) and Griffiths (2003) among others, that emotions attempt to fit the world to our mental attitude (Nussbaum 2001: 48). She argues instead that they respond to the way the world already is. If it is uncomfortable or fills me with fear, I do not pretend it is other than frightening, but I may try to make it into a place which does not arouse fear (Nussbaum 2001: 48–9). In such a case, emotions become actions.[3]

It is clear that these philosophers who focus on emotions as forms of cognition are less concerned to make the link with morality (as I did in Josephides 2003a, 2003b). For Kant, it is precisely the relation between emotions and morality that makes us truly human.[4] Kant (1960: 21–3) outlines the elements of human personality: animateness is the psychological element, which is the ground of our animality; rationality is the transcendental element, which is the ground of our humanity; but human personality could not be complete without morality, which makes us into responsible, accountable beings (Heidegger 1988 [1932]: 131). In the insight that what is crucial is how feeling reveals the self, Kant shows that feeling is not a simple reflection upon oneself 'but rather a feeling of *self* in having a feeling *for* something' (Heidegger 1988: 132, original emphasis). Kant's moral self-consciousness is not mediated by sense-experience; on the contrary, the moral law thwarts all our inclinations, understood as sensible feelings, and strikes at the root of self-conceit. Respect for it is therefore a feeling produced by an intellectual ground. This respect is a revelation of my own self as agent, an active ego who is not defined by 'self-conceit and self-love'. When I subject myself to my own self as the free self, this is a 'submissive self-elevation of myself to myself', which discloses me to myself 'in my *dignity*' (Heidegger 1988: 134–5, original emphasis). Two sentences from Heidegger (Heidegger 1988: 135–6) encapsulate the connections between emotion, the self and morality which support the central arguments of this chapter: 'Respect is the mode of the ego's being-with-itself [*Bei-sich-selbst-sein*] according to which it does not disparage the hero in its soul. The moral feeling, as respect for the law, is nothing but the self's being responsible to itself and for itself.'

From Anthropology

While philosophers contrast cognitivist with non-cognitivist approaches, anthropologists concentrate on the physicalist and culturalist divide. Recent calls to theorize emotions in anthropology arise from a double perception: that in ethnographic monographs, which study systems of meaning in the form of culture (Lyon 1995), emotions are made incidental to other descriptions, and that theory-building exercises marginalize emotions even more. Despite this perceived lack, the 1980s and 1990s saw a sizeable literature on emotions appear in print.[5] The perspectives found there parallel to some extent those of functionalism versus interpretivism in older theoretical literature. The physicalist approach considers emotions to be physical feelings susceptible to explanation. The culturalist approach sees emotions as ideas in the mind, a form of cognition whose social and cultural meaning is to be interpreted. Moreover, the meaning so interpreted is social and cultural, no longer purely individual and innerly. Leavitt warns against three easy assumptions: that human phenomena pertain either to biology or to a specific sociocultural tradition, that emotions are inward and private while words and meanings are public, and that ideas can be interpreted while emotions cannot. These dichotomies, he argues, originate in a Western distinction between an expressive freedom thought to characterize our minds, and a determinism thought to characterize our bodies (Leavitt 1996: 515). In this chapter I take it as given that emotions pertain both to physical feelings and cultural meanings, and agree with Lyon that 'emotion cannot be conceived as entirely separate from either psychophysiological *or* social phenomena' (Lyon 1995: 257, original emphasis).

Cultural constructionists developed the anthropological insight that emotions have meaning and are social in character. My own work demonstrates that emotions are forms of communicative practices, or, as Lutz and Abu-Lughod (1990: 11) put it, 'pragmatic acts and communicative performances', inseparable from social activity (quoted in Leavitt 1996: 523). I use the category of 'elicitation' to denote a particular type of emotional communication. It was exemplified in the exchange between Rimbu's anger and Ragunanu's resentment, when each elicited from the other information on the limits of each other's tolerance. But the same example also showed that emotions are more than just forms of discourse. Rimbu's anger and Ragunanu's resentment expressed internal states which moved them to act. Against the claims of cultural constructionists (e.g. Lutz and White 1986), I read my ethnography as demonstrating that emotions are also expressive vehicles for internal states or passions; with Nussbaum (2001), I observe that emotions can also be actions.

The argument about emotions as internal states or passions also counters claims that emotions are constructed by language alone. While language and emotion are intertwined and impossible to separate as vehicles of meaning and communication, several exchanges which I recorded could not be adequately understood by reference to language alone. For some, meaning and intent resided in the pragmatics of the 'unsaid' (see Josephides 2001). Language did however make an appearance as a troublesome trickster in cases of cohabitation: people who live together talk more, and talk always runs a risk of hurting someone's feelings.

To theorize emotions in anthropology means also to think of them comparatively and cross-culturally. It means to ask such questions as: if people in different cultures respond with different outward emotion to the same event, should it be assumed that they actually feel differently? Or is the external response not to be taken at face value? When the expression of an emotion is culturally prescribed or proscribed, does it then follow that the emotion is felt more strongly or more weakly? As Wikan (1990) has demonstrated exhaustively in her work in Bali, ethnographers should beware of ready-made assumptions about the fit between outward appearance of emotion and inward feeling, or facial expressions and emotional or psychological states. Wikan's ethnographic study on the apparent dissonance between the demonstration of grief and the felt emotion was complex, demonstrating that emotions, their expression, and cultural meanings defied perfect pairings and easy categorizations.

As a rebuff to lingering propensities for functionalist homogeneity, the results of anthropological studies on emotion also question assumptions about the uniformity of emotional responses in one society. Consider the emotional responses of two people to a similar event to which they have the same relationship. Are the differences emotional or behavioural? An example from my own fieldwork concerns the reactions of Kiru and Hapkas to the death of their newborn babies. Kiru appeared detached and uncaring, Hapkas was sombre and resentful of his brothers' failure to observe the event. To some extent, the different responses might be explained in terms of the men's different personalities. But closer attention to the ethnography can make more insights available. Hapkas's expression of resentment was caused by more than grief for his baby's death. It was exacerbated by other personal, psychological and political feelings of perceived neglect and lack of esteem. Another example is easier to explain in terms of cultural exemplars. When Michael responded with violence to a perceived slight but Rimbu analysed the incident in a manner that removed the slight, Michael's and Rimbu's heads can simply be seen to fit different hats: the hothead warrior's in the first case, the dispute-mediating big man's in the second.

If emotions are more than 'pragmatic acts and communicative performances', and more than just forms of discourse exchanging cultural meaning, they are also more than cognitions, or culturally informed interpretations (Lyon 1995: 247). Philosophers such as Nussbaum and Prinz and neuroscientists such as Damasio have already pointed to the importance of emotions for our well-being. In the next section I turn to an examination of the Kewa emotional landscape and ask, following Rosaldo (1984: 146), 'Where is the deepest sense of Kewa self located?'

Emotions and the Kewa Self

I want to identify two referents for the word 'emotion': the analytic category or concept to be theorized, and the ethnographic description of emotions as felt and expressed. When I consider emotion as an analytic category I make no attempt to theorize it as a functionalist one, designed to replace another such category as an explanation for a particular cultural group's mode of understanding and expressing its distinctiveness. Thus the chapter is not about one big complex of emotions, such as love or fear, that can be shown to play a significant role in the determining structure of people's culture or identity. My intention is at the same time more general and more particular: particular because I look at the minutiae of everyday emotions, and general because I argue that at their small-scale level emotions are always and everywhere active in the construction of the lived world. *inteeeisrity?*

By 'emotions as felt and expressed' I intend to signal an interest in the 'innerliness' of emotions, how they affect, impinge on and motivate the actor or agent. Physicalists and cultural constructivists alike have neglected this aspect of inwardness or innerliness. Cultural constructionists in particular cannot conceive of emotion without an immediate external referent. In their theorization, emotion must be relative to another before it can be treated as culturally constructed and concerned with cognition, meaning and communication (Lyon 1995). Yet not all emotions experienced are 'relative to another' in an obvious or direct way. My account of resentment experienced 'as an arrow to the heart' develops, in a provisional way, an understanding of this sort of 'innerliness'.

This is not to suggest that I do not consider emotions as feelings that unite or exist between persons. It is simply that here I am more interested in the aspect of people's concerns about their own feelings as mood-inducing action-motivators, and as evaluators, diagnosticians and interpreters of social standing. Thus I do not discuss altruistic feelings of love or other sentiments that may be analysed as performing functionalist roles in society, for instance by working towards stability, equilibrium, conflict resolution, and generally towards social reproduction and 'the common good'. In their emotion-driven actions people may perform all these things, but still nurse a feeling of personal hurt and resentment. My focus is on how feelings spring from the needs of the inner self or the social self, but always from the perspective of that self, especially in contexts where people feel hurt or slighted (see Nussbaum's (2001) insistence that my emotions focus on *my* goals). My argument is that perceived slights are experienced 'as arrows to the heart', not as breaches of norms and rules enjoined by kinship structures or political stratification. The hurt felt at not being accorded respect is personal. What responds to the slight is not the knowledge that 'brothers should not be treated this way', or that ego should be accorded the respect attached to a specific role (as elder, wife, big man, brother, father, mother). Rather, what responds is one's *amour-propre*, in the form of a feeling of personal slight. 'Lack of respect' is recognized and described, physically and emotionally, as a deep personal injury, not as a cerebral realization that some rule has been broken. The perceived damage to one's own social worth as a person is what drives the outraged feeling to leap out of the body and demand restitution.

The power of emotions in this society is openly acknowledged. They determine people's movements and place of residence, the shape of the village itself and its pulsating character. Rather than subordinate emotions to something called 'reason' (*kone*, opinion or understanding, is the nearest Kewa equivalent), people are more likely to temper their actions by taking into account the debilitating effect of some emotions, if unleashed, on other emotions. Expression of emotions and being swayed by emotions is not considered a sign of weakness but a sign of strength. Or it may be truer to say that it is good to be overcome by certain emotions that weaken one's resolve, because it reinforces the moral basis of humanity. This attitude may not be extended to all emotions. Sexual love is considered weakening and a man can be enfeebled and be brought close to death – or at best lose his mind – if he indulges in too much sexual activity. Having many children may serve as evidence that a man is mad. Furthermore, it is said that if a husband shows his wife love (in the form of indulgence) it could make her lazy and lead to insubordination. If sexual love is in a different category from other emotions, it is also the one that gives rise to most resentment, as examples show. Rather than argue that Kewa consider the expression of emotions and being swayed by emotions as a sign of strength, it may be more accurate to suggest that they treat emotions as legitimate sources and causes of action.

For the argument of this chapter, the most pertinent connections to emerge from the ethnographic vignettes were those between emotions and a person's self-image. While people's emotions did not rebel against wasted journeys and uneconomic use of time, they protested when such failed arrangements suggested lack of respect for the person thus let down; the emotional use of time was more compelling than its economic use. Emotions can show a person's spirited independence, as when Liame refused to restrict herself to women's work but went out hunting for herself when her husband slighted her by withholding game from her. Her action was a sort of *rawa*, competitive and destructive exchange practised by men in a payback spirit. Emotions can also be manipulated, used to put people in their place, as when a person is shamed in public. In such a case, awareness of being wrong deprives a person of the power of speech and she (or he) 'hangs her head'. While people may manipulate the emotions of others, they also use their own emotions to account for actions that may additionally have other pragmatic or political motives. It was not clear, for instance, when Wata was leaving the settlement and Rimbu called her back because he was moved by her sentiments, who was manipulating whom and who was being pragmatic.

A brief consideration of the occasions when people are overcome by emotion will highlight the connection with the moral basis of humanity. Grief at funerals is the most striking example. Dirges accompany the dead (or dying) on their journey, displaying in their exhibition of strong emotion the value of the departing person. The visible outlay of emotion becomes accrued as value to the mourner's own social personhood. Others remember it and allow it to affect their own emotions and influence their decisions, as was seen in Wata's case. Wata's mourning of Wapa's death is almost a text book demonstration of the moral law as outlined by Kant. Being a newcomer, Wata was not linked to Wapa by old ties of affection. But she knew how to behave with respect and dignity. Her own self-respect, as a responsible person who does not act merely out of self-conceit and self-love, was the font of her respect for the moral law to which she must subject herself in order to maintain this self-image. This subjection, originating in self-respect, was in effect the subjection of herself to her own self, as a free self. Thus the feeling she experienced as a mourner, who knew and acted upon the proper way to behave, was a feeling for the law as both sign and origin of her own dignity.[6] Heidegger (1988: 135) paraphrases Kant in a sentence that captures the quintessential Kewa concern with respect for the self: 'Respect is the mode of the ego's being-with-itself [...] according to which it does not disparage the hero in its soul.' Resentment follows if this respect and dignity are not acknowledged, as I discuss below.

In her analysis of Ilongot emotions, Rosaldo (1984: 146) locates the deepest sense of the Ilongot self in a set of actions that display the 'energy' or 'anger' that gives shape to all healthy human hearts. Ilongot are 'autonomous and equal members of a group' who do not oppose 'self' and 'person' in separate public and private domains, thus their actions do not separate the individual from the group (Rosaldo 1984: 147). While Kewa exhibit a similar healthy energy and anger in their demands to be treated with respect as persons, their appeals to be acknowledged as persons worthy of respect often mean that they must shape their prestigious selves, or worthy selves, *against* others. This by no means inhibits them from claiming authenticity for their actions, as being correct interpretations of cultural practices. As the ethnography demonstrates, all demands or appeals for recognition of one's worth are tied to such claims to authenticity.

On a similar quest as Rosaldo, Lutz (1985: 39) considers the salience or resonance of particular 'emotion' words within the knowledge system of the Ifaluk. By contrast, I have given prominence to expressions that stamped themselves on my memory as I observed and interacted with the Kewa. Even if Kewa do not use the expression 'an arrow to the heart' to describe an action that wounded their self-esteem, the English expression came forcefully to mind when I looked at their faces and listened to their voices and read their body language. Other regular words for culturally salient emotions are well recorded: anger is *rono*, grief is *yara*, shame is *yala*. These words, which are often on people's lips, can be said to 'link characteristics of persons to situational and social-moral considerations', as Lutz (1985: 68) has argued for the Ifaluk. Does it follow from this that '[t]he traits of a good person are those that create valued emotions in others and otherwise serve social ends' (Lutz 1985: 68), and, by corollary, that the emotions are not the private property of the self? Lutz relies for this conclusion on linguistic evidence, which links emotion words, and plural pronouns that imply interconnectedness of self and other (Lutz 1985: 44), to the allocentric nature of morality. Kewa also use dual and plural pronouns which work on a nuanced register of inclusion and exclusion.

Saa, 'you and I', excludes the others in whose presence we are speaking, yet does not unite us, while *naa*, 'we', is inclusive but excludes others elsewhere – or, when followed by a clan name, excludes all non-clan members. In the Kewa case, then, the presence of plural nouns is not evidence that the emotions are not the private property of the self.

Kewa ethnography is similarly unable to give a straightforward answer to the question whether 'the traits of a good person are those that create valued emotions in others and otherwise serve social ends' (Lutz 1985: 68). My examination of Kant's moral law revealed a different understanding of moral action, as starting from the self and self-respect. As discussed earlier, all Kewa claim that the emotions on which they act reflect cultural values that serve social ends; but their specific actions diverge. Does that mean that Kewa simply fit the world to their mental attitude, as Griffiths (2003) would have it? I would argue instead that through her emotions a person attempts to understand the world and others, and to convince others that hers is a true understanding of the world. There is room here for negotiation, but my emotions pursue my own goals, are my property and inward, though they incorporate external objects in the scheme of my goals. As Nussbaum (2001: 49) puts it, emotions 'view the world from the point of view of my own scheme of goals and projects, the things to which I attach value in a conception of what it is for me to live well.' With such a focus, I am bound to become resentful when I remain unacknowledged; or, in Heidegger's (1988: 135) words, when the hero in my soul is disparaged.

Resentment

As my ethnographic account turned into longer, coherent anecdotes, one emotion emerged as the locus of the deepest sense of Kewa self. This was resentment.[7] Rero's attack on Yadi, Liame's hunting trip, Rarapalu's desertion, Rika's bitter outbursts, all were attempts to compel another person to reflect back the desired personhood.

In their work in Hagen in the Highlands of Papua New Guinea, Andrew Strathern and Marilyn Strathern report on a similar emotion, called *popokl*. *Popokl* is defined as frustration, helpless anger, desire for revenge; it can weaken a man and leave him prey to sickness (A. Strathern 1971: 77). Just as with Kewa resentment, *popokl* can be lethal if concealed, and must be expressed in order to gain redress (Strathern and Stewart 2000: 154). Marilyn Strathern (1972) records its presence especially in marital relations. As resentment (M. Strathern 1972: 96, 131), vengeance anger and protest anger, *popokl* results from neglect and thwart (M. Strathern 1972: 145, 308). It can lead to sickness or revenge, but may also 'contain an appeal that the relationship be restored to one of reciprocity' (M. Strathern 1972: 309). The fact that women 'are said to die with *popokl* in their hearts' (M. Strathern 1972: 143) can be read as an acknowledgement that women never feel fulfilled.

Kewa resentment at not being treated with respect was always explained in terms of some act of omission or commission ('my husband put the coffee bags in her room, not mine'), not just in terms of perceived feelings ('he never shows me affection'). Whether expression of resentment has social support cannot be determined at the outset, without investigation of the specific case. Schieffelin (1985: 179) observes for the Kaluli that grief has social support whereas shame does not. In the case of the Kewa it is necessary to distinguish between different kinds of grief. Only grief for a death enjoys complete social support; but even this grief is not a pure feeling of bereavement, unalloyed by other feelings that concern one's own personhood, such as anger, resentment and fear. The sorrow expressed by the woman who was neglected by her husband did not draw sympathy, nor enjoy social support. Rarapalu alienated potential support because of her own personality, but also because of the attitude that marital differences were the affair of the couple. To some extent, my ethnography dissolves the analytic distinction between emotional response, such as sympathy, and predetermined norms, suggesting instead that social and moral norms are manipulated labels that are no less liable than personal responses to be influenced by feelings and perceptions.

The primary feeling on which most studies focus is anger. Prinz (2003: 72) argues that anger is 'an evaluative judgement that construes an event as an offence'. What he means is that there are not two moments and two judgements, the experience and evaluation of an event followed by an emotion which judges that event to be an offence. Emotions are rather 'embodied appraisals' (Prinz 2003: 79–80). Solomon stretches the event further, arguing that anger '*is* the interpretation plus the view of a cause ... and consequent behaviour' (Solomon 1984: 249, original emphasis). He stresses that anger is an interpretation of the world, not of a feeling, though a feeling may also be present. For him, anger is not an inner phenomenon so much as a way of being-in-the-world, a relation to one's situation, the experience of interpreting the world in a particular way. Moreover, it is essentially a *judgemental* emotion, a perception of an offence (as Aristotle argued in *Rhetoric*). It involves the concept of blame, thus to express anger is at the same time to make an indictment (Solomon 1984: 250). For Solomon, the evaluations involved in making the indictment are learned. This is the requirement of the cognitive theory of emotions, which takes emotions to be composed by concepts, perceptions, judgements and beliefs. As these cognitions are learned, they are also taken to be public and not private phenomena.[8]

Resentment is close to anger, but it differs from it in being specifically concerned with perceptions pertaining to one's sense of self. The examples of resentment in the ethnography are responses to real situations in which Kewa persons felt unappreciated and disadvantaged, at risk of losing respect and damaging their position in society (this reveals an element of fear; see note 5). Is resentment an interpretation of the world in the way that Solomon and Prinz have argued for anger? It certainly interprets an act of omission or commission as being injurious to oneself. Thus the concern is not with the relationship in general, which for Lutz determines that emotions are social rather than personal, but with how oneself was constructed in that relationship. While it is true that among the Kewa resentment is a judgemental emotion which is on the lookout for a slight or an offence, it is also experienced as deep personal pain. In so far as emotions have the power to elicit comparable ones (see, for example, how Wata's sorrow moved Rimbu), they are also actions. They are actions *as* emotions, because they have the capacity to move others, not only as interpretations of meanings of social events.

Conclusion

I have argued that the most commonly encountered emotional response in the ethnographic vignettes presented here is that of resentment. People feel resentment at being slighted, cheated, deceived, exploited, singled out for blame, prevented from participating equally in distributions and more generally from exercising a controlling influence over affairs that concern them. The cumulative effect of such perceived slights is the feeling that respect has been withheld and one's opinions have been ignored. This is experienced as an arrow to the heart and draws an immediate response, often violent and resulting in considerable physical injury. Resentment is such a strong feeling that if left unexpressed it can kill the person who has caused it. Everybody is constantly on the lookout for possible neglect, lack of appreciation, or offences against one's person. As expected, resentment is more likely to be experienced by those in a politically weak position, and because of its potentially lethal consequences big men are especially wary of giving rise to such a feeling (A. Strathern 1971: 77). In a limited sense, resentment might be called the weak person's witchcraft, or a weapon of the weak. Local concepts of male egalitarianism and what is due to a person (whether male or female) provide a powerful incentive for such fears, keeping in check more open expressions of contempt and disdain.

The insight with which I conclude after the analysis of Kewa emotion in this chapter is something like this: it is not so much that resentment is the emotion that defines the structure of people's culture and identity, as that it is the mode of constructing the self everywhere; it is a manifestation of what Kant has described as respect for the self as the origin for respect for the law, which shrinks from disparaging the hero in one's soul. Since my emotions view the world from the perspective of my goals and projects, it is not strange that I should become resentful when my goals do not achieve their ends. Resentment is the feeling of not being acknowledged. What gives rise to the feeling, as action, is the (psychological) need for such acknowledgment in order to flourish as a person. Elicitation is the strategy for drawing forth such acknowledgment; it is based on negotiation and a willingness to compromise.

How is my argument different from that of the cognitivists and the cultural constructionists? My ethnography highlights the multiple input from emotions in people's everyday lives: they discover meaning, they interpret situations and the intentions and emotions of others, they act as appraisals and judgements, and without them communication would be impossible. But passions and inwardness cannot be left out. Emotions make these links between the self and others because they are part of our very selves, not simply constructs of social conventions. Had they been such conventions, what culture or society constructed my emotions when I understood the Kewa, theirs or mine? Lutz (1985: 69) writes that psychology, like anthropology, is 'a culturally constituted enterprise', articulating particular psychologies with other aspects of culture. Yet the basis of my understanding of the Kewa as persons and as human beings did not follow on a prior understanding of other aspects of their culture. I was a cultural outsider, but my own emotions made my understanding of the Kewa possible. This is what gives this chapter its dual character: it describes the generation of ethnographic knowledge through an understanding of the role of emotions in social dynamics, and simultaneously shows how emotions participate in the local production of cultural knowledge. Furthermore, my emotions had acted as Kantian judgements, not only helping me understand the Kewa but also creating links from emotion to empathy and morality. This would have been possible only if my own emotions were at the same time feelings and cognitions.[9]

Notes

1. This section is adapted from Josephides n.d.

2. These questions are discussed at length in Josephides 1998.

3. Griffiths cites Sartre (1962) on emotions as 'a form of bad faith, in which people reject reality out of "mental weakness"' (Griffiths 2003: 60). Emotions are intrinsically pathological, Sartre claims; they alter the perception of reality and are 'used to make our pretences real to ourselves and to others' (Griffiths 2003: 60). Griffiths is thus disposed to understand emotions as self-serving and Machiavellian, interpreted in any way that suits the agent. This Machiavellian emotional intelligence shows 'an evolved sensitivity to strategically significant aspects of the organism's social context' (Griffiths 2003: 59).

4. My reading of Kant is filtered through Heidegger (1988).

5. Among others, see Shweder and LeVine (1984); Lutz (1985); White and Kirkpatrick (1985); Lutz and White (1986); Lutz (1988); Myers (1988); Lutz and Abu-Lughod (1990); Wikan (1990); Schwartz, White and Lutz (1992); Shore (1993); Parish (1994); Leavitt (1996); James (1997); Reddy (1997, 1999, 2001); Overing and Passes (2000).

6. Paraphrased from Heidegger (1988: 135–6).

7. There is no single Kewa word for resentment, but this absence should not throw doubt on the presence of the emotion. Resentment is a key emotion among the Yoruba, yet the Yoruba language, so rich in vocabulary, also does not have a word for it (personal communication, Marc Schiltz). A common alternative word in Kewa is *rono* (anger). Another alternative is *ni gipia* ('I am fed up/tired of/can't be bothered with': the expression also denotes reluctance, dislike, even aversion). Kewa tend to favour understatement and a studied show of nonchalance when they are deeply affected. More commonly, people use longer descriptions or figurative expressions.

8. Solomon (2003: 13) now agrees that feelings were left out of the cognitive account.

9. Like Solomon (2003: 2), I do not suggest that emotions are necessarily conscious – or even more strongly, 'self-conscious – reflective, articulate judgements'.

References

Damasio, A. (1994), *Descartes' Error: Emotion, Reason, and the Human Brain*, New York: Putnam.

—— (1999), *The Feeling of What Happens: Body and Emotion in the Making of Consciousness*, London: William Heinemann.

Griffiths, P. E. (2003), 'Basic Emotions, Complex Emotions, Machiavellian Emotions', in A. Hatzimoysis (ed.), *Philosophy and the Emotions*, Cambridge: Cambridge University Press.

Heidegger, M. (1988 [1982]), *The Basic Problems of Phenomenology*, translation, introduction and lexicon by Albert Hofstadter, revised edn, Bloomington, IN: Indiana University Press.

James, W. (1997), 'The Names of Fear: Memory, History, and the Ethnography of Feeling Among Uduk Refugees, *Journal of the Royal Anthropological Institute* (NS) 3 (1): 115–31.

Josephides, L. (1985), *The Production of Inequality*, London: Tavistock.

—— (1998), 'Biographies of Social Action: Excessive Portraits', in V. Keck (ed.), *Common Worlds and Single Lives: Constituting Knowledge in Pacific Societies*, Oxford: Berg.

—— (2001), 'Straight Talk, Hidden Talk, and Modernity: Shifts in Discourse Strategies in Highland New Guinea', in J. Hendry and C. W. Watson (eds), *The Anthropology of Indirect Communication*, London: Routledge.

—— (2003a) 'Being There: The Magic of Presence of the Metaphysics of Morality', in P. Caplan (ed.), *The Ethics of Anthropology: Debates and Dilemmas*, London: Routledge.

—— (2003b), 'The Rights of Being Human', in R. Wilson and J. Mitchell (eds), *Human Rights in Global Perspective: Anthropological Studies in Rights, Claims and Entitlements*, London: Routledge.

—— n.d., 'Elicitations: From Narratives of Self to Ethnographic Mimesis', unpublished manuscript.

Kant, I. (1960), *Religion within the Limits of Reason Alone*, New York and London: Harper and Row.

Leavitt, J. (1996), 'Meaning and Feeling in the Anthropology of Emotions', *American Ethnologist* 23 (3): 514–39.

Lutz, C. (1985), 'Ethnopsychology Compared to What? Explaining Behaviour and Consciousness among the Ifaluk', in G. M. White and J. Kirkpatrick (eds), *Person, Self, and Experience: Exploring Pacific Ethnopsychologies*, Berkeley, LA: University of California Press.

—— (1988), *Unnatural Emotions: Everyday Sentiments on a Micronesian Atoll and their Challenge to Western Theory*, Chicago and London: University of Chicago Press.

—— and Abu-Lughod, L. (eds) (1990), *Language and the Politics of Emotion*, Cambridge: Cambridge University Press.

—— and White, G. M. (1986), 'The Anthropology of Emotions', *Annual Reviews of Anthropology* 15: 405–36.

Lyon, M. L. (1995), 'Missing Emotion: the Limitations of Cultural Constructionism in the Study of Emotion', *Cultural Anthropology* 10 (2): 244–63.

Myers, F. R. (1988), 'The Logic and Meaning of Anger among Pintupi Aborigines', *Man* 23 (3): 589–610.

Nussbaum, M. (2001), *Upheavals of Thought: the Intelligence of Emotions*, Cambridge: Cambridge University Press.

Overing, J. and Passes, A. (eds) (2000), *The Anthropology of Love and Anger: The Aesthetics of Conviviality in Native Amazonia*, London: Routledge.

Parish, S. M. (1994), *Moral Knowing in a Hindu Sacred City: An Exploration of Mind, Emotion and Self*, New York: Columbia University Press.

Prinz, J. (2003), 'Emotion, Psychosemantics, and Embodied Appraisals', in A. Hatzimoysis (ed.), *Philosophy and the Emotions*, Cambridge: Cambridge University Press.

Reddy, W. M. (1997), 'Against constructionism: The Historical Ethnography of Emotions', *Current Anthropology* 38 (3): 327–51.

—— (1999), 'Emotional liberty: Politics and History in the Anthropology of Emotions, *Cultural Anthropology* 14 (2): 256–88.

—— (2001), *The Navigation of Feeling: A Framework for the History of Emotions*, Cambridge University Press.

Roberts, R. C. (2003), *Emotions: An Essay in Aid of Moral Psychology*, Cambridge: Cambridge University Press.

Rosaldo, M. Z. (1984), 'Toward an Anthropology of Self and Feeling', in R. A.

Shweder and R. A. LeVine (eds), *Culture Theory: Essay on Mind, Self, Emotion*, Cambridge: Cambridge University Press.

Sartre, J-P. (1962), *Sketch for a Theory of the Emotions*, trans. P. Mairet. London: Methuen.

Schieffelin, E. L. (1985) 'Anger, Grief, and Shame: Toward a Kaluli Ethnopsychology', in G. M. White and J. Kirkpatrick (eds), *Person, Self, and Experience: Exploring Pacific Ethnopsychologies*, Berkeley, CA: University of California Press.

Schwartz, T., White, G. M. and Lutz, C. (eds) (1992), *New Directions in Psychological Anthropology*, Cambridge: Cambridge University Press.

Shore, B. (1993), 'Emotion: Culture, Psychology, Being', *Ethos* 21: 357–63.

Shweder, R. and LeVine, R. (eds) (1984), *Culture Theory: Essays on Mind, Self, and Emotion*, Cambridge: Cambridge University Press.

Solomon, R. C. (1984) 'Getting Angry: The Jamesian Theory of Emotion in Anthropology', in R. A. Shweder and R. A. LeVine (eds), *Culture Theory: Essay on Mind, Self, Emotion*, Cambridge: Cambridge University Press.

—— (2003) 'Emotions, Thoughts and Feelings: What is a "Cognitive Theory" of the Emotions and does it Neglect Affectivity?', in A. Hatzimoysis (ed.), *Philosophy and the Emotions*, Cambridge: Cambridge University Press.

Strathern, A. (1971), *The Rope of Moka*, Cambridge: Cambridge University Press.

—— and Stewart, P. J. (2000), *Arrow Talk: Transaction, Transition and Contradiction in New Guinea Highlands History*, Kent, OH: Kent State University Press.

Strathern, M. (1972), *Women in Between*, London and New York: Seminar Press.

White, G. M. and Kirkpatrick, J. (eds) (1985), *Person, Self, and Experience: Exploring Pacific Ethnopsychologies*, Berkeley, CA: University of California Press.

Wikan, U. (1990), *Managing Turbulent Hearts: A Balinese Formula for Living*, Chicago: University of Chicago Press.

Wollheim, R. (1999), *On the Emotions*, New Haven, CT: Yale University Press.

–5–

Emotion, Memory and Religious Rituals: An Assessment of Two Theories

Harvey Whitehouse

Introduction

In order for rituals to be passed on from one generation to the next, the procedures they entail must be successfully remembered, and at least some participants in the tradition must be motivated to continue carrying them out. But how are these conditions satisfied? Recent research points to the presence of two modes of transmission that are caused by alternative patterns of remembering, thinking and emotional arousal. Investigation of these is currently focused around two closely related theories, which consider, respectively, the frequency with which rituals are performed (Whitehouse 1992, 1995, 2000, 2004) and the forms they take (McCauley and Lawson 2002). Both theories propose that variations in levels of emotional arousal are crucial in explaining the transmission of religious rituals. This chapter assesses some key features of the two theories and examines their scope of application.

Ritual and Emotion: What Exactly are We Talking About?

To talk about the role of emotion in the transmission of rituals presupposes a notion of what ritual is – what defines it as a distinctive phenomenon or domain. In a brilliant and path-breaking treatise on the nature of ritualization, Humphrey and Laidlaw (1994) have argued that rituals are actions that lack intrinsic intentional meaning. Whereas a non-ritual action is understood to be the expression of intentional states arising from the performing agent, rituals simply cannot be understood that way – and might in fact be attributed any of a great range of possible meanings, or no meaning at all. Ritual meaning is not intrinsic to the ritual actions themselves. This is an insight that Bloch (2004) has more recently embraced, and extended to incorporate theoretical developments in cognitive psychology, concerning the way people normally attribute intentions to agents. When people observe an action, they naturally make assumptions about the intentions of the actor. The psychological mechanisms involved in this process are commonly referred to as 'mind-reading' or 'theory of mind' capacities.[1]

Confronted with ritualized behaviours, however, these mechanisms run into difficulties (see Bloch 2004). Clearly the ritual actor is not constructing his or her movements and utterances with reference to internally generated intentional states, but rather is rehearsing stereotyped procedures that have been fixed by others in advance. The hunt for intentional meaning is therefore deflected. Are the participants to look for the intentional origins of the ritual action in the minds of previous performers? If so, how far back should they go; to their elders and ritual experts, to mythical ancestors, to messianic founders, or to whom? Much may depend on what sources of authoritative interpretation are available to the participants. Are these rituals performed as part of a tradition that provides a standard explication of its practices, or are people required to work out these unspoken meanings for themselves? If they are left to their own devices in the search for meaning, then what pressures (if any) are brought to bear on the exercise of their imaginations? Confronted with the challenges of exegetical interpretation, mind-reading mechanisms may simply give up the ghost. After all, some rituals, as any anthropologist can attest, seem to attract no exegesis at all, and the eager researcher is fobbed off with statements such as 'that's just how we do it (end of story)'.

The different ways in which people respond to problems of ritual interpretation would seem to be influenced decisively by a small number of variables, of which one of the most prominent is emotional arousal. But before we can address that issue, we first we have to sort out another can of worms: what is 'emotional arousal'?

In talking about emotional arousal, as a general human capacity, just as when discussing the role of 'theory of mind' mechanisms in ritualization, my aim is to mark off features of human thought and behaviour that can be abstracted from most of the culturally particular circumstances of their activation. This chapter is concerned with emotion in a way that might seem odd to many students of culture. For social and cultural anthropologists in particular, a primary focus of interest is the way emotions are 'culturally constructed' or 'mediated' through social interactions. Such scholars seldom ask how universal features of the human emotional system might help to explain cultural transmission, but more typically they ask how locally distinctive sociocultural dynamics might 'shape' (and might in turn be 'shaped by') distinctive emotional landscapes.[2] This latter strategy is entirely appropriate, of course. It is partly thanks to fine-grained ethnographic research that we now know as much as we do about variations in human emotional experience and expression, and their close connections with locally variable (and sometimes rapidly transforming) institutional conditions. We need to be able to characterize more precisely the limits of variation in emotional experience, and we should strive to take this project further still. It is perfectly possible, for instance, that the grieving patterns of Spanish gypsies (Gay y Blasco, Chapter 9 in this volume) are adopted by other marginalized populations, with similar sociopolitical consequences, or that the emotional strategies of Sudeten Germans described by Svašek (Chapter 11 in this volume) are adopted by other populations forcibly displaced from their homelands. To develop such hypotheses persuasively, however, would require more than just inspiring metaphor and thematic association. It would require a precise rendering of the hypotheses and of the conditions under which they might be falsified. That is a challenge that might perhaps be taken up by others. My objective in this chapter is rather different.

I am not concerned here with what is locally distinctive about emotional expression and meaning. While it is clear that parts of the human emotional repertoire can be suppressed or exaggerated by locally distinctive ecology, it seems equally clear that the repertoire itself, like the limitations of the human vocal range, is much the same in humans everywhere. True, the emotional tone of certain forms of gift exchange in the New Guinea village where I conducted fieldwork were initially hard for me to grasp (see Whitehouse 1995), just as the diphthongs of Norwegian are difficult for an English speaker to master, but sentiments are forged within a biologically constrained space of emotional possibilities, just as my utterances (like those of Scandinavians) are located within the space afforded by a limited set of 'cardinal vowels'. Extreme relativism on this topic, as espoused for instance by Harré (1986), Heelas (1986) and Lutz (1988), has been systematically debunked by more rigorous scientific cross-cultural research on emotions (e.g. Ekman 1989; Brown 1991; Shaver, Wu and Schwartz 1992). But even in the absence of such fine-grained empirical work, the relativist position must blind itself to the high degree of mutual intelligibility of core emotions (such as love, anger, happiness and sadness) across cultures, and to global commonalities in the way these emotions are inscribed in people's facial expressions. Still, if the emotional repertoire is *roughly* the same for humans everywhere, then how might this impact on other aspects of human thinking and behaviour, for instance a domain like 'ritual', that are also cross-culturally recurrent? The question *complements* rather than conflicts with those being asked in other chapters of this book.

Arousal and the Frequency Hypothesis

Some human learning strategies are common to a wide range of complex animals. This has been shown particularly clearly in the study of certain aspects of memory. For instance, mammalian brains depend heavily on two methods for reinforcing inputs, so that they can be recalled in future. One of these is repetition. Humans, in common with many other animals, learn particular skills (from walking and running to finding food and recognizing enemies) through *practice*, that is by repeating particular patterns of behaviour in response to regularized cues. This kind of rehearsal is vital to what psychologists sometimes call 'procedural learning' (following Cohen and Squire 1980) – that is, the embodied skills that eventually become second nature to us, in the sense that we can carry them out without consciously representing the knowledge we have acquired. An obvious example to be observed in many contemporary human environments would be the skill required to ride a bicycle. Much of the knowledge involved in peddling, balancing, steering and braking is activated implicitly, with little or no need for conscious control. But repetition also underpins certain forms of learning at the level of explicit (that is, statable) cognition. Humans are capable of learning large amounts of explicit information (what we might refer to as 'general knowledge') simply by being exposed to it enough times. Knowledge of this kind, often referred to by psychologists as 'semantic memory' (following Tulving 1972), can be quite easily expressed in words; we can consciously compare the terrain of separate geographical regions, for instance, or draw parallels between road maps and our aspirations for a peace process in some troubled region. But much of the information available to us in this form is not tied to a particular moment of acquisition. That is, we often cannot recall where or when we first learned a chunk of semantic knowledge, such as the shape of our country or the words of our national anthem.

The other main way of reinforcing inputs, and thus of acquiring new information, depends upon elevated emotional arousal. Again, versions of this general strategy are adopted by a wide range of complex organisms. If a novel input is associated with sufficiently heightened affective responses (whether of an unpleasant kind, like fear, or more positively charged, for instance in the case of ecstasy or joy) then we are likely to recall salient features of that input. In mammals at least, it seems appropriate to refer to such memory as 'episodic' (again, following Tulving 1972), in the sense that any future stimulus that sufficiently resembles the initial, highly emotional one, will activate various aspects of the original encoding experience (that is, activate recall of certain details of the original episode). Once bitten, twice shy. In humans, this kind of memory operates largely at an explicit level, enabling us to comment verbally on the details of things we have personally experienced in our lives. Not all such episodes available to self-report in this fashion are associated with strong emotions, but the general rule of thumb is that if an experience is novel and emotionally arousing, it will most likely be recalled episodically, perhaps for many years to come. Not surprisingly, we find that both of these mechanisms – repetition and arousal – are prominently deployed in processes of cultural transmission. A distinguished American neuroscientist, James L. McGaugh (2003), put it like this:

Scientific studies of memory, started only a little over a century ago, have amply confirmed the conclusion that practice makes perfect. We all know that rehearsal of information or skills creates stronger memories. Much education is, of course, based on this general principle, but there is another way to make strong memories of experiences ... [which] has been long known but only recently the subject of scientific enquiry. In medieval times, before writing was used to keep historical records, other means had to be found to maintain records of important events such as the granting of land to a township, an important wedding or negotiations between powerful families. To accomplish this, a young child about seven years old was selected, instructed to observe the proceedings carefully, and then thrown into a river. In this way, it was said, the memory of the event would be impressed on the child and the record of the event maintained for the child's lifetime ... Research from many laboratories has revealed that there ... [is] a promiscuous system that enabled the lasting memory of the medieval child thrown into the river. Emotional arousal activates stress hormones that, in turn, stimulate a specific brain system that regulates the consolidation of recently acquired information to other brain regions. (McGaugh 2003: ix–x)

In the domain of ritual, repetition and arousal can both play a very prominent role. In the world's religious traditions, a general bifurcation has long been observed such that rituals tend to be either highly repetitive (high-frequency) or relatively rare but intensely emotional (high-arousal). One of the earliest attempts to build a systematic body of theory around this empirical observation is to be found in Max Weber's (1930) contrast between routinized and 'charismatic' forms of religiosity, but many other dichotomous theories have since been developed along similar lines (e.g. Benedict 1935; Goody 1968; Gellner 1969, 1986; Barth 1990).[3] The main reason for the bifurcation of ritual types appears to be that repetition and arousal are a bit like oil and water, they do not mix. A substantially novel event is by definition very low in frequency and, as noted above, if the event has a strong enough emotional charge, then it is likely to persist in episodic memory. For instance, people generally remember such things as their first kiss, the day war broke out, or the first time they saw a complete solar eclipse. Those experiences have a special emotional intensity and distinctiveness. But if those experiences are repeated very frequently they are likely to *lose* these qualities. Many people enjoy kissing, but if you kiss the same person every day it is not quite the same as kissing them for the first time, or after a substantial period apart. Likewise, if your country declared war every week, or if solar eclipses were a daily occurrence, the emotional intensity of these experiences would be greatly reduced. In other words, as a general rule of thumb, *frequency varies inversely with arousal.*

Low-frequency rituals are usually very emotional events. Rites of passage furnish a particularly rich source of illustrations. For groups of novices undergoing initiation rituals the experience is likely to be highly arousing. Beatings, scarification and other forms of physical torture are common features of such rituals, and often these physical shocks are linked with various kinds of psychologically arduous ordeals. By contrast, high-frequency rituals are typically much lower in emotional intensity. Examples of highly routinized patterns of ritual behaviour are to be found in all the world religions and most regionally dispersed traditions as well. Such rituals are often richly coloured by emotions but they seldom elicit the extremes of emotion we find in initiation rites. Rare exceptions might include routinized rituals that involve life-threatening behaviour (e.g. handling of poisonous snakes), although we have no clear evidence that arousal levels do not diminish over time among participants in such rituals. It is similarly possible that the somewhat exuberant services of many Evangelical Christian churches deliver declining levels of arousal over time (old hands experiencing lower intensities of excitement than new recruits), but this has yet to be properly tested. What does appear to be clear from the ethnographic record is that high-frequency rituals deliver relatively lower levels of arousal, in general, than low-frequency rituals (see Whitehouse and Laidlaw 2004), and many high-frequency rituals elicit such low levels of emotional stimulation that they become frankly tedious, and so may impact negatively on morale and motivation among religious adherents (see Whitehouse 2000).

These comments, however, potentially raise a clamour of questions. How do we distinguish high and low frequency or high and low levels of arousal? Even if we grant that such distinctions can be made and that the postulated bifurcation is 'out there' in the real world of religious ritual practices, then *why* is it there? What are the mechanisms that have brought it about? To say that we have two basic strategies for memory enhancement – repetition and arousal – is not sufficient to explain why rituals should be either highly routinized or emotionally exciting. After all, rituals are often quite simple clusters of procedures that could, surely, be quite easily remembered without the need of any special mnemonic tricks. Let us take these points in turn.

Distinguishing high and low frequency in relation to ritual performances raises the question, 'frequency for whom?' For a religious leader who presides over the rituals of a substantial community, participation in rites of passage may be a very frequent experience. Rites of passage are generally only low in frequency for the patients of those rituals: the novices being initiated, the bride and groom being joined in wedlock, and so on. And the mnemonic effects on the patients of some rites of passage can range from negligible (e.g. for infants undergoing a naming ceremony) to non-existent (e.g. for corpses at funerals). Consequently, not all rites of passage are low in frequency or high in arousal for all or even some participants. The point, then, is that it is not rituals *per se* that are low or high in arousal, but rather the experiences that particular categories of people have of those rituals. For certain categories of persons some specifiable types of ritual experiences are low in frequency, and the general rule of thumb is that such experiences will be accompanied by exceptionally high levels of arousal. This largely holds true, not only for the conscious patients of rites of passage, but also for participants in rituals of all types that are rarely performed in the society or religious tradition as a whole. As

Atran (2002: 158) has pointed out, it is extremely difficult to find examples of rituals that are low in frequency for a significant category of persons and yet are not also exceptionally emotional experiences for those persons.

Of course terms like 'low' and 'high' are approximate rather than precise measures. We are dealing here with relative rather than absolute levels of arousal and frequency. Very few people can recall the surface areas of Australia and England, but they know perfectly well that Australia is the larger of the two countries.[4] Similarly, we do not need to be able to measure precisely the levels of stress experienced by novices in New Guinea initiation rites to realize that the tortures they endure are vastly more arousing than people's experiences of routinized worship in a temple, mosque or church.[5] We could perhaps be a little more precise about what constitutes high or low frequency, however. Certainly, a ritual that is performed more frequently than once a month would qualify as relatively high in frequency, whereas a ritual that occurs no more frequently than once a year would be relatively low in frequency. The key point is that, in general, ritual cycles in any given ritual tradition tend to cluster around the relatively high-frequency and/or the relatively low-frequency ends of this spectrum. That is, most rituals occur either in cycles of less than a week or in cycles of more than eleven months. Rituals of intermediate frequency are much less common. And as frequency drops, so emotional arousal tends to rise. Annual rituals are often quite highly arousing – but rituals experienced only once in a lifetime tend to carry an extremely powerful emotional 'punch', and to have a lasting impact on our lives. These general arguments (first set out in Whitehouse 1992) have come to be known as the 'ritual frequency hypothesis'.

According to the ritual frequency hypothesis, most rituals are either relatively low in frequency and high in arousal or relatively high in frequency and low in arousal. But why? To put it more concretely, why is it that when people are initiated into the religious cults of aboriginal Australia, tribal Africa, Amazonia, Melanesia and many other traditions (including many of the esoteric cults of Europe, both ancient and modern), are they required to undergo extremely arousing (typically terrifying) experiences? Why are rarely performed rituals – the great feasts, fertility rites, millenarian vigils and so on – generally accompanied by relatively high states of emotional excitement? And, conversely, why do we find so many religious rituals around the world repeated day in and day out, or week in and week out, to the accompaniment of relatively lower levels of affective stimulation and general fanfare? In particular, why are such rituals so commonly repeated to the point of *routinization*?

It could be argued that diffusion has had a role to play in all of this. But if so it must have been a rather limited role, for we are talking about tendencies in ritual traditions distributed across all the continents over very long periods of time (see Whitehouse and Martin 2004). But whether by diffusion or independent invention (and we may be dealing with elements of both in many cases), the bifurcation of ritual forms, in terms of frequency and arousal, has not only become established around the globe, but also become *entrenched*. This entrenchment is probably best explained in terms of processes of *selection*. Certain high-frequency/low-arousal and low-frequency/high-arousal rituals are culturally fitter than those in an intermediate position.

When I first advanced this argument (Whitehouse 1992), it seemed to me that ritual procedures were more easily remembered if they were either frequently repeated or somewhat shocking and arousing, and that this in turn made it more likely that they would be transmitted in future. I have since largely abandoned this view on the grounds that frequent rituals are far more frequent than would be necessary to ensure that people will remember the procedures, and that infrequent rituals are seldom reconstructed mainly on the basis of episodic recall (for discussions of this topic see, for instance, Barth 2002; Whitehouse 2002). It seems likely, however, that variations in frequency and arousal have decisive effects on the way ritual *meaning* is constructed and transmitted, and particularly on its motivational effects.

Recall that rituals present problems for our 'theory of mind' mechanisms. Confronted with the behaviour of any kind of agent, humans naturally (and largely at a tacit, automatic level) generate inferences about the agent's intentions, but in the case of ritual actions none of these inferences is satisfactory. Plainly, the procedures carried out by the ritual actor are not his or her inventions, but originate elsewhere. The original intentions behind the procedures, however, are hard to pin down. Why does the ritual action have to be like this, rather than that? Why must a particular sequence be followed, when plenty of other sequences would be possible? Sometimes, such questions are answered by figures of authority in the religious tradition. High-frequency ritual repetition provides optimal conditions for the transmission of official exegesis of this kind. Indeed it is only in conditions of frequent rehearsal that complex orthodoxies can be transmitted at all. In practice, we find that stable, authoritative exegesis flourishes in conditions of religious routinization, where the motivation to participate in rituals depends on techniques of verbal persuasion via specialized forms of public oratory.[6] By contrast, intermediate or low-frequency speech-making is incapable of transmitting complex, interlocking religious teachings in a stable form. Nevertheless, low-frequency rituals that are also highly arousing can bring about other, equally impressive, effects.

Ritual experiences that are encoded as enduring and vivid episodic memories stimulate high rates of 'spontaneous exegetical reflection'. Again, we need to remind ourselves that rituals are psychologically rather peculiar actions. In the case of high-frequency rituals, 'theory of mind' mechanisms are activated but then effectively switched off as the actions themselves become habituated, and as a ready source of authoritative ritual exegesis is provided. Such conditions are conducive to relatively low rates of spontaneous reflection of matters of ritual meaning.[7] By contrast, low-frequency/high-arousal rituals are not subject to habituation, the conditions do not allow verbal transmission of authoritative exegesis (teachings presented at such low frequencies would be subject to massive distortion and decay), and yet the need to supply some kind of exegesis does not go away. In part, this is because one's recall for high-arousal life experiences, especially of a traumatic kind, has an intrusive and haunting quality. Even when it comes to life-changing experiences of a non-ritual kind, people frequently dwell on issues of meaning: why did this happen to me and what does it signify? Teleological reasoning, that hunts for designs in such events, no matter how apparently random, is readily activated (see Pillemer, Rinehart and White 1986). Think how much more intensive such processes become when we are dealing with ritual events: unique episodes in people's lives that we know are supposed to have meanings and designs but which remain obscure in the absence of authoritative exegesis. Ethnographic evidence suggests that these conditions are conducive to long-term rumination, and it is through these elongated processes of spontaneous reflection that the esoteric knowledge of ritual elders and experts is generated. Such religious knowledge delivers motivational effects that are at least as powerful as the kind of doctrinal knowledge acquired through processes of verbal persuasion – and may in some ways be rather more powerful, as we shall presently see.

The Ritual Form Hypothesis

In *Bringing Ritual to Mind* (2002), McCauley and Lawson set out 'the ritual form hypothesis' – a theory that explicitly builds upon what they dub the 'Whitehouse frequency hypothesis'. Like me, they argue that rituals tend to cluster around two opposing attractor positions: low-frequency/high arousal and high-frequency/low arousal. But they argue that the frequency hypothesis fails to specify the underlying *causes* of variations in performance frequency. To do that, McCauley and Lawson (2002) maintain, we need to take into account the structure or 'form' of rituals, and the roles presumed to be taken in these rituals by culturally postulated superhuman agents (hereafter referred to more economically as 'the gods').[8]

McCauley and Lawson's starting point is that rituals are *actions*, and as such they possess a distinctive structure linking agents, actions, instruments and patients into a connected whole. Imagine a waiter placing food in front of a hungry diner. Your representation of this action can be broken down into certain key elements: an agent (the waiter), an instrument or artefact (the plate of food), the action (presentation of the food) and a patient or recipient of the action (the diner). You may visualize other features of this scenario (the decor of the restaurant, the colour of the table cloth, the suit worn by the waiter, and so on), but the four elements specified above (agent, instrument, action and patient) have special importance in determining the structure of the action. A significant change to any one of these elements radically alters the nature of the action, producing new scenarios that might be either absurd (e.g. the diner presenting food to the waiter, where agent and patient roles are reversed, or the waiter presenting a plate of coal, where the instrument is substituted), or simply an altogether different kind of action (e.g. the waiter clearing the table, where the action itself is simply reversed). Religious rituals, like all other actions, involve agents, instruments, actions and patients, whose relations can be formally mapped, but here there is another factor to take into account, namely, the intervention of the gods. In religious rituals, the gods might be seen as acting through the ritual's agent, as is clearly the case in rites of ordination, in weddings and in initiations. Here, the patients of the ritual are being permanently transformed through the intervention of a deity, associated with the agent role. McCauley and Lawson (2002) refer to these as 'special agent rituals'. The gods might, however, be seen as acting through the instrument of the ritual, as for instance in a blessing where the holy water is most closely linked to the supernatural being. Or, alternatively, the gods might be associated with the patient role, as in the making of offerings and the performance of sacrificial acts. McCauley and Lawson refer to these as 'special instrument' and 'special patient' rituals respectively.

Now, according to McCauley and Lawson (2002), these differences in the way supernatural agents are implicated in religious rituals, have a series of important consequences. To simplify somewhat,[9] we can distinguish three main kinds of consequences of ritual form, concerning repeatability, reversibility and levels of sensory pageantry. Where the involvement of the gods is most closely associated with the agent role in the form of the ritual (as in 'special agent rituals') the predictions are as follows:

1. Such a ritual should not be repeatable (it should ideally be performed once only on a given patient).
2. The effects of the ritual can be 'undone' in principle through reversing rituals (where gods might again intervene in an agentive role, for instance in rites of defrocking or divorce).
3. Levels of bodily stimulation, or what McCauley and Lawson refer to as 'sensory pageantry', will be relatively high.

By contrast, where the involvement of the gods is most closely associated with either the patient or instrument role in the form of the ritual (as in 'special patient rituals' and 'special instrument rituals') it is predicted that:

1. The rituals will be repeatable (the same actions, performed with the same agents, instruments and patients, can be carried out over and over again).

2. The rituals will be irreversible (there will be no mechanism for ritually 'undoing' the effects of previous performances).
3. Levels of sensory pageantry will be relatively low.

According to McCauley and Lawson, the above considerations drive variations in frequency that the ritual frequency hypothesis *presupposes* but (on their view) is insufficient to explain. What makes a ritual low in frequency, they argue, is the especially close association between the gods and the agent position in the ritual representation system. To put it crudely, in special agent rituals the gods are in the driving seat and what the gods have accomplished is assumed to be permanent (unless or until the gods undertake to reverse the ritual's effects). By contrast, in special patient and special instrument rituals, the gods are seen as the recipients or facilitators of actions undertaken by merely human agents, whose effects are impermanent, necessitating further repetition. This, argue McCauley and Lawson, should serve to make rituals of this kind more frequent. As they put it,

> We are arguing that participants' representations of how CPS-agents ['the gods'] are implicated in their religious rituals, ultimately, determine whether or not religious rituals are repeatable as well as the mnemonic dynamics those rituals enlist. Consequently, those representations also determine the rituals' performance frequencies and their levels of sensory pageantry'. (McCauley and Lawson 2002: 43)

Assessing the Two Theories

According to McCauley and Lawson (2002), frequency is the unexplained independent variable in the Whitehouse frequency hypothesis. They argue, in short, that their ritual form hypothesis is capable of explaining the tendency for rituals to cluster around contrasting positions on the frequency scale. My own view is that the explanatory potential of the ritual form hypothesis is somewhat exaggerated in this context, and that of the ritual frequency hypothesis underestimated. Considerations of ritual form may suffice to ensure that most participants in special agent rituals assume the patient role once only, or at least very infrequently. But even if we accept that participation in special patient/instrument rituals is capable of being repeated, there is nothing in the ritual form hypothesis to explain why such rituals are typically repeated as frequently as they are. The real challenge is to explain, not repeatability, but extensive *routinization*. On this front, the ritual frequency hypothesis fares rather better than its rival. The former maintains that rituals of intermediate frequency and arousal provide inadequate foundations either for the transmission of authoritative exegesis or for the generation of spontaneous exegetical reflection. As such, unless some very special conditions apply (as outlined in the next section), such rituals will become extinct. This provides a way of explaining variations of frequency according to selectional mechanisms, which the ritual form hypothesis cannot.

The ritual form hypothesis maintains not only that form drives frequency but also that it determines relative levels of sensory pageantry. The grounds for this last claim are similar but not identical to those proposed by the frequency hypothesis. In the first place, 'sensory pageantry' is not exactly the same thing as emotional arousal (and recall that the frequency hypothesis makes claims primarily about arousal rather than sensory stimulation). An arguable merit of the McCauley–Lawson strategy is the fact that sensory pageantry is more readily accessible to empirical observation than is the internalized experience of arousal. Nevertheless, McCauley and Lawson are at times incautious in treating levels of sensory pageantry as a reliable index of emotional arousal. Some rituals stimulate a broad spectrum of sensations (sight, sounds, smell, taste, etc.) without necessarily triggering heightened emotional responses. And if sensory pageantry is to be measured in terms of intensity rather than variety, then how is that to be calibrated, even in relative rather than absolute terms? Is louder music more 'intense' than softer music, or brighter colours indicative of greater pageantry than duller ones? Again, it is difficult to map these things directly onto levels of emotional arousal. Indeed, some of the most intensely emotional rituals might be based upon the withholding of sensory stimulation rather than its intensification.

On McCauley and Lawson's view, people expect their special agent rituals to elicit higher sensory pageantry because these are rituals in which the gods are taking a leading role. Acts of the gods intuitively demand suitable fanfare, both to mark the gravity and power of the agency at work and to encourage participants to pay attention to what is happening, to take it seriously. This allegedly has a dual effect. On the one hand, it increases levels of religious motivation, by convincing people that the gods really are intervening in their lives. But McCauley and Lawson also endorse my earlier argument that heightened arousal (which on their view is occasioned by elevated sensory pageantry) helps to trigger episodic recall for the ritual procedures themselves. By making it easier for people to remember the ritual procedures, the emotionality of special agent rituals contributes to their transmissive success. Note, however, that the ritual frequency hypothesis advances a somewhat different claim with regard to the role of episodic memory in ritual transmission. Whereas some of my earlier publications proposed, as McCauley and Lawson have now also done, that episodic recall for rare, climactic rituals played an important role in the preservation of ritual procedures (e.g. Whitehouse 1992), my more recent work in this area has suggested that the ritual procedures are transmitted substantially via other mechanisms of memory, and that the importance of episodic encoding lies mainly in the production of spontaneous thinking about issues of ritual meaning. Private rumination, and the esoteric religious knowledge resulting from this, is the principal motivational engine driving subsequent transmission of low-frequency, high-arousal rituals.

Form and Frequency: Towards a Synthesis of Competing Models

The transmission of complex religious knowledge requires special supports for learning and memory – and the two most obvious supports are, as indicated at the outset, *repetition* and *arousal*. In order for a corpus of elaborate orthodox teachings to be transmitted, a regime of heavy repetition is indispensable – both in order to learn the teachings, and also in order to ensure that people continue to remember them over time, without garbling or forgetting crucial portions of their content. In a religious tradition based around rarely performed rituals, verbal transmission of authoritative exegesis and doctrine is simply not an option. But elaborate, highly motivating religious knowledge can be constructed by other means, for instance by increasing levels of emotional arousal and thus triggering elongated processes of private rumination pertaining to the significance of religious experiences. Either way, considerations of ritual form are problematized.

In the case of highly routinized rituals, the procedures often take the form of automated habits, stored in implicit, procedural memory (see above). Once this happens, conscious reflection on ritual scripts and meanings (the 'hows' and 'whys' of ritual performance) is inevitably reduced. 'Theory of mind' mechanisms can be more or less effectively bypassed, leading to a suppression of spontaneous interpretation and a greater vulnerability to any official exegesis that may be on offer. If so, we should expect other tacit mechanisms to exercise a diminishing influence, including people's intuitions about ritual form. I have elsewhere presented ethnographic evidence in support of this argument, based on my studies of absolution rites among Pomio Kivung followers in Papua New Guinea (Whitehouse 2004), and more recent experimental evidence concerning intuitive judgements of ritual form among Christians, Hindus, Jews and Muslims, points in much the same direction (Malley and Barrett 2003).

In the case of low-frequency, high-arousal rituals we are likely to get more or less the opposite effect. Here, reflection on matters of ritual procedure and meaning is driven by explicit episodic memories, and the analogical reasoning that progressively gives rise to personal exegetical insight is somewhat detached from tacit, intuitive judgements. The emphasis is on an unveiling of layers of meaning that are ever more remote from both commonsense and intuitive evaluations. In short, the kinds of intuitive judgements upon which the predictions of the ritual form hypothesis depend, may not figure at all significantly in many religious traditions. If so, does that make the McCauley–Lawson theory redundant? I do not think so.

Where the ritual form hypothesis may be more helpful is in explaining the transmission of rituals that attract neither elaborate authoritative exegesis nor high levels of 'spontaneous exegetical reflection'. If such rituals are to survive at all, they must have significant intuitive appeal, free from the dampening effects of habituation and the overriding effects of explicit rumination. I have elsewhere described such rituals as 'cognitively optimal' in the sense that they owe their survival to pan-human cognitive susceptibilities rather than to the presence of elaborate and highly motivating explicit religious knowledge of the sort generated via strategies of repetition and arousal (Whitehouse 2004). The nature of these susceptibilities or 'natural propensities' has been explored in a growing body of recent research, particularly by Justin Barrett (2000, 2004), of a technically complex nature which it is beyond the scope of the present discussion to consider in any detail. But we can note that a striking feature of this new research is that it shows how magical rituals, for instance, can be constructed around such intuitively appealing premises that there is no need to develop elaborate exegetical justifications for them, in order to ensure their subsequent transmission. This would also imply that such rituals do not need to fall into the attractor positions indicated above; that is, they can be of intermediate frequency and elicit almost any level of arousal without this having any significant consequences for their cultural survival. And these are, by and large, precisely the kinds of rituals that proliferate in the intermediate position. Moreover, predictably, they are not associated with elaborate orthodox exegesis and do not give rise to significant levels of spontaneous reflection on questions of ritual meaning (see Lewis 2004; see also Whitehouse 2004, for a response). *Nevertheless*, we do find that a portion of cognitively optimal rituals migrates towards our two attractor positions, tending to be either low-frequency/high-arousal or high-frequency/low-arousal, rather than evenly spread across the spectrum. Although the ritual frequency hypothesis as currently constituted cannot explain this observation vis-à-vis cognitively optimal rituals, the ritual form hypothesis might.

Considerations of ritual form may well come into play decisively in determining levels of sensory pageantry (whether or not these correspond to arousal levels) in cognitively optimal rituals, and largely for the reasons McCauley and Lawson (2002) propose. In the case of special agent rituals, people intuitively expect higher levels of sensory pageantry to mark the intervention of the gods, whereas no such requirement is present in the case of special patient/instrument rituals. The same theory can also explain the low frequency of special patient rituals and it can at least help to account for the relatively higher performance frequencies of special patient/instrument rituals. If some of the latter become routinized, this may be because they are modelled on the rituals of religious orthodoxies, rather than because they need to be routinized in order to survive. All such hypotheses are potentially capable of being tested via a combination of experimental and ethnographic investigations across a range of ritual traditions.

Conclusion

Rituals associated with elaborate bodies of exegetical knowledge depend for their survival on strategies of either repetition or emotional arousal, or some combination of both in different domains of the ritual repertoire. The ritual frequency hypothesis is well equipped to explain the cross-cultural recurrence of religious traditions organized on the basis of such strategies. The ritual form hypothesis, although explicitly intended to explain the same phenomena, would seem to be better placed to account for the character and survival of rituals that derive their appeal from intuitive mechanisms rather than from elaborate explicit religious knowledge. The two theories, taken together, hold out the prospect of a testable theory of religious transmission, capable in principle of generalization regardless of the particularities of local cultural/ecological conditions.

Notes

1. Classic work on this topic includes Astington, Harris and Olson (1988); Harris (1989); Wellman (1990); Baron-Cohen (1995).

2. What causal relations, if any, are proposed by a metaphor of mutual shaping (and others like it) is not, however, clear to me.

3. For a discussion of comparable theories, see Whitehouse (1995); Laidlaw (2004); Peel (2004).

4. McCauley and Lawson (2002) make the same point using a different example.

5. Nevertheless, such major differences in levels of arousal are in principle measurable, for instance using galvanic skin response tests or even via less invasive techniques based on the analysis of saliva samples.

6. A much more detailed account of the relationship between ritual routinization and religious persuasion is set out in Whitehouse (2004).

7. Again, this is a relative claim. Some participants in routinized rituals may exhibit high levels of 'spontaneous exegetical reflection', for all kinds of reasons that are unnecessary to discuss here, but the general pattern at a population level is that levels of reflexivity correlate inversely with frequency and directly with arousal.

8. McCauley and Lawson (2002) present a precise and carefully thought-out definition of 'culturally postulated superhuman agents' (or CPS agents for short), based on Boyer's (2002) highly sophisticated theory of the cognitive foundations of representations of extranatural agency. Space does not permit an adequate summary of these arguments, but the general idea is that what makes certain culturally postulated agents 'super' (in the sense of 'superhuman') is that they violate our universal (largely tacit) expectations based on intuitive ontological knowledge

in various domains. For instance, ghosts may conform to standard intuitive psychological expectations, but violate intuitive physics by being able to pass through walls or defy gravity. Ancestors may additionally violate some intuitive psychological expectations, by being able to read people's thoughts, or to cause people to behave in ways that are contrary to their intentions. Referring to CPS agents simply as 'the gods' is intended merely to make the present summary more easily digestible, but readers should bear in mind that our category of 'the gods' includes all kinds of concepts of superhuman agents (from ghosts and spirits to ancestors and God) and that a fuller justification of this lumping together of such concepts may be found elsewhere (especially Lawson and McCauley 1990; Boyer 2001; McCauley and Lawson 2002).

9. The ritual form hypothesis incorporates a number of additional arguments concerning the structural depth and immediacy of the gods' involvement in rituals, impacting in various ways on their classification of rituals in terms of the special agent and special patient/instrument categories. These technical considerations must be taken into account in any detailed consideration of the empirical productivity of the McCauley-Lawson model, but such lacunae are set aside here because of space limitations.

References

Astington, J. W., Harris, P. L. and Olson, D. (eds.) (1988), *Developing Theories of Mind*, Cambridge: Cambridge University Press.

Atran, S. (2002), *In Gods We Trust*, New York: Oxford University Press.

Baron-Cohen, S. (1995), *Mindblindness: An Essay on Autism and Theory of Mind*, Cambridge, MA: MIT Press.

Barrett, J. L. (2000), 'Exploring the Natural Foundations of Religion', *Trends in the Cognitive Sciences* 4: 29–34.

—— (2004), *Why Would Anyone Believe in God?* Walnut Creek, CA: AltaMira Press.

Barth, F. (1990), 'The Guru and the Conjurer: Transactions in Knowledge and the Shaping of Culture in Southeast Asia and Melanesia', *Man* (NS) 25: 640–53.

—— (2002), 'Review of *Arguments and Icons: Divergent Modes of Religiosity* (Harvey Whitehouse, Oxford Univ. Press, 2000)', *Journal of Ritual Studies* (2) 16: 14–17.

Benedict, R. (1935), *Patterns of Culture*, London: Routledge and Kegan Paul.

Bloch, M. (2004), 'Ritual and Deference', in H. Whitehouse and J. A. Laidlaw (eds), *The New Comparative Ethnography of Religion: Anthropological Debates on Modes of Religiosity*, Lanham, MD: AltaMira Press.

Boyer, P. (2001), *Religion Explained: The Evolutionary Origins of Religious Thought*, New York: Basic Books.

Brown, D. E. (1991), *Human Universals*, Philadelphia, PA: Temple University Press.

Cohen, N. J. and Squire, L. R. (1980), 'Preserving Learning and Retention of Pattern Learning Skill in Amnesia: Dissociation of Knowing How and Knowing That', *Science* 210: 207–10.

Ekman, P. (1989), 'The Argument and Evidence about Universals in Facial Expressions of Emotion', in H. Wagner and A. Manstead (eds), *Handbook of Social Psychophysiology*, Chichester: Wiley.

Gellner, E. (1969), 'A Pendulum-Swing Theory of Islam', in R. Robertson (ed.), *Sociology of Religion: Selected Readings*, Harmondsworth: Penguin Education.

Goody, J. (1968), 'Introduction', in J. Goody (ed.), *Literacy in Traditional Societies*, Cambridge: Cambridge University Press.

—— (1986), *The Logic of Writing and the Organization of Society*, Cambridge: Cambridge University Press.

Harré, R. (1986), 'The Social Constructionist Viewpoint', in R. Harré (ed.), *The Social Construction of Emotions*, Oxford: Blackwell.

Harris, P. L. (1989), *Children and Emotion: The Development of Psychological Understanding*, Oxford: Blackwell.

Heelas, P. (1986), 'Emotion Talk across Cultures', in R. Harré (ed.) *The Social Construction of Emotions*, Oxford: Blackwell.

Humphrey, C. and Laidlaw, J. (1994), *The Archetypal Actions of Ritual: A Theory of Ritual Illustrated by the Jain Rite of Worship*, Oxford: Oxford University Press.

Laidlaw, J. (2004), 'Embedded Modes of Religiosity in Indic Renouncer Religions', in H. Whitehouse and J. Laidlaw (eds), *Ritual and Memory: Towards a Comparative Anthropology of Religion*, Walnut Creek, CA: AltaMira Press.

Lawson, E. T. and McCauley, R. N. (1990), *Rethinking Religion*, Cambridge: Cambridge University Press.

Lewis, G. (2004), 'Religious Doctrine or Experience: A Matter of Seeing, Learning, or Doing', in H. Whitehouse and J. A. Laidlaw (eds), *Ritual and Memory: A New Comparative Anthropology of Religion*, Walnut Creek, CA: AltaMira Press.

Lutz, C. A. (1988), *Unnatural Emotions: Everyday Sentiments on a Micronesian Atoll and their Challenge to Western Theory*, Chicago: University of Chicago Press.

McCauley, R. N. and Lawson, E. T. (2002), *Bringing Ritual to Mind: Psychological Foundations of Cultural Forms*, New York: Cambridge University Press.

McGaugh, J. L. (2003), *Memory and Emotion: The Making of Lasting Memories*, London: Weidenfeld and Nicolson.

Malinowski, B. (1944), *A Scientific Theory of Culture*, Chapel Hill, NC: University of North Carolina Press.

Malley, B. and Barrett, J. L. (2003), 'Can Ritual Form be Predicted from Religious Belief? A Test of the Lawson–McCauley Hypothesis', *Journal of Ritual Studies* 19 (2): 1–14.

Peel, J. (2004), 'Modes of Religiosity and Dichotomous Theories of Religion', in H. Whitehouse and J. Laidlaw (eds), *Ritual and Memory: A New Comparative Anthropology of Religion*, Walnut Creek, CA: AltaMira Press.

Pillemer, D. B., Rinehart, E. D. and White, S. H. (1986), 'Memories of Life Transitions: The First Year in College', *Human Learning* 5: 109–23.

Shaver, P. R., Wu, S. and Schwartz, J. C. (1992), 'Cross Cultural Similarities and Differences in Emotion and its Representation', in M. S. Clark (ed.), *Review of Personality and Social Psychology, Volume 13, Emotion*, Newbury Park, CA: Sage.

Tulving, E. (1972), 'Episodic and Semantic Memory', in E. Tulving and W. Donaldson (eds), *Organization of Memory*, New York: Academic Press.

Weber, M. (1930), *The Protestant Ethic and the Spirit of Capitalism*, London: George Allen and Unwin.

Wellman, H. (1990), *The Child's Theory of Mind*, Cambridge, MA: MIT Press.

Whitehouse, H. (1992), 'Memorable Religions: Transmission, Codification, and Change in Divergent Melanesian Contexts', *Man* (NS) 27: 777–97.

—— (1995), *Inside the Cult: Religious Innovation and Transmission in Papua New Guinea*, Oxford: Oxford University Press.

—— (2000), *Arguments and Icons: Divergent Modes of Religiosity*, Oxford: Oxford University Press.

—— (2002), 'Conjectures, Refutations, and Verification: Towards a Testable Theory of Modes of Religiosity', *Journal of Ritual Studies* 16 (2): 44–59.

—— (2004), *Modes of Religiosity: A Cognitive Theory of Religious Transmission*, Walnut Creek, CA: AltaMira Press.

—— and Laidlaw, J. A. (eds) (2004), *Ritual and Memory: A New Comparative Anthropology of Religion*, Walnut Creek, CA: AltaMira Press.

—— and Martin, L. H. (eds) (2004) *Theorizing the Past: Historical and Archaeological Perspectives*, Walnut Creek, CA: AltaMira Press.

–6–

When Intuitive Knowledge Fails: Emotion, Art and Resolution

Paul Sant Cassia

Introduction: Art, Emotion and Cognition

In this chapter I explore emotion partly, but not exclusively, in terms of its cognitive dimension. I am interested in emotion in terms of its relationship to thought, and the impossibilities or difficulties in following logical reasoning through to its inevitable conclusions. My starting point is some observations by Aristotle. In his writings on rhetoric, poetry and tragedy, Aristotle (1999) suggested, *contra* Plato, that thought played a central role in emotion. Aristotle was interested not in emotions *per se*, but rather in affective effects, especially through the operations of rhetoric, poetry (and in a more complex form with tragedy, where he introduces the notions of *mimesis* and *katharsis*), in short with the *affects* on an audience or a receiving public. He suggests that the effectiveness of rhetoric and poetry is that they move us through thought, which alters or stimulates our emotions. I wish to explore some of these insights, but give my interpretation a more anthropological turn. I suggest that emotions, as in the situation I shall be dealing with (the traumas surrounding missing persons in Cyprus), are embedded in social frameworks that set limits to, as well as providing common interpretative frameworks for, the cognitive linkages that are made.

The two particular sets of emotions I am interested in are grief and desire, hope and fear. I am interested in how these pathic states are refracted and reflected in, and through, popular art. Although emotion has received attention by anthropologists, the general focus has tended to concentrate on communities of communication. In this chapter I explore the emotional situation of a specific social group (relatives of Greek Cypriot missing persons) by reference to a particularly powerful set of murals in a church dedicated to missing persons. I follow Aristotle's hint that emotions occur 'because of' (*dia*) thought, and I suggest that such thoughts, stimulated as they are by exposure to these paintings, follow a mimetic narrative that helps sustain certain sets of emotions. I explore the relationship between emotions (specifically hope and fear) and religion, and suggest that in certain situations, because formal religion (in this case Greek Orthodoxy) cannot offer any resolution to certain cognitive aporias, art can have an important cathartic role in enabling individuals to deal with their emotional predicaments. By 'aporia', I mean an insoluble conflict between rhetoric on the one hand, and reasonable experience on the other. The example upon which my account is based, that of relatives of missing persons, is an admittedly particular case, and is therefore not necessarily generalizable. Nevertheless, we can see perhaps more clearly in such situations how the study of emotions requires recourse to both cognitive elements and social frameworks.

Ritual and Emotion: An Infernal Couple?

In a widely quoted article, Renato Rosaldo (1984) tackled the problematical relationship between emotion and ritual. Following the accidental death of his wife he wrote a semi-autobiographical article suggesting that emotion is prior to, and more dominant than, ritual: 'Just as the intense emotions of bereavement do not explain obligatory ritual acts, so obligatory ritual acts do not explain the intense emotions of bereavement' (Rosaldo 1984: 187). 'Funeral rituals, for example, do not contain the entire process of mourning. It is a mistake to collapse the two because neither ritual nor mourning fully encapsulates or fully explains the other' (Rosaldo 1984: 192). If we were to follow this suggestion then we could see rituals as an occasionally inadequate means to legitimize and control emotions. Rituals, therefore, do not necessarily provide 'closure', to use a bland word that has been adopted by therapists in the Western world. We therefore need to explore other means of coming to terms with emotions.

Rosaldo identified anger and action (including rage) as means to resolve and provide expression to emotion (grief). Yet his account does not address one problem, and bypasses another. First, although, as he says, we find it difficult to understand and explain why an Ilongot man from the Philippines facing the loss of someone dear is impelled by his rage to kill his fellow human being and toss his head away, most of us can probably understand why Achilles drags the body of Hector around the walls of Troy following the slaying of his friend, Patroclus, or why Ajax cuts the head of Imbrios from his slender neck and hurls it like a ball to roll in the dust. I have selected two similar situations (revenge at the loss of a loved one and desecration of the body) to explain why one set of actions can seem understandable or comprehensible and another not. The difference is not merely that one culture (Ancient Greece) may be familiar and the other not. This explains nothing, except the fact of difference. I think it is due to another factor. The Classics deal with characters and their emotions, and anthropology rarely does so. Characters

create stories: 'a character is the one who performs the action in the narrative...
characters are themselves plots' (Ricoeur 1992: 143). Their emotions become
more understandable. Their actions sometimes say much more about what they
feel than their words. This gives us a handle on the force of emotion. Often because
it is tragedy it is an imitation of actions and of life: 'Tragedy is essentially an imitation not of persons but *of actions and life*, of happiness and misery. All human
happiness or misery takes the form of action; the end for which we live is a certain
kind of activity, not a quality... a tragedy is impossible without action, but there
may be one without Character' (Aristotle's *Poetics*, quoted in Ricoeur 1992: 143).
Although tragedy is impossible without action, *understanding* tragedy (such as
bereavement) is probably impossible without embeddedness in characters.

This is what may be missing in Rosaldo's (1984) account. This lacuna is not
Rosaldo's *per se*, but stems from the way anthropology has traditionally charted
out its problematic. We rarely deal with tragedy, which we consider to be a one-off
occurrence, inimical to our concentration on structure, society or culture. Rosaldo
attempts to chart a way through this unknown territory by criticizing the tendency
of anthropologists to see all practice as spectacle, and augurs that, as anthropologists, we should not write about death as if we were 'positioned as uninvolved
spectators who have no lived experience that could provide knowledge about the
cultural force of emotions' (Rosaldo 1984: 193). This is salutary. We should culti-
vate empathy for the pathic states of our informants. However, my understanding
of the etymology of 'spectacle' is not merely *spectaculum* (show, sight and spectacle), but also *speculum* (a looking-glass or mirror). Through their (sometimes
'excessive') actions, individuals do not just vent their emotions, but resolve them
precisely by re-presenting them as *specula* (mirrors) to their rage to be viewed by
others as 'spectacle'. Achilles' grief and rage is assuaged not just by killing and
dragging Hector's body around the walls of Troy, but also by *presenting it as a
spectacle of his own internal state*. He does not serve revenge cold, but white-hot
'like flaming fire or the rising sun' (Homer, *Iliad*, 22.370-1). In matters of high
emotion, display and re-presentation, even spectacle, are critical.

The case I explore in this chapter is both similar and different. It deals with the
loss of loved ones, but there is no body to mourn. Individuals therefore find it difficult to express their emotions by 'conventional' means, either through 'ritual',
however inadequate, or through spectacles, however cathartic they may be. In such
situations we are obliged to concentrate on representation as a means to work
through emotions. Briefly, I deal with the art used to represent missing persons,
people who, following interethnic hostilities, and war and invasion, are in all prob-
ability dead, but who cannot be dispatched through mortuary rituals. I raise the
possibility that popular art, partly because it may be seen as 'naïve' or 'simplistic'
by political and artistic elites whose tastes are generally oriented towards the
European metropolis, and partly because its religious emplotting contradicts

rationalism, can be used to resolve contradictions in the relationship between emotions that are so strong that they become beliefs (for example, hope that a missing person might still be alive after a disappearance of some thirty years) and intuitive knowledge (for example, that the person must have long been dead).

A Brief History of Disappearances in Cyprus

Cyprus, an island with a population of 78 per cent Greeks and 18 per cent Turks, became independent of Britain in 1960 following an armed uprising in favour of union with Greece (*enosis*). Between 1963 and 1974 over 2,000 persons, both Greek and Turkish Cypriot, disappeared in Cyprus. They disappeared in the course of hostilities between Greek and Turkish Cypriots between 1963 and 1967, and during the mainland Greece backed coup and the subsequent Turkish invasion in 1974. Responsibility for the disappearances appears straightforward in some cases, more murky in others. Few bodies have been officially recovered. There are major differences in the manner in which Greek and Turkish Cypriots regard their missing. Briefly put, whereas the Turkish Cypriots regard their missing as *kayipler* (as disappeared/dead/lost), the Greek Cypriots regard their missing as of unknown *agnoumeni* (fate), as not (yet) recovered either as living prisoners at best, or at worst as concealed bodies requiring proper and suitable burials. Turkish Cypriots claim they have lost a considerable number of civilians who disappeared between 1963 and 1974. By contrast, the majority of Greek Cypriot missing persons date from the 1974 Turkish invasion. Officially the Turkish Cypriots claim 803 missing persons and the Greek Cypriots claim 1,619. The latter further claim that their missing were captured by the Turkish army, that they disappeared in captivity, and that the Turkish and Turkish Cypriot claims that these individuals are dead, goes against the evidence as they want to close the issue and not accept responsibility.

There are further differences in perception. The Turkish Cypriots have long been encouraged by their leaders to perceive their missing as dead, desiring to distance the Turkish Cypriot community from the Greek Cypriots, whom they blame as the culprits. For the Turkish Cypriot leadership it is important that the missing are dead, while for the Greek Cypriots it is important that they may still be alive, and that the main culprits are not the Turkish Cypriots (with whom they claim they coexisted peacefully in the past) but the Turkish army occupying some 38 per cent of the island. Thus, whereas the Turkish Cypriots appear to wish the matter closed in its present manifestation, but keep the memory and memorials of their oppression alive, the Greek Cypriots wish to maintain the issue as open in a present continuous tense, as an issue that is very much alive and will be buried only when the missing are finally returned and their bodies laid to rest. The issue is far from closed and continues to poison relations between the two groups. (For a fuller discussion of the issue, see Santa Cassia 2000.)

Painting an Aporia

It is important to draw attention to the representational difficulties attendant upon the concept of 'Disappearance'. 'Disappearance' pre-empts the possibility of representation. Clearly, the representation of the *action* of disappearance is non-realizable, while the representation of what has disappeared as object or subject is an *exercise of recall*. As the philosopher Patrice Loraux notes, 'Pour comprendre les difficultés de la représentation, il faut comprendre quelque chose à l'anaesthésie; pour comprendre quelque chose à l'anaesthésie, il faut comprendre quelque chose au trauma et, pour comprendre quelque chose au trauma, il faut comprendre quelque chose au disparaitre' (Loraux 2001: 47) ('To understand the difficulties of representation, it is necessary to understand something about anaesthesia; to understand something about anaesthesia it is necessary to understand something about trauma; to understand something about trauma, it is necessary to understand something about disappearance').

Anaesthesia of sentiments, trauma of recall; these are conditions one has to apprehend when precursing relatives of missing persons. The situation in Cyprus is rendered even more problematic because until very recently Greek Cypriots refused to accept that their missing were dead. The problematic of representation of disappearances is thus rendered even more acute. We are not in the presence of the representation of disappearance as (permanent) *loss*, but as a (potentially 'recoverable') *absence of what has been disappeared*. We are therefore in the presence of an aporia – an insoluble conflict between rhetoric on the one hand, and reasonable experience on the other. Representationally, the aporia can therefore be expressed as a riddle: when can an absence not be presented a loss? How can one conceal disappearances-as-losses, as absences, and yet conjure them through presences? This is no mere word play. Greek Cypriot society has been traumatized by the 1974 disappearances following the Turkish invasion. These disappearances have not been officially accepted as final by the Greek Cypriot authorities and by their relatives. For many years Greek Cypriot missing persons have been treated as lost (i.e. potentially recoverable) rather than dead (i.e. absent and non-recoverable). Aporias emerge out of the disarticulation between experience/knowledge, hope/fear and belief. This chapter explores how popular art has been employed to resolve these insoluble tensions.

The Alexandros Papachristophorou Church for Missing Persons outside Nicosia is a major pilgrimage centre, a place of remembrance expressing the continued trauma of relatives of missing persons. It is also a place where relatives of missing persons meet visiting dignitaries and politicians. It thus brings together private emotions and its public representation. As one woman told me,

This is a place that represents our wound (*travma*). We try to prevent the problem of the missing from being sealed, because according to Mr Denktash (the Turkish Cypriot leader), none are alive. We cannot accept that they are dead. We don't accept this erasure by official conjecture. We insist the fate of every missing person be clarified officially in detail.

The west side of the church facing the iconostasis consists of a wall completely covered by little windows each containing a photograph of a missing person. To the right of the church is the *House of the Missing Persons* (*Oikos ton Agnooumenon*). This contains an art gallery of murals representing the story of the missing and their drama. An analysis of these murals provides a useful insight into the symbolism of the narratives of loss and absence. To refined aesthetic sensibilities these murals could be dismissed as kitsch. Yet the church receives many visitors and pilgrims, and many commented to me how touched they were by them. Their apparent naivety and directness conceals as much as they display. An analysis of their iconography can help us understand that these pictures are an attempt to resolve a number of contradictions between the political treatment of the missing (the formal ideology that unless there is documentation of their death the state considers them still alive) and private experience and 'intuitive' knowledge that they are lost forever. I discuss the murals below, giving them titles that best capture their iconography, as well as their time frame. I hope that the reader will forgive the absence of illustrations in this chapter, but as I hope to show, what is important are the *themes* which can be expressed in words, rather than their actual pictorial or aesthetic significance.

1. *The Long March*: The struggle of the relatives to obtain information on their missing. This is by far the largest picture. The style is in the tradition of social realism and shows people marching. Some of the poses are clearly taken from Bernardo Bertolucci's film *1900*, which in turn was based upon the famous painting called *The Fourth Estate*, by Giuseppe Pelizza de Volpedo, painted between 1898 and 1901 (Milan, Galleria Civica d'Arte Moderna). Time frame: present.
2. *Saviour Mother Church*: Allegory of the Church as represented by the *Panayia* (Mother of God) reaching out to save a sinking boat. Time frame: past–present–future.
3. *Early Christian Martyrs*: A scene in a dungeon representing imprisoned Missing Persons. The words 'KYPROS' (Cyprus) and 'ELEFTHERIA' (freedom) incised on the walls. Time frame: past.
4. *The Cross of the Missing*: Allegory of a mother and daughter carrying a cross with the number 1619 in place of the INRI sign with faces of the missing carved out of the rock resembling Mount Rushmore. Time frame: past–present–future.
5. *The Meeting with the Risen Christ*: A family of a missing person clearly

mourning his loss suddenly meeting him. Here the symbolism seems closely modelled on the disciples meeting the risen Christ. The missing son, bare-chested, and wearing army fatigue trousers, seems as surprised by their mourning him as they are by his appearing to them. Interestingly the two groups (the living relatives on the one hand, and the Risen Christ/*Agnoumenos*) do not touch. A physical gap between the two groups symbolizes that the two groups occupy different time zones: the family in the here and now, the risen son in the future. Time frame: future.

6. *The Inconsolable Family*: A family consisting of a father, mother and daughter at the dinner table waiting for their son/brother who will never return. Symbolizes incompleteness. Time frame: present.

Sophistication through 'Naiveté'?

The analysis that follows relies more on the iconography than on what people said about these pictures. The murals are too direct to allow anyone to say much. They empty or nullify conversation. One cannot ask people what they mean for they wear their emotions on their sleeve, so to speak. Nor can one directly challenge their message because this would be to question what Taussig calls 'the public secret', 'that which is generally known but cannot be spoken' (Taussig 1999: 50), the public secret here being the fear that the missing persons are dead, but which cannot be aired openly.

The symbolism therefore could not be more unambiguous. Indeed their very naivety raises questions not so much about their 'propagandistic' purpose, but rather how such a relatively politically sophisticated culture and society could sustain such direct, unambiguous, unproblematic messages. We are amazed by such paintings because they seem to have been painted 'out of time'. There appears to be little personal interpretation by the artists. This is odd because Cyprus possesses a vibrant and sophisticated artistic community.

The closest one can get to understanding these pictures is that they appear to resemble social realism, in that no doubts, ambiguity, personal interpretations, or alternative voices are allowed to intrude. There is a 'smoothness' and 'complete-ness' about these images that excludes the personal or even the local. The collec-tion of murals suggests a faith not so much in images *per se*, in their ability to convey an unambiguous message, but rather an absolute confidence in how to view and interpret the problem of the missing persons. The narrative appears to be mono-phonic rather than antiphonic, or even polyphonic. But is that confidence so strongly grounded? I suggest not. Behind the apparent certainty lies a plethora of questions and emotions we have to decipher. I suggest that, while these murals seem to depict unambiguous messages, they conceal a number of contradictions, and an immense emotional uncertainty. In this respect, the murals are quite different to icons, the dominant pictographic tradition in Orthodoxy. Although they utilize a Christian symbolism, their very naivety suggests an attempt to provide a resolution that cannot be offered by the theodicies of formal religion. We are in the presence of a millenarianism, for the murals, like myth, depict a time outside time where anything can happen. They operate in what Minkowski (1968) called 'mediated futures'. And like Lévi-Strauss' notion of myth, they encode a basic set of contradictions that formal religious beliefs cannot resolve because of political exigencies.

According to Lévi-Strauss' (1963) celebrated definition, through being told, narrated or in this case depicted, myths attempt (ultimately unsuccessfully) to resolve underlying contradictions. Although these murals appear similar to social realism in their apparent boundless certainty, they are in fact different. Social realist art operates in an unambiguous, unified, time frame – that of the constructed past and a realizable future. By contrast, these paintings operate in two irreconcilable time frames: that of the here and now, and that of religious time, in other words time beyond time, time out of this world. Here, as in myth, 'anything can happen' – the missing can appear as early Christian martyrs, or as shadowing the risen Christ. The attempt to employ religious iconography to express (and resolve) what is recognizably a political problem on a societal level, and an existential one on the personal level, is thus vitiated.

The main tension the paintings try to resolve is that between political powerlessness and religious certainty, or at least the certainty that religion aims to offer. Put differently, the murals attempt unsuccessfully to resolve the main contradictions between the political treatment of the missing (the formal ideology) which holds that the missing should be assumed to be alive unless their mode of death is clarified – in short that they are *absent* – and private experience and 'intuitive' knowledge that they are *lost* – that is, it is reasonable to assume they are dead. By displaying a monophonic security, the paintings conceal a profound insecurity. They betray a fear that the missing are lost forever, which can only be transcended through a popular religious soteriology (theory of salvation). The contradiction these murals express is the following: how can one reclaim these people who have politically been kept alive and whose death has not been faced by the state, nor recognized by society, when all logic and experience suggests that they may well be dead? And the only 'resolution' that can be offered to this predicament is that they are alive outside time. Rather than becoming absent, these missing are still lost. Thus they can even represent 'us'. Recovery of the missing is tantamount to the recovery of self. Ultimately, therefore, these pictures address the problem and tension between loss and absence.

Absence and Loss

Here some insights of Dominick LaCapra may be useful. He suggests we should tease out the differences between absence and loss: 'the difference (or nonidentity) between absence and loss is often elided, and the two are conflated with confusing and dubious results. This conflation tends to take place so rapidly that it escapes notice and seems natural or necessary' (LaCapra 1999: 700). He relates absence to structural trauma, and loss with historical trauma: 'In an obvious and restricted sense losses may entail absences but the converse need not be the case' (1999: 700).[1]

LaCapra situates absence on a trans-historical level and loss on a historical level. By trans-historical he means 'that which arises or is asserted in a contingent or particular historical setting but which is postulated as trans-historical' (LaCapra 1999: 700, note 7). Here one could refer to the mural *Early Christian Martyrs*. An event that arose out of a particular historical setting is transformed into a proto-typical scene of a transhistorical early Christian martyrdom. Absence and loss can in some senses almost be seen as opposed. They also have different aetiologies, not just in the way the past is interpreted, but also in the way the past is dealt with, and in the means adopted to transcend or recover that loss or absence.

Let us begin by observing that both Greek and Turkish Cypriots faced a problem of the 'absence' of loved ones. How both groups responded to that fact varied. Initially, as with situations of death and trauma to which they certainly approximated, both groups were faced with two sets of experiences: absence and loss. In 'normal' mourning processes, the initial experience of sudden absence (of a loved one) is worked through as a loss, which in turn leads to a fuller acceptance of absence. I wish to suggest that, on a societal level, Greek Cypriots have never fully worked out the relationship between the two. This could be interpreted as a chronic case of melancholia, and this is indeed what the psychoanalyst Vamik Volkan has suggested (Volkan and Itzkowitz 2000).

LaCapra (1999: 700) suggests that, 'When absence is converted into loss, one increases the likelihood of misplaced nostalgia or utopian politics in quest of a new totality or fully unified community'. This applies particularly to the Greek Cypriots. The recovery of the missing is viewed as a means to recover not just lost territory but also heralding a type of reunification of the living with their missing loved ones.

I suggest that Greek and Turkish Cypriots responded to their losses/absences differently. Simply put, the Greek Cypriot experience of loss was of a sudden, massive, widespread societal dislocation, in a *war situation* that created a common solidarity and group awareness *qua* group and predisposed the survivors to fear the worse. Their initial experience was that of loss (of loved ones, land, etc.) rather than absence. They transformed those real losses into symbols of absence. By contrast, Turkish Cypriot experiences in the 1963-4 period were much more individual, spread over a longer period, and in a situation of reciprocal hostage taking where the relatives may well have 'reasonably' expected to get their loved ones back, as indeed did happen to a certain extent. This does not make their suffering any less serious, nor less worthy of our sympathy. Indeed in some senses the very fabrication and simulation of normality by the Greek Cypriot authorities who controlled the state after 1963, renders Turkish Cypriot experiences more horrific and traumatizable. Nevertheless, it is important to note that their experiences and expectations then were more oriented towards the pole of absences. They subsequently transformed their real absences into symbols of losses.

For Greek Cypriots the private experiences of loss were transformed on the societal level into symbols of absence. They became markers of a structural trauma, which can probably never be resolved. As LaCapra (1999: 698) notes, 'when loss is converted into (or encrypted in an indiscriminately generalized rhetoric of) absence, one faces the impasses of endless melancholy, impossible mourning and interminable aporia in which any process of working through the past and its historical losses is foreclosed or prematurely aborted'. A good example of this is the mural of the mother and her daughter carrying *The Cross of the Missing*. The mother and daughter are condemned to carry the cross of the missing for the living/society for all time. The switch from Christ to the mother/wife of the missing person as the person carrying the cross is a further demonstration of identification of permanently enacted suffering. LaCapra (1999: 707) suggests that 'the anxiety attendant upon absence may never be entirely eliminated or overcome but must be lived with in various ways. Avoidance of this anxiety is one basis for the typical projection of blame for a putative loss onto identifiable others, thereby inviting the generation of scapegoating or sacrificial scenarios'. We can represent the process in the following way:

Loss → → → → Absence: endless aporia: Carrying the Cross (Collective)

Yet on the private, individual level as the society did not provide the institutional means to resolve the trauma of absence, to provide closure, and because the issue was kept alive on a political level, the private experience of absence has been transformed into an unending experience of loss. I suggest we are witnessing here the beginnings of the creation of sacrality. As Georges Bataille (1998: 70) observed, 'Sacred things are established through a labour of loss: in particular the success of Christianity must be explained by the significance of the theme of the appalling crucifixion of the Son of God, which takes human anguish to the point of a representation of loss and unlimited decline'.

A good example of how the private experience of absence has been transformed into an unending experience of loss is the mural of *The Inconsolable Family* waiting for their missing son to come to the dinner table. Here the overriding sentiment is that of despair. As LaCapra (1999: 707) notes, 'the conversion of absence into loss gives anxiety an identifiable object – the lost object – and generates the hope that anxiety may be eliminated or overcome'. The emphasis on the symbols of absence – the empty chair and dinner setting, the substitution of the son by the photograph above, the uneaten bowl of fruit, suggest a self-conscious exploration of the symbols of melancholia. He suggests, 'when mourning turns to absence and absence is conflated with loss, then mourning becomes impossible, endless, quasi-transcendental grieving, scarcely distinguishable (if at all) from interminable melancholy' (LaCapra 1999: 716).

This theme merits further attention. The empty dinner place is clearly a trope of absence. Without having seen this picture, many Greek Cypriots often described this imaginary scene to me as an indication of the pain and suffering experienced by the families and the fact that they still hoped for the return of their loved ones. Interestingly, however, I have never come across such an actual practice among the families of the missing. It is clear that this represents a *symbolism* of absence, rather than a literal practice. Relatives adopted other actions (such as retaining items of clothing), but these were closer to *momento mori*. There is certain self-awareness here in the use of the popular symbolism of melancholia that should alert us to the fact that something subtle is taking place. It is precisely because of this self-awareness that certain psychoanalytical attempts to describe the predicament of the Greek Cypriots as a refusal to face reality and to persist in melancholia (e.g. Volkan and Itzkowitz 2000) seem unsatisfactory.

From a cultural perspective in terms of the representation of Greek dining rooms, something is missing in this picture which gives us a clue as to the relationship between sentiments and faith. There is a total absence of any religious element in the living room, such as icons, etc. I believe this is not fortuitous. Christian theology considers sadness a sin. Of all the paintings, this is the most lacking in hope, and therefore problematic from a Christian perspective. As Kristeva elliptically notes, 'The depressed person is a radical, sullen atheist' (Kristeva 1989: 5). These pictures are subversive of formal Orthodox notions of *engarteresis* (the acceptance of suffering through patience and forbearance). Writing on depression and melancholia, Kristeva explores the feelings associated with the word 'disconsolate'. It suggests a 'paradoxical temporality: the one who speaks has not been solaced in the past, and the effect of that frustration leads up to the present … "Disconsolate" turns the present into the past when the trauma was experienced. The present is beyond repair, without the slightest solace' (Kristeva 1989: 148). This mural, like the photographs to which it approximates in style and origin (for these murals are illustrations of staged photographs, rather than based upon sketches from life), suggests an unresolved absence experienced as a permanent state of loss. How is the tension between loss and recovery anticipated and resolved?

The mural of *The Meeting with the Risen Christ* gives some suggestion of a 'solution'. Yet this is not fully a recovery. A returning soldier appears as a risen figure, almost as a phantasm, even in a manner similar to the period between

Christ's Resurrection and Ascension – a transitional period, for the missing are located betwixt and between in Turner's felicitous phrase. In this mural he encounters his family, but both groups cannot believe whom they are seeing: the son that his family could be mourning, the family that he could (re)appear. There is no joy, just amazement. This is a Resurrection picture. The recovery anticipated here is not a collective but a familial one. The murals thus represent a collective struggle and problem, but they portray individual, familial loss, and suggest a familially based recovery. The nature, timing, and aetiology of such recovery is left vague. The viewer is not guided to visualize whether this will be an individual real homecoming or a symbolic one. Like the family in *The Meeting with the Risen Christ*, we are never sure whether the recovered missing person is our phantasm. He is perfect, like a saint, or a *levendis*, an unblemished, handsome, resplendent eternally young man.

It is clear that these murals are designed to express and reflect the emotions experienced by the relatives of the missing. As we are dealing with an extraordinary situation (the resistance by a society to accept that persons missing since 1974 are dead), it proved difficult to explore directly the complex of emotions with relatives beyond a certain level. I discovered that direct engagement with the relatives on their emotional states to be fraught with practical, epistemological, ethical and methodological difficulties. They were certainly 'emotional' about the political issue of missing persons, but there was also an understandable weariness in talking about their own personal feelings after so many years of frustration and political activism. Loraux would term this a type of (self-imposed) emotional anaesthesia, suggesting: 'L'anesthésie implique, d'abord, la disjonction d'un sentir et d'un ressentir' (Loraux 2001: 47).[2] So I tended to approach the issue elliptically. In this chapter I therefore complement the insights obtained through discussions with relatives with a concentration on another form of language, that of popular art. The advantage of this approach is that such art is intended to be reflective of emotional states. Clearly there is an element of artifice, but the artifice here is that of a lack of artifice. This is not high art and it does not lend itself to the rigours of art criticism. But it is eminently suitable for anthropological analysis. We are in the presence of emotions, or more precisely the representation of pathic states: hope and fear (e.g. *The Meeting with the Risen Christ*), grief and desire (e.g. *The Inconsolable Family*). As one woman protested, 'Listen, every being wants its young! The dog, its puppy! The cat, its kitten! Why can't we want our own returned to us?'

Here some thoughts of Vincent Crapanzano (2004) might be useful. He notes that hope as a category of experience and analysis has been ignored in anthropology. Crapanzano is acutely aware that hope as an emotion cannot be approached independently of religion, and unsurprisingly finds it difficult to disentangle the two. Instead he concentrates more on the mystification that is inherent in hope. He begins by comparing hope and desire: 'hope is intimately related to desire. It is desire's passive counterpart... Desire is effective. It presupposes human agency... while desire presumes a psychology, hope presupposes a metaphysics. Both require an ethics – of expectation, constraint, and resignation' (Crapanzano 2004: 100). Hope shares the same direction as *attente* (expectation) – toward the future-present: 'Unlike desire, which is continuous, hope assumes a moment of arrest' (Crapanzano 2004: 104), a condition that certainly applies to the relatives of the missing. He then points to the dimensions of hope: 'imaginative stimulus; vague hope; effective desire... and dreams, waking dreams, daydreams, and illusion; anticipation, expectation, and possibility; the future; patience and waiting; doubt, fear, and joy; revolution, utopia, and apocalypse; and *a quantity of theological terms like salvation, redemption, and of course, expiation*' (Crapanzano 2004: 100, my emphasis). These are terms that certainly apply to these murals, and I am interested in the last sets of terms. On one level, the symbols provided by religion provide a useful way for Greek Cypriots to 'resolve' their emotional predicaments. It provides them with a ready and obvious iconography. But on another level, these murals also indicate that the theodicies of formal orthodoxy cannot offer much relief or consolation. Holst-Warhaft (1992) has suggested that in contrast to Catholicism, orthodoxy cannot offer much consolation to people's feelings as it lacks the rituals which closely follow and replicate the passage of the individual through life to deal with extreme crises. Indeed, these pictures veer more towards popular Catholicism, rather than formal Orthodoxy in their freedom of expression. The result is therefore something that *appears* to be religious art, but is actually something more: a series of emotional *mises en scenes* (dramatic presentations) utilizing iconographies provided by religion, because they are the only ones imaginatively available, to 'resolve' an aporia: an insoluble conflict between rhetoric (that the missing are recoverable, because they might be still alive to be returned to their loved ones) and reasonable experience on the other (that they are dead and thus non-recoverable). The murals project imagined futures for an unimaginable reality.

In his study of myth, Lévi-Strauss (1963) suggested that myths have three features: one, that in myth anything could happen; two, that myths are unsuccessful attempts to resolve contradictions or aporias; and three, that the mythic value of a myth emerges in spite of the worst translation (in contrast to poetry). These features are applicable to these murals. First, as in myth, anything could happen in these paintings: the Mother of God saving the missing; a young soldier returning like the Risen Christ to meet his loved ones; a missing person returning to join a family meal. Anything *could* happen, except 'we' know that these are precisely the things that will *not* happen. But who is the 'we' here? The readers of this chapter or viewers of the murals, or the relatives of the missing? This partly depends on the contingency of emotions, and highlights the difficulty in conveying and communicating emotions felt by others except through some form of representation – which is where the ideas of Aristotle might be useful. Second, these paintings attempt unsuccessfully to resolve a contradiction between hope and desire on the one hand and reasonable expectations on the other. This contradiction is repeated in various forms in all the murals. In short, they are all variations on the same theme. The viewers, like the missing persons in the murals, are in the words of Crapanzano, 'caught in the *structure* of waiting' (2004: 115, my emphasis). Waiting is a structure, rather than a (temporary) condition, because in this case what is waited for is unrealizable. Finally, the mythic values of these paintings emerge in spite of their very coarseness of execution and would not be enhanced through a more refined rendition (indeed one could argue that their coarseness re-enforces their distance from logical presumption). Could we not therefore entertain the possibility that modern contemporary societies also employ some forms of mythic thought when dealing with traumatic emotions, while being alerted to the possibility that desire may have a politics and politics a desire – in short, that certain segments of society may well have benefited from the harvesting of the mystification of hope? I explore the latter part of this question in my conclusion. Here I am interested in the homology between such art and mythic thought. Indeed, it is precisely their very naivety in their narrative structure, their day-dream quality, their anticipation, expectation and possibility, which suggests the murals are attempting to express mythic messages. Our sensibilities are challenged precisely through the disjuncture between medium and message, for they employ a medium (representative art) to say things which we (and most Cypriots) would not normally culturally associate with such a medium. And although both Orthodox and Catholic religious art depict miracles, these are associated with the lives of saints or holy personages *in the past*, not (as in these murals) with the anticipated outcomes *in the future* of the fates of ordinary people who disappeared in the course of violent conflict. It is not the lives of these people that were miraculous, it is their non-deaths or redemption from a death that cannot be faced that is thaumaturgical (miracle producing).

LaCapra (1999: 716) has suggested, 'in acting-out, the past is performatively regenerated or relived as if it were fully present rather than represented in memory and inscription, and it hauntingly returns as the repressed ... [ ] to the extent someone is possessed by the past and acting out a repetition compulsion, he or she may be incapable of ethically responsible behaviour'. He suggests that 'with respect to traumatic losses, acting-out may well be a necessary condition of working-through, at least for victims' (LaCapra 1999: 717).[3]

Conclusion: The Social Frameworks of Emotional Cognition

In this chapter I have been interested in the role of popular art to convey a complex alloy of emotions (grief and desire, hope and fear) that cannot be uncoupled without incurring symbolic collapse. The products of the imagination, such as myth in 'simple' societies, or certain forms of literary and artistic creation in more 'complex' literate ones, serve to resolve the tensions between epistemological intuitions and emotional states. These murals act as a societal counter-depressant. They have both aesthetic and cathartic dimensions. Aesthetically, they utilize the soteriological symbols and discourse provided by religion in an imaginary fictional mode to resolve some of the problems experienced by relatives of the missing. And they have a cathartic functional effectiveness whereby pilgrims can explore their predicament in a condition of symbolic collapse (the object of desire has disappeared and is a cause of pain). Some support for this view comes from Kristeva (1989), who writes:

> Aesthetic and particularly literary creation, and also religious discourse in its imaginary, fictional essence, set forth a device whose prosodic economy, interaction of characters, and implicit symbolism constitute a very faithful semiological representation of the subject's battle with symbolic collapse. Such a literary representation is not an *elaboration* in the sense of 'becoming aware' of the inter- and intrapsychic causes of moral suffering; that is where it diverges from the psychoanalytic course, which aims at dissolving the symptom. Nevertheless, the literary and religious representation possesses a real and imaginary effectiveness that comes closer to catharsis than to elaboration; it is a therapeutic device used in all societies throughout the ages. (Kristeva 1989: 24-5, original emphasis)

Kristeva's reference to catharsis enables us to approach emotions by reference to two things: first, their expression and elaboration, and second, their reception. Here some of Aristotle's insights might be useful. Aristotle had suggested that emotions, far from being irrational, have a cognitive dimension. This enables him to show how emotions are central to the effective and affective workings of poetry, ethics and politics. Products of the imagination, such as rhetoric, poetry and art, move us by altering or stimulating our emotions. They do so through the human proclivity for mimesis, which is part of human experience. All humans derive pleasure from learning and inference. Tragedy is particularly powerful because the emotions represented and evoked are pity and fear. Pity is felt towards those who suffer an undeserved misfortune; fear is evoked through the intuition that such misfortune could happen to anyone, like us. I suggest that it is through such dual processes that these works of art operate. They link the relatives of missing persons with the wider society through the *mise en scene* of their tragedy to a wider audience, and create a national political community of suffering. But the catharsis involved here is not a psychoanalytic one of exposure of, and to, the underlying causes, the cathartic abreaction ('a discharge of emotion attaching to a previously repressed experience,' Rycroft 1972: 1). Rather, it is a semiological representation of the subject's battle with symbolic collapse through an endless repetition of expectation or *attente* towards the future-present.

Why such art does not ultimately provide closure to personal and national emotional traumas is related to politics. Greek Cypriot society has long refused to accept that the missing are dead. In short that these were losses, because the loss of the missing symbolically represents the loss of the north of the island, still under Turkish occupation. Rather, it has conjured the missing as absences, to be (potentially) recovered, at least in terms of their *leipsana* (remains) which they are currently prevented from reclaiming because of 'Turkish intransigence'. This has been sustained by a whole scaffolding of laws (such as those which maintain that the missing, not having been declared dead by the state, require that their legal rights be protected) and by propaganda. This helps maintain what Taussig (1999) had called the 'public secret', something that most people recognize but refuse to admit. Emotions, therefore, are socially framed. The anthropology of emotions may require us to recognize that emotions have their own politics, and politics have their own emotions.

Acknowledgements

Earlier versions of this chapter were presented at Queen's University Belfast and the University of Greenwich. Fieldwork was conducted intermittently in Cyprus since 1997. I should like to thank the University of Durham for its generous support, and the participants at the university seminars mentioned above for their comments.

Notes

1. There is a huge literature on the processes of mourning; see, for example, Bowlby (1961); Doka (1989); Freud (1984 [1917]); Parkes (1995).

2. This sentence is difficult to translate, not least because of the multiple and subtle meanings of the verb *sentir*. An approximate, though not entirely satisfactory, translation would be: 'Anaesthesia implies, above all, a disjunction between feelings/experiences and reflection on those feelings/experiences.'

3. For an interesting philosophical treatment of the contemporary difficulties of representation, see Rose (1996).

References

Aristotle (1999), *Poetics*, New York: Longman.

Bataille, G. (1998), *Essential Writings*, ed. by M. Richardson, London: Sage.

Bowlby, J. (1961), 'Processes of Mourning', *International Journal of Psychoanalysis* 44: 431–53.

Crapanzano, V. (2004), *Imaginative Horizons*, Chicago: University of Chicago Press.

Doka, K. (ed.) (1989), *Disenfranchised Grief*, Lexington, MA: Lexington Books.

Freud, S. (1984 [1917]), *On Metapsychology*, vol. 11, London: Pelican.

Holst-Warhaft, G. (1992), *Dangerous Voices, Women's Laments and Greek Literature*, London: Routledge.

Kristeva, J. (1989), *Black Sun: Depression and Melancholy*, New York: Columbia University Press.

LaCapra, D. (1999), 'Trauma, Absence, Loss', *Critical Enquiry* 25 (4): 696–727.

Lévi-Strauss, C. (1963), *Structural Anthropology*, New York: Basic Books.

Loraux, P. (2001), 'Les Disparus', in J-L. Nancy (ed.), *L'Art et la mémoire des camps. Représenter, Exterminer*, Paris: Seuil, Le genre humain.

Minkowski, E. (1968), *Le Temps vécu*, Neuchâtel: Delachaux & Niestlé.

Parkes, C. M. (1995 [1972]), *Bereavement: Studies of Grief in Adult Life*, London: Penguin.

Ricoeur, P. (1992), *Oneself as Another*, Chicago: University of Chicago Press.

Rosaldo, R. (1984), 'Grief and a Headhunter's Rage: On the Cultural Force of Emotion', in E. Bruner (ed), *Text, Play, and Story*, Prospect Heights, IL: Waveland Press.

Rose, G. (1996), *Mourning Becomes the Law: Philosophy and Representation*, Cambridge: Cambridge University Press.

Rycroft, C. (1972), *A Critical Dictionary of Psychoanalysis*, Harmondsworth: Penguin.

Sant Cassia, P. (2000), 'Statist Imperatives and Ethical Dilemmas in the Representation of Missing Persons in Cyprus', in I. Pardo (ed.), *Morals of Legitimacy: Between Agency and System*, Oxford: Berghahn.

Taussig, M. (1999), *Defacement: Public Secrecy and the Labour of the Negative*, Stanford, CA: Stanford University Press.

Volkan, V. and Itzkowitz, N. (2000), 'Modern Greek and Turkish Identities and the Psychodynamics of Greek–Turkish Relations', in A. Robben and M. Suarez-Orozco (eds), *Cultures under Siege: Collective Violence and Trauma*, Cambridge: Cambridge University Press.

7

'Catholics, Protestants and Office Workers from the Town': The Experience and Negotiation of Fear in Northern Ireland

Karen D. Lysaght

Introduction

While violence and conflict have been dominant concerns for researchers on Northern Ireland for several decades, the closely allied theme of fear has remained largely absent from the academic debate. This chapter attempts to fill this gap by describing how residents in Northern Ireland live with and manage fear in their daily lives. The lack of attention paid to fear in previous research is due in part to the methodological leanings of the majority of commentators, who display a distinct quantitative bias.[1] They have focused, for instance, on the identification of the most dangerous locations and the most vulnerable population categories in Northern Ireland,[2] on the measurement of the scale and nature of population segregation,[3] and on the social-psychological impact of violence on survivors and on those who have witnessed violent attacks.[4] As a whole, this body of work concentrates on the interpretation of census records, police statistical data and psychological questionnaires in order to provide snapshot profiles of Northern Irish society. Fear rarely receives explicit treatment, being seen as an aspect of specific violent incidents, and as implicated merely in one-off decisions such as that of moving job or home as a result of direct intimidation.

On the other hand, there has been a burgeoning interest in the topic of fear of violence in recent years, especially within the disciplines of criminology, sociology, urban planning and human geography (see reviews of this literature by S. J. Smyth 1987; Pain 1991, 2000). Although a feature of more recent work is a discernible shift toward more qualitative and ethnographic approaches, the mainstay of this literature continues to be quantitative work where emphasis is placed upon similar exercises to those outlined above, of enumerating and locating violent incidents, and cataloguing the social characteristics of victims. The findings from police statistics and crime surveys are assessed and analysis provided as to the accuracy of the fears experienced by particular social categories, whether these be women, men, gay men, lesbians, ethnic minorities, elderly people, children or disabled people. Surveys are used to catalogue subjective fears and to quantify the degree of fear to which particular social categories attest. This information is then judged against the 'real' level of victimization of these predefined social categories in order to assess how realistic particular groups are with respect to the relative threat faced. The social geographer, Rachel Pain, describes this focus as the 'risk/fear debate' (Pain 2000: 366).

This work draws clearly upon a framework which understands fear as being either realistic or unrealistic given examination of the objective indices. The emphasis is placed on a judgement of the reasonableness of fear, where the fears of women and the elderly are continuously shown to be disproportionate to the actual threat which exists, while men continuously fail to report personal feelings of fear on crime surveys and demonstrate greater freedom of movement in public space despite higher 'actual' levels of violent victimization (Valentine 1989; Stanko 1990; Walklate 1995). The emphasis upon 'objective reality' draws clearly upon a dualistic appreciation of the topic in which the emotional and fearful are viewed as subjective, chaotic, uncontrolled and, at their most extreme, neurotic. Moran et al. (2003) note that, in the literature on fear of crime, the body is continuously foregrounded as the key location of fear, with the implication that 'fear is personalized and individualized. In its association with the body, fear is understood predominantly in this literature as unreason and irrationality' (Moran et al. 2003).

It is clear from this brief review that the work on violence in Northern Ireland and the literature on fear of violence are underpinned by the same theoretical and methodological concerns. There is a preference for 'objective' data, which tends to create static representations of urban space, and a sense that subjective material merely documents the irrational, the misguided, or indeed an active attempt on the part of the researched to mislead the researcher. This chapter, which uses a qualitative rather than a quantitative approach, treats subjective expressions of fear as indications of significant influences in people's daily lives, and, in so doing, illustrates how fear is implicated in the dynamism of city life.

While Belfast is necessarily characterized by divided territories and regular acts of sectarian/political violence, it is equally a city typified by the dynamics of work, transport, schooling, social life and shopping, among other activities. Such mundane tasks take residents of these segregated residential districts over and across the seemingly set boundaries of the city in furtherance of their daily routines. While placing an emphasis upon everyday activities creates a more complex and nuanced picture of life in the divided city, it is important not to create a false sense of 'normality', which obscures the way in which the dividedness of the city proves a crucial aspect of the daily negotiation and management of life in these politicized urban spaces. It is necessary, therefore, to find the middle ground between a static sense of the city as violent and 'abnormal' and an equally skewed picture of the city typified by the 'normality' of everyday routines and untouched by the violence which necessarily exits.

This middle ground can be reached through the adoption of an ethnographic perspective to the issue of fear. This chapter presents a case study of the generation and management of fear in the divided city of Belfast. By focusing upon the actual experience of residents, it is possible to discern a highly attuned sense of fear which bears little relationship to the dualistic juxtaposition of 'real threat' against irrational groundless fear. Instead, fear is shown to be not merely individualized and personalized, but also intersubjectively shared, situationally specific, socially constituted and indeed socially constituting. The case study focuses particularly on districts where people live in highly segregated working-class areas, as a strategy for avoiding sectarian assault. Their residential choices have created a whole series of boundary zones between the segregated spaces, which provide particular challenges for safe usage. These spaces are characterized by high levels of violent activity, in the form of rioting, intimidation, sectarian or political attacks and killings. This chapter draws upon the narratives of residents of these inner-city communities in order to illustrate how fear is both generated and negotiated within the context of daily life. The material is presented in terms of 'combatant' and 'non-combatant' narratives, in order to reveal how the experience of those directly involved in the violence differs from, or is similar to, the experience of those not so involved.

Fear and the Divided City: A Case Study of the Generation and Management of Fear

The way in which the experience of fear shapes the daily dynamic of life in Belfast has been overlooked, not merely as a result of the emphasis upon quantitative examinations, but also as a result of the relative invisibility of the topic to academic onlookers. The reason for this myopia is due in part to the rare self-conscious articulation of the topic by residents of districts characterized by division and boundary violence, where the issue is treated as a tacit unproblematic body of information. As one resident notes, it is the case that 'people are so used to living like that, that it seems normal to them and it's only when you jerk their memories that all of this starts coming out … 'cause it's just your life'. It is precisely the 'normality' and casual mundanity of the topic which leads it to be overlooked by academic observers of Northern Ireland. In order to provide a context for the narratives presented in this chapter, I shall begin by illustrating the nature of the feared violence through a brief vignette which outlines a series of violent incidents which occurred over a twenty-four hour-period in the year 2000. The timing of these incidents is significant, occurring as they did six years after the initial paramilitary cease-fires of 1994, which led to reduced levels of violence twinned with a protracted period of political negotiations in search of a possible settlement to the conflict. Despite the cessation of hostilities, however, this period was not untouched by acts of violence, whether the result of sectarian or political attack or indeed internecine feuding between the illegal paramilitary groups.

> In December 2000, a 30-year-old Catholic builder, Gary Moore, from the small market town of Limavady, 58 miles north of Belfast, was employed on a building site in a local corporation housing estate with a near-exclusively Protestant population on the northern outskirts of Belfast. In the late afternoon of Wednesday 4 December he was approached by two men who shot him, wounding him fatally. Within hours of this shooting, another Catholic man, in his early twenties, Paul Scullion, was sitting in his taxi outside his depot on the Oldpark Road in North Belfast when he was shot several times by a pillion passenger on a motorcycle. The two shootings were determined to have been carried out by the Ulster Defence Association as revenge attacks for the killing the previous evening of a Protestant taxi driver: 35-year-old Trevor Kell was shot dead when he answered a bogus call to a house on the Hesketh Road, on the Protestant side of a highly tense interface in the north of the city. Initially the police blamed Republican elements for the shooting, but given their adamant denial, questions were raised as to whether the shootings might instead have been carried out by Loyalist paramilitaries in an attempt to provide the justification for a series of revenge attacks.

This series of events raises several pertinent questions about the nature of fear experienced by individuals resident in communities where such violence is experienced. The three shootings appear to be merely the result of random, unpredictable and indiscriminate targeting of victims in tit-for-tat violent exchanges carried out during the course of the working day on individuals who are clearly non-combatant. The violence appears to be relatively chaotic and disorganized. Such a pattern of violence begs the question of how ordinary citizens live lives which are not entirely disabled and paralysed by fear of violent assault. As already mentioned, however, the city is characterized by those normal daily flows of employment, schooling, shopping and socializing which are common to all large urban spaces. Residents clearly do not live lives which are immobilized by fear of random acts of violence. Instead, they negotiate the city in a myriad of complex ways which are underpinned by a reading of the violence which attempts to find pattern, and by extension order, in the events which threaten to disrupt their lives.

An example of such a reading of violence was provided several days after the series of events described above, when I interviewed an individual linked to one of the leading Loyalist paramilitary organizations. While we carried out the interview in a community centre in a small Loyalist district in Belfast, a workman visited the building in order to repair a faulty lift. This incident led us into a discussion of the shootings several days before, and in particular of the case of the young builder killed in Monkstown in the north of the city. I questioned the interviewee as to whether the workman visiting his building could be viewed as a potential threat, or indeed could be in potential danger. I have chosen to include substantial sections of the transcript, as the exchange illuminates many of the key ways in which violence is read and represented by those coming from a paramilitary background.

INTERVIEWEE (I/E): A single guy like that coming in to fix a lift would be all right … when it's Housing Executive [agency for public housing] working on people's homes, then they are suspicious and they check out the firms before they get into homes.

INTERVIEWER (I/R): Because they would get to know the layout of houses?

I/E: Because many of the builders would be Catholic, much of the time they would be put off site or the contractor was not welcome.

I/R: Was that because they were seen to be a potential threat letting them into houses?

I/E: Yes.

I/R: Is that why a lot of Catholics on building sites have been targeted, because they are seen to be spying?

I/E: Yes, I would say so.

I/R: I mean, some of them would be building houses though, like your man in Monkstown?

I/E: No, he wasn't building houses, he was repairing houses.

I/R: Would you say, was he seen as dodgier than others on the site?

I/E: No, I think he was just unfortunate, that guy was in the wrong place at the wrong time, [killed] by people trying to break the peace process. That guy probably didn't do anyone any harm in his life.

I/R: What would you think about his decision to work on those building sites?

I/E: You will find that a lot of Catholics work in building and they are not from the city, they are from the country, these boys travel miles.

I/R: Does that make a difference, that guy was from Limavady, does that make a difference that he was from the country?

I/E: No, not really.

I/R: Do you think he would have taken that job if he were from Ardoyne [Catholic district in North Belfast]?

I/E: No, because that is part of North Belfast, because Protestants would know you, because you were on the interface [rioting or merely posturing] and you are travelling all the time and you get to know people and faces and names.

I/R: But at the same time, that didn't save his life. They still knew who he was?

I/E: They knew he was a Catholic, and that is all they wanted to know.

I/R: Do you think that there were others on the site and he was the unlucky one?

I/E: Yes, I have no doubt about it.

I/R: Do you think he was wise to take the job?

I/E: I am sure that the contractors sought assurances.

I/R: Do they normally?

I/E: When they go into Nationalist or Loyalist areas, the contractors would be checked out. Most contractors would be told in certain areas, especially when the troubles were on, that 'there will be no Catholics working in here', but since the cease-fire it has got a bit more lax, and because they were country boys they weren't really a threat. I think that guy [contractor] was given assurances, but I think because of the [Loyalist] feud at that time, they were out to kill a Catholic and that poor guy got it.

…

I/R: Do you think that your man felt safe in Monkstown?

I/E: I think he probably did, the problem with these areas [is] if there is an incident somewhere else and it has nothing to do with you or anyone, if they are going to retaliate they pick on an easy target.

I/R: Why?

I/E: Because it is easy and you are guaranteed to get away.

I/R: But would it not be better if you are going to get somebody, to try and get someone you really want, as opposed to a nobody.

I/E: That is very difficult and it takes a lot of time and preparation.

I/R: Because they are harder to get at?

I/E: Because, for example, a high-profile Loyalist very rarely goes out of a Loyalist area, he would never take the same route, he is always watching his movements.

I/R: He would move from Loyalist area to Loyalist area, is that by car?

I/E: It would be, but it might not always be the same car, he might get a lift with people and it will never be at the same time or the same day.

…

I/R: The senior guys, or anyone who is in an organization, who could be recognized, they are the ones who are not going to be in same place every week and they are going to be watching their movements, what about people who would be less worried, who are not in organizations but are tarred with the same brush because they are from the same areas, would they change their movements?

I/E: Many of them would just head off to work, I would say during the troubles, for the first few years they would change it and vary it as much as possible.

I/R: And what kind of ways can people change their movements? For example, if you are leaving Grangefield [home community] and you going to Shorts [large factory in the city], and you start work at eight and work through to four, how can you change that when they know that you have to be at work for eight every day?

I/E: They can get you outside, you mean? The problem for them, would be that there might be a thousand or two thousand people going to work all at the same time, so there is loads of witnesses and as Jimmy Jowlan [Ulster Volunteer Force commander] said, and he said it to a good friend of mine about three or four weeks before he was murdered [in the Loyalist feud], the only place they could get to him is either leaving home or going home, because he varied his route and he was working in different places. And Jimmy knew that he had to go in to the house and he had to come out of the house and that is where they got him, going into the house, so if people really want to get you, they would get you.

I/R: If you did work over in Shorts at eight o'clock in the morning can you vary your movements?

I/E: You can just vary your movements by taking a different route into work. The easiest way from here is to go along the thoroughfare through Slatersville (Catholic district), but you would only go through Slatersville once a week, on a different day and then you would go up Abercrombie Road and then you would go in around the town.

I/R: And people would actually do that?

I/E: Yes, and they would arrange lifts with people as well.

I/R: And this is people that aren't involved in anything?

I/E: No, not so much now, but at the height of the troubles, yes.

I/R: People would have felt that they could have been mistaken for someone in an organization?

I/E: When the troubles are on and it still goes on over the summer, there is always some sort of incident between our community and Slatersville, but it is people that are not in anything, and they might be sitting in a bar having a drink and they hear that the Catholics are coming in and everybody runs out, so you get involved, whether you are in a paramilitary organization or not, you still get involved because you think your community is getting violated. It is not because a certain area is linked to a group, it is because it is a loyalist area and you will do anything to keep that.

I/R: If you thought about Slatersville, would you know that x, y, and z are involved in things, but the chances are those guys aren't involved in anything.

I/E: The major players would be recognized and a lot of the foot soldiers would be known.

I/R: And would that be both ways?

I/E: Yes, it's common knowledge.

Embedded within these extracts there is a very clear reading of the violence, where incidents are viewed as neither random nor chaotic, but rather as relatively patterned and comprehensible. Some of the key themes which emerge from this individual's deliberations include a highly spatialized understanding of the violence, its patterns and by extension its avoidance. This spatialized reading of violence is found not merely in his detailed knowledge of the segregated landscape and tense boundaries, but also in a range of complex spatial strategies he outlines to offset the possibility of victimization. In addition, he draws a clear spatial distinction between those urban (politicized) Catholics and those from rural areas (viewed as non-politicized), but also in the distinction drawn between work carried out in public (building new houses) as opposed to private space (renovating private occupied homes with the implication of information-gathering) as an assessment of the degree of danger posed.

The interviewee also outlines certain mechanisms which are utilized in the attempt to reduce danger by those in high-risk professions such as the construction industry, when he outlines the common practice of contractors seeking assurances of safe passage for their workers from paramilitary bosses in local areas. He also acknowledges, however, that such assurances are ultimately little protection when a soft target is sought in a tit-for-tat revenge attack or merely in an attempt to create general political instability. Targeting, he reveals, appears to be predominantly guided by the all-engrossing necessity to escape arrest. In a conflict in which engagement is criminalized, the prospect of long-term imprisonment is a factor in determining a choice of victim. The result is that those killed are often the 'softest' of targets. Indeed, builders and taxi drivers have proven to be at particularly high risk in Northern Ireland. Their extreme vulnerability relates to their occupying roles which involve crossing boundaries and working in open, relatively isolated locations.

While the interviewee acknowledges that senior paramilitary personnel could be targeted, their avoidance of routine and constant surveillance ensure that they are rarely victims of successful murder bids. Ultimately, while the individual interviewed does acknowledge that the two communities possess significant knowledge about the identity of both paramilitary leaders and foot soldiers in one another's communities, his words also demonstrate the ultimate blurring of categories, where entire communities are viewed as politicized and complicit with the illegal armies which live among their number. Members and sympathizers, those who riot and posture on the interface or those who only appear when the community is under a direct assault from a riotous mob, are viewed as part of a continuum in which the degree of politicization of the individual is largely irrelevant. In his estimation, these are politicized spaces and politicized populations, where targeting is more a matter of categories determined by age and gender than it is by known or suspected paramilitary membership.

In his final comment, the interviewee makes the interesting observation that there is a body of what he refers to as 'common knowledge' available on the nature and operation of the violence in Northern Ireland. Necessarily, this particular script is provided by an individual closely associated with one of the leading Loyalist paramilitary groups in Northern Ireland. It begs the question, however, as to whether this is merely a combatant reading, or whether such interpretations have filtered into a more general shared social script within the wider population. In order to explore whether non-combatants do in fact echo these themes, I shall draw upon a range of individuals who were interviewed as part of the Violence Research Programme's study of the impact of the fear of violent sectarian attack among Belfast residents.[5]

Social Scripts of Fear in Belfast

As noted earlier, the residents of Belfast's inner-city districts live in residential areas characterized by high degrees of religious segregation. Movement outside of local residential areas therefore necessitates the navigation of a complex topography of politicized space. The following comments were made by two men who express some of the feelings triggered by engaging in such daily negotiations.

> I honestly think fear is a factor … there will be a fear factor, who I'm working with, there's a suspicion. Anybody, honestly, I really do think if you're born and bred in Belfast, I truly believe there's a suspicion. It's almost a gene! 'Right, you can't work in north Belfast', 'you can't work in west Belfast', 'you can't work in east Belfast'. It automatically clicks in and then the fear starts and you're sweating … I remember going for an interview in the Upper Springfield, and Jesus, that was the worst day of my life … I didn't feel safe … it was the area … I don't know that area, didn't know the people, didn't know the geography. You're going into somewhere strange, that's my opinion. (Jack, Protestant male, mid-twenties)

> [That bus stop] is not that commonly used. A lot of people would walk into town first to get the bus [rather] than stand there on the road [an interface] [or] you'd find a lot of people they try to time it, so that they are only standing there maybe two or three minutes. They would hang about in [our community], maybe in the corner or they would stand on this side of the road where they feel safe and then move across [the road] when the bus is due to come around the corner. I mean, you look at who is passing. If there's two or three young men coming up, then you would feel threatened and your heart would start pumping a bit until they were eventually passed. (Gary, Protestant male, mid-thirties)

In their statements both Jack and Gary echo the paramilitary-associated interviewee above, in drawing upon a highly defined understanding of the threat of violence. This reading provides both known categories and known locations which trigger physical feelings of fear. Echoing the paramilitary script, Gary in particular speaks of a distinct social category, young men, as those most likely to trigger a sense of fear. As mentioned previously, young men represent the group who have suffered the highest number of deaths in the conflict, and, as demonstrated through this remark, the group who are seen by members of the local population as those who pose the greatest threat. The random targeting of young men from specific politicized districts has been a common feature of the conflict, regardless of whether or not these men were members of paramilitary groups. They are viewed by many in these localities as the social category most likely to be paramilitary members, to sympathize with the organizations or to engage, themselves, in politicized street violence.

Coming through in these scripts is a definite spatial locatedness of threat and a series of spatial practices designed to avoid becoming victims of attack, which depend upon the accurate interpretation of the situation. The spatial practices outlined by the young men above involve avoiding unknown spaces where the boundaries are unfamiliar and difficult to read, or using known dangerous spaces in ways which are highly defined. These practices necessitate the reading of space in highly intricate ways, in a situation in which all space is identified as either 'ours' or 'theirs' and given a sectarian complexion.

> See that road there, well, the Catholics they walk on the other side of the road, they're the only ones that use that side, and then us Protestants use this side, and the office workers from the town. (George, Protestant man, mid-thirties)

While this remark illustrates the highly specific detailing of the spatial divisions, which divide streets into 'safe sides' and 'unsafe sides', it also illuminates an interesting feature of fear of sectarian violence. George points to the use of the Protestant side of the street by those invisible others whom he refers to as the 'office workers from the town'. These individuals do not come without their own religious identities, whether Catholic or Protestant, but for George, and indeed for the many others who echo his thoughts, they appear to exist outside the framework of fear and threat. Most city residents adopt spatial practices which avoid whole swathes of the city which they view as politicized residential territories with established negative reputations, but for the majority of people there is little reason to visit these residential communities. The difference highlighted by George's remark is that the space for which he provides his sectarianized reading is a major thoroughfare into the city centre, through which thousands of individuals enter and exit the central business district on a daily basis. This intricate spatial detailing and the highly patterned use of space is not, therefore, commonly shared among all residents of the city. This situation illustrates the necessarily partial nature of this script for Belfast's residents. This is not a shared body of information, but instead it represents a highly local corpus of knowledge. Indeed the office workers from the town would probably be quite surprised to know that they are daily walking through such highly defined 'sectarianized space' (Lysaght and Basten 2002); the Protestant side of the street just happens to be the quickest route.

The adoption of a spatial tactic of utilizing a predefined side of the street is most clearly connected to a sense of being recognized or recognizable when moving on the community boundaries. This could be the result of local faces being identifiable, bodies being read (according to criteria such as clothing or signs of class background which distinguish the local working-class population from the passing middle-class 'office workers') or through the reading of spatial movements, in particular those of entering or exiting the segregated space of one or other of the residential communities which border the thoroughfare. While this local spatial patterning is clearly shared and of long-standing duration, it is also subject to continuous modification with the addition of new information, new dangers and new strategies. Warnings, rumours and advice are a central part of local communication. In the following quotation, Terry outlines the best strategy for walking into or out of the city centre at night, a route which involves passing in the vicinity of a particularly volatile interface.

> The only problems that our people have had in the last while back is people going in or out of town late at night walking when the buses have not been on, and getting badly beaten going by Slatersville or coming back past it. Once they knew you weren't a Catholic, you'd run for your life. The way it is … that's Slatersville [referring to a map], and see here, that brings you on up the Prendergast Road, and once you come past this point there's people watching. They see you coming up. Most of them know their own community down there because it's a very small community. We've always told our people, 'Come up Birchill Street', because Birchill Street goes up and brings you round this way. We always tell our people, 'If you're going into town go in that way if you want, and when you're coming home, try and come home the other way … and cut across, because it means if you're walking down the far side you have a better chance of running up the bypass even, and round into Freyne Street if you see anything there'.
> (Terry, Protestant man, late forties)

Terry's remarks point to a highly intricate spatial detailing which is shared by those living in a particular locality, whether through direct instruction or merely through hearing numerous stories of local incidents of violence. Such stories provide local people with the knowledge of what it is that they should learn to fear. Knowing what to fear is critical to actually experiencing fear. While several of the respondents above detail the physical manifestations of fear, of sweating bodies and pumping hearts, what they relate is necessarily learnt and intersubjectively shaped. Cultural factors do play a role, and it is only through awareness that a particular thing represents a threat, that individuals actually experience fear. In this sense, 'space is always discursive space; for the individual, it cannot be known beyond the information that is used to make sense of it' (Moran et al. 2003: 133). This is clearly demonstrated by the following narrative from Arthur, a Protestant man in his late forties, living near an interface in Belfast, who speaks of the 'distress' he experiences, which is triggered by a specific chain of events.

> I remember one night my son didn't come in, and me and my wife got very distressed, and went down to Clarence Road [the interface] because he wasn't home. It wasn't like him, he was only 16 at the time. And the night before a Catholic had been killed. We were so convinced that something had happened to him. When we went down there was a guy on a stretcher getting put into the ambulance. I was hoping it was him because

this guy was still moving. Eventually my son came home, he had gone to his mate's house. (Arthur, Protestant male, late forties)

For Arthur, fear was triggered by the fact that his son failed to return home as expected, but clearly within the context of a killing the previous evening of a Catholic man. His comment draws upon the pattern of tit-for-tat killings which have been a common feature of the conflict. He acknowledges in his statement that at some times, such as those of political tension, there are more reasons to be anxious than at others. There is a learned element, also, in his reaction, in visiting the interface between his own residential community and that of his Catholic neighbours. These spaces have a long history of concentrated political and sec-tarian violence (Feldman 1991). This spatio-temporal emphasis is a common feature of the discussion of fear in Belfast. It is echoed clearly by Simon, a young Catholic man living directly on a volatile interface associated with recurrent vio-lence and tension. Such violence is particularly intense during the summer months and the most controversial points in the marching season, such as the conflict over the right to march at Drumcree each July.[6] His narrative reveals how his commu-nity reads the potential threat in any given incident, and chooses either to ignore or to react on the basis of this reading.

> After dark … any serious things that have happened within the district have happened three or four in the morning. I live beside one of the interfaces and I mean you get woke up and … you're astonished at what time you hear people coming home drunk and wants to shout for his cause down the street. From both sides now you can hear people shouting, whether it's, 'you dirty Fenian B' or whatever, 'you dirty Orange B', you know, that type of thing. Whether they're standing in the street shouting 'Kill the Pope!', 'God save the Queen!' I've heard some mad obscenities being shouted, like. Mostly it's down to drunkenness … most of the time it's drunks and they're standing at the top of the street shouting, and a crowd comes out and off they go back up the road and it's all forgot about. Most of the times it's an individual just drunk … no audience whatsoever and probably that's what the problem is … once they get an audience … But it's different when somebody is drunk … I mean it's not as harmful as when it's the summer period whereby people only use alcohol to fire up their emotions. You know, people do come down and they're sober and they are fully conscious of what they're doing and they're causing trouble. Well, you always know … Sometimes it could be orchestrated … the likes of Drumcree over the summer marching season, things like that tend to be more orchestrated. 'If we want to do something we'll go down into the district, we'll go down into Clarence Road' [the interface], 'we'll do this or we'll do that'. But when you're talking drunks coming home, you know there isn't going to be a serious problem … most people know that they are drunk and just let him go on up to where he belongs and it's the same up there. He'll go, he'll get tired of hearing himself shouting and away he'll go. (Simon, Catholic man, early twenties)

For residents like Simon, there is an interpretation of such situations, and the decision is made as to whether there is anything to fear, or whether they should merely remain in their beds and ignore the incident. The decision is based on the wider context within which the incident occurs, whether political or seasonal. Given the supposed predictability of violence, individuals can judge particular incidents as they arise. They judge these occurrences, and those which are deemed unusual are sometimes rejected as 'not sounding right', or 'making no sense', and dismissed as merely rumour or supposition. In addition to analysing particular violent incidents, individuals also judge the spatial decisions of others. The following comment was made by Andrew, remarking on Protestant men he has recognized walking on a particular thoroughfare adjacent to the interface with a Catholic district:

> Very dangerous ... anybody ... if you ever see anybody walking ... the first thing you say is, 'Look at that idiot ... he's going to end up dead' ... [night time], day time as well ... well it would be very dodgy for anybody. (Andrew, Protestant man, late thirties)

The natural extension to such a judgement is made by the young Catholic man, Simon, who has very clear thoughts on safe spatial practice and on the judgement of those who do not act in ways which are fully cognizant of the fear of violence.

> Driving and walking, you know, you wouldn't do the same thing at the same time every day, you know, people do have that mentality and it's because they saw how easy it is if you do something in a routine, you'll end up getting yourself shot. People in these areas do watch themselves more ... You do get people that say, 'Why would I get shot? I mean I don't do anybody any harm', and they're the ones that end up getting shot, because they go wherever they want. Well some people say, not that he deserved to be shot but he should have had more sense not to work in one of these types of places [employer in a Protestant district], or whatever. I know that's harsh to say, but when you go to work in one of these places you're taking a risk, and they're fully conscious of where they're going. (Simon, Catholic man, early twenties)

In his spatial practices, Simon mirrors the safety strategy of the leading Loyalists referred to in the interview extract above, in avoiding the formation of routine in his daily activities. For Simon, those who ignore the shared understanding that spatial freedoms need to be limited for the sake of safety, are foolish in the extreme. Thus, while negative assessments are made of those who are overly fearful, equally disapproving comments are directed at those who fail to live their everyday lives in ways that are fully cognizant of the very real dangers which exist.

Conclusion

From the comparison of the combatant and non-combatant scripts, it is clear that both are echoing the same overriding themes. From the ethnographic detail presented, it is possible to see that both categories have very definite patterns to their reading of the violence of the Northern Irish conflict. Order and predictability are credited to the violence in terms of victim-choice, spatial, temporal, seasonal and political influences. Tacit agreement exists on the nature of the violence and on the relative threat posed by various situations. Just as violence and threat are read intersubjectively, so too a variety of spatial strategies are shared, which offset potential danger. These strategies involve complex mapping processes, whereby space is carved into safe and unsafe zones, where both macro and micro-territorial considerations exist, involving respectively the 'other side of town' or the 'other side of the street'.

Predictability ensures that palpable fear levels are reduced, and events are catalogued under merely 'normal' for this time of year, as no cause for undue concern or indeed as just cause for worry, distress and action. Just as specific violent incidents are interpreted by local onlookers, so too the spatial choices of others are examined and judged by community members, who view unsafe movements negatively, and often credit the individual with naivety, stupidity or foolishness. Fear is shown to be normalized and routinized in a range of daily practices. This is not an articulation of fear as neurotic, paranoid or immobilized. It is rather the complex appreciation of the very real dangers in the local environment and the development and sharing of a range of practices designed to offset the possibility of victimization.

This case study directly challenges an overly personalized and individualized reading of fear. The categories of 'real' as opposed to 'un-real' or irrational fears are shown to have little use within a case study which examines the practical impact of fear of violent assault in the daily negotiation of the mundane acts of shopping, working or socializing. Ultimately, fear is shown to be highly spatialized, with the sense of both threat and fear related to the occupation and use of space. In fact, in both combatant and non-combatant scripts there is a clear spatialization of identity, where there is an acute blurring of the individual into place. The quantitative appreciation of distinct social categories and the measurement of their respective level of risk would be difficult to ground in the realities of these blurred politicized readings, where presence in space and place can come to be a more important factor than an individual's political affiliation or sympathies. There is a blurring of the categories of the political and the non-political, and space comes to define the person moving through it.

Notes

1. See Lysaght and Basten (2002) for an examination of this literature and the advancement of an argument for a more dynamic approach to examining everyday life in the divided city.

2. See Murray 1982; Poole 1983; O'Duffy and O'Leary 1990; Poole 1990; White 1993; O' Duffy 1995; Fay, Morrissey and Smyth 1999.

3. See Boal 1969; Darby 1971; Boal 1978, 1981, 1982; Boal and Livingstone 1983; Darby 1986, 1990; Boal 1987, 1993, 1994; Murtagh 1993; Doherty and Poole 1995; Poole and Doherty 1996.

4. See, for instance, Cairns (1987) and Smyth (1998) on the impact of violence on children.

5. The initial field research for this chapter was undertaken as part of an Economic and Social Research Council funded project, 'Mapping the spaces of fear: the socio-spatial processes of violence in Northern Ireland', award no. L133251007 carried out by the Centre for Spatial and Territorial Analysis and Research at Queen's University Belfast as part of the 'Violence Research Programme', led by Professor Elizabeth Stanko, and written up as part of the Strand III study of 'Young People's Experiences of Crime in Ireland' at the Centre for Social and Educational Research at the Dublin Institute of Technology.

6. Marches by Loyalist organizations take place regularly throughout the summer; one, at Drumcree in Portadown (30 miles south-west of Belfast), became particularly controversial during the 1990s.

References

Boal, F. (1969), 'Territoriality on the Shankill-Falls Divide, Belfast', *Irish Geography* 6: 30–50.

—— (1978), 'Territoriality on the Shankill-Falls Divide, Belfast: The Perspective from 1976', in D. Lanegrin and R. Palm (eds), *An Invitation to Geography*, New York: McGraw-Hill.

—— (1981), 'Residential Segregation and Mixing in a Situation of Ethnic and National Conflict: Belfast', in P. Compton (ed.), *The Contemporary Population of Northern Ireland and Population-related Issues*, Belfast: Queen's University Belfast Institute of Irish Studies.

—— (1982), 'Segregating and Mixing: Space and Residence in Belfast', in F. Boal and J. N. H. Dougals (eds), *Integration and Division: Geographical Perspectives on the Northern Ireland Problem*, London: Academic Press.

—— (1987), 'Segregation,' in M. Pacione (ed.), *Social Geography: Progress and Prospect*, London: Croom Helm.

—— (1993), 'Between Too Much and Me', in B. Murtagh (ed.), *Planning and*

Ethnic Space in Belfast, Belfast: University of Ulster Centre for Policy Research.

—— (1994), 'Encapsulation: Urban Dimensions of National Conflict', in S. Dunn (ed.), *Managing Divided Cities*, Keele: Keele University Press.

—— and Livingstone, D. (1983), 'The International Frontier in Microcosm: The Shankill-Falls Divide, Belfast', in N. Kliot and S. Waterman (eds), *Pluralism and Political Geography: People, Territory and State*, London: Croom Helm.

Cairns, E. (1987), *Caught in Crossfire: Children and the Northern Ireland Conflict*, London: Appletree Press.

Darby, J. (1971), *FLIGHT: A Report on Population Movement in Belfast during August 1971*, Belfast: Community Relations Commission.

—— (1986), *Intimidation and the Control of Conflict in Northern Ireland*, Dublin: Gill and Macmillan.

—— (1990), 'Intimidation and Interaction in a Small Belfast Community: The Water and the Fish', in J. Darby, N. Dodge and A. C. Hepburn (eds), *Political Violence: Ireland in a Comparative Perspective*, Belfast: Appletree Press.

Doherty, P. and Poole, M. (1995), *Ethnic Residential Segregation in Belfast*, Coleraine: University of Ulster Centre for the Study of Conflict.

Fay, M-T., Morrissey, M. and Smyth, M. (1999), *Northern Ireland's Troubles: The Human Cost*, London: Pluto Press.

Feldman, A. (1991), *Formations of Violence: The Narrative of the Body and Political Terror in Northern Ireland*, Chicago: University of Chicago Press.

Lysaght, K. and Basten, A. (2002), 'Violence, Fear and the Everyday: Negotiating Spatial Practice in the City of Belfast', in E. Stanko (ed.), *The Meanings of Violence*, London: Routledge.

Moran, L. J., Skeggs, B., Tyrer, P. and Corteen, K. (2003), 'The Constitution of Fear in Gay Space', in E. Stanko (ed.), *The Meanings of Violence*, London: Routledge.

Murray, R. (1982), 'Political Violence in Northern Ireland 1969–1977', in F. Boal and J. N. H. Douglas (eds), *Integration and Division: Geographical Perspectives on the Northern Ireland Problem*, London: Academic Press.

Murtagh, B. (ed.) (1993), *Planning and Ethnic Space in Belfast*, Belfast: University of Ulster Centre for Policy Research.

O'Duffy, B. (1995), 'Violence in Northern Ireland 1969–1994: Sectarian or Ethno-National', *Ethnic and Racial Studies* 18: 740–72.

—— and O'Leary, B. (1990), 'Violence in Northern Ireland: 1969–June 1989', in J. McGarry and B. O'Leary (eds), *The Future of Northern Ireland*, Oxford: Clarendon.

Pain, R. (1991), 'Space, Sexual Violence and Social Control: Integrating Geographical and Feminist Analyses of Women's Fear of Crime', *Progress in Human Geography* 15: 415–31.

—— (2000), 'Place, Social Relations and the Fear of Crime: A Review', *Progress in Human Geography* 24: 365–87.

Poole, M. A. (1983), 'The Demography of Violence', in J. Darby (ed.), *Northern Ireland: The Background to the Conflict*, Belfast: Appletree Press.

—— (1990), 'The Geographical Location of Political Violence in Northern Ireland', in J. Darby, N. Dodge and A. C. Hepburn (eds), *Political Violence: Northern Ireland in a Comparative Perspective*, Belfast: Appletree Press.

—— and Doherty, P. (1996), *Ethnic Residential Segregation in Northern Ireland*, Coleraine: University of Ulster's Centre for the Study of Conflict.

Smyth, M. (1998), *Half the Battle: Understanding the Impact of the 'Troubles' on Children and Young People in Northern Ireland*, Coleraine: Incore.

Smyth, S. J. (1987), 'Fear of Crime: Beyond a Geography of Deviance', *Progress in Human Geography* 11: 1–23.

Stanko, E. A. (1990), *Everyday Violence: Women's and Men's Experience of Personal Danger*, London: Pandora.

Valentine, G. (1989), 'The Geography of Women's Fear', *Area* 21: 385–90.

Walklate, S. (1995) *Gender and Crime: An Introduction*, London: Prentice-Hall.

White, R. W. (1993), 'On Measuring Political Violence: Northern Ireland 1969–1980', *American Sociological Review* 58: 575–85.

8

'As if someone dear to me had died': Intimate Landscapes, Political Subjectivity and the Problem of a Park in Sardinia

Tracey Heatherington

Introduction: Conservation Debates

A lively political debate took place through the spring of 1998 on the immanent creation of the Gennargentu National Park in central Sardinia, Italy. It was a rational and reasonable plan, quite in tune with mainstream philosophies of modern ecological management coupled with economic growth. With the support of the Italian government, the European Union and high-profile conservation groups such as the World Wide Fund for Nature, the regional government of Sardinia saw considerable advantage in the project. Yet in a number of rural towns designated to contribute large areas of their traditional commons to the project, when news emerged that the agreement to set up the park had been ratified, there was an overwhelmingly negative popular response to the news. This was forceful enough to result in the organization of grassroots demonstrations, and throw the legislation into question. In the town of Orgosolo, where I carried out ethnographic fieldwork during the late 1990s, local action to oppose a national park had precedents in the 1960s. This resistance has been interpreted by outsiders largely on the basis of perceived cultural psychology, rather than treated as an organized, critically informed initiative. The emotional expressions embedded in the Sardinian anti-park movement were primitivized and dismissed by Italian politicians as unsuitable to civilized political process. This chapter examines the strategic implications of the imagined divide between thinking and feeling as it has played out in scholarly and political discourses associated with ecodevelopment in central Sardinia.

My discussion explores the sociopolitical life of narratives of emotion – and embodied experience more generally – to reflect critically upon the political anthropology of emotion, and the problem of a park in Sardinia. I argue that one can use insights from Begoña Aretxaga's (1997) post-structuralist feminist model of political subjectivity to frame an alternative approach to understanding local sentiments vis-à-vis certain environmental initiatives in Sardinia. According to Aretxaga, the articulation of marginal subject positions can draw force, meaning and coherence from the evocation of embodied states. Here I also draw upon anthropological discussions of historical consciousness 'embodied' through daily experience and social practices, whether strategic or habitual, which contribute to shared subjectivity (see Merleau-Ponty 1964; Bourdieu 1977; Jackson 1983; de Certeau 1984; Csordas 1990; Herzfeld 2003; see also Svašek, Chapter 11 in this volume). In making sense of my fieldwork on Sardinian 'resistance' to the park, I vigorously reject a false opposition between reason and emotion that demeans the intelligence of anyone whose stand is passionate. On the contrary, emotions can summarize and symbolically condense 'rational' or literal thought (see for example Leavitt 1996; Strathern 1996; Stoller 1997). When I report that people in Orgosolo felt deeply about communal landownership, I mean to highlight the extent to which self-conscious conceptual work conditioned this embodied experience and vice versa, so that a distasteful political debate became an aesthetically unpleasant experience, and an impending legal disempowerment provoked personal grief, or personal anger.

How should we construe the role of emotion associated with both ardent 'resistance' and the apparent *cultural attachment* to specific landscapes that paradoxically underlies opposition to the national park in Sardinia? The feminist scholars (see for example Rosaldo 1984; Abu-Lughod 1986; Lutz 1988) who first turned to the cultural study of emotion taught us to value and respect the emotive self-expressions of informants. Their ethnographically informed insights emphasized that emotional subjectivity is never predetermined by biological functions, but is inherently engaged with a dynamic play of social and material, intrinsically meaningful relationships. By attending to ethnographic conversations, we can refute claims that devotion to the commons, as well as 'resistance' to a national park, are the outcome of an unreflexive, backward cultural psychology. Instead, we can examine the experiential basis of the meanings and emotions attached to the future of the commons. Kay Milton (2002) suggested that people who choose to participate in environmentalist movements typically come to identify with and value the non-human beings, things and relationships associated with the natural world when they are able to recognize them as 'contributing sense, pattern and meaning to their lives as a whole' (Milton 2002: 105). This is precisely how we may also better understand rural Sardinian 'love' for the commons. Although it tends to converge only awkwardly with the global orientation preferred by some environmentalists (Milton 1996), who are more likely to define abstract 'nature' as the proper object of care and devotion, this sense of sincere and encompassing intimacy with particular landscapes informed de facto local conservation practices (Meloni 1984) long before environmental values entered fashionable discourses of governmentality in modern nation-states.

In rural Sardinia, metaphors of kinship, interdependence and affection are extended by townspeople to the communal territory as they explain their own negative reactions to the planned Gennargentu National Park. These metaphors affirm that common lands are, in Orgosolo, an intrinsic part of the community and a basis for appropriate development. Meaning and feeling are blended both in the sense of intimate connection to the landscape, and also in the sense of how the embodied experience of environmental politics is enmeshed with local identity and the boundaries of social belonging. The social memory of marginality, scarcity and hardship in the past is narrativized in relationship to the experience of transhumant herding and other forms of agricultural work. In this context, social agency is imagined as the product of intimate ties to both the community and the landscape of the town commons. Conversely, defending against the dismantling or appropriation of the commons – as in the case of the planned park – is explained as the outcome of a natural, historically rooted affinity for the land and is positively defined as a defence of traditional values. Contestation against a national park in Sardinia thus entailed not only a reappropriation of 'the environment' as a sphere of political discourse, but also a fundamental reframing of debates to take account of alternative frameworks of embodied moral authority.

Primordial Attachments?

The starkly beautiful mountain plateaux of central Sardinia were targeted for ecological preservation in the 1930s, by politicians inspired by the national parks model in the United States. Legislative initiatives in favour of a 'Gennargentu National Park' emerged in the 1960s, in tandem with the rebuilding and development of post-war Europe. These initiatives were defeated by local opposition in highland Sardinia, including left-wing youth activists from the highland towns of Baunei and Orgosolo, which organized demonstrations against the park. In 1969, Orgosolo herders and their entire families joined with youth activists to demonstrate against the appropriation of their common lands for the establishment of a NATO base, staging the occupation of areas designated for artillery practice over the course of four days.[1] Opposition was consolidated and the project was set aside until the late 1980s. When a second period of planning and development studies culminated in the announcement that new park legislation had been ratified in 1998, a flurry of anxious debate followed in the towns whose lands were targeted for inclusion. In Orgosolo, the significant erosion of local control over the traditional territory of the commons had sweeping implications, and town meetings were called several nights in a row. In the midst of this, the mayor of Orgosolo came into the local library one morning to use the phone, announcing her intention to call higher authorities and 'get angry' over the liberties taken with centralized park planning. 'What they're not counting on', she said, 'is the primordial attachment of Orgolesi [residents of Orgosolo] to the land.'

The link she presumed between common lands and collective action in rural highland Sardinia bears some reflection, because many authors have noted precedents for both social unrest and unified political initiative when control over the communal territory has been threatened. The idea of indigenous Sardinian 'resistance' to colonization and 'neocolonialism' has been affirmed as a mark of positive cultural distinction in many ethnonationalist narratives (Schweizer 1988). Orgosolo is, for example, particularly celebrated for its historical insubordination to the Piedmontese enclosure movement of the early nineteenth century. Orgolese intellectual Giovanni Battista Salis claims that despite Piedmont's policies to eradicate free range herding on communal territories and institute 'perfect property,' neither the *Editto Sopra le Chiudende* of 1820 nor subsequent laws to abolish feudal landownership structures had any effect in Orgosolo (1990: 100).[2] As anthropologist Franco Cagnetta once noted with fanciful appreciation, 'Not one enclosure was constructed at Orgosolo by virtue of the collective refusal by the herders, who saw themselves being despoiled of their most ancient communal pastures' (Cagnetta 1975 [1954]: 152; my translation).

Such historical narratives have developed over time to attribute a nearly legendary status to the traces of collective action regarding the commons in Orgosolo. Spano's treatise on 'the Sardinian question' says that after 1860, many communities in Sardinia were forced to sell their territories to speculators in order to pay high taxes to the demanding new Italian state, and only a few highland communities such as Orgosolo, isolated from the seats of administration in the urban centres, managed to preserve their forests (1922 in Del Piano 1979: 9). Cagnetta relates that Sardinian communities during this period came under increasing fiscal pressure, the levying of troops, and a systematic despoiling of communal lands and forests which contributed to a growing phenomenon of endemic banditry (Cagnetta 1975: 152).[3] Orgosolo was, according to him, the principal site of resistance to the political-economic penetration of the state into highland Sardinia at this time. In the late nineteenth century, however, Orgosolo was forced to cede over 4,500 ha of its communal territory to the crown in payment of debt. Del Piano (1979: 16) remarked that 'tumults and agitations' arose because the pastoralists of Orgosolo felt themselves unjustly deprived of their lands by the crown forestry enterprise.

Although government-managed forestry activities eventually became an important factor in the local economy, Orgosolo residents vigorously opposed a plan in 1931 by the Azienda Foreste Demaniali (State Forestry Enterprise) to take over more communal pastures. Salis (1990) wrote that despite the risk involved in challenging the police during the fascist period, when people heard news of the decision, 'the Orgolese population [did] not hesitate a moment to go out into the plaza to protest' (Salis 1990: 119). While Corda (1989: 209) noted the centrality of the commons to the herding-based local economy at the time, Salis claimed that this action illuminated something fundamental about the enduring 'character', 'mentality' and 'culture' of the residents of Orgosolo. He told the story of the 'uprising of 1931' in dramatic present tense, but used remote past verbs to describe how the authorities backed down from their decision to take over the communal territory. These subtle linguistic devices organized the narrative as though the act of protest were eternal and the successful outcome always already decided:

> One morning in April, when the women, as always, go to the nearby fountain to fill their water-jars, they read a written message: 'Wake up, sleeping people, the commons is sold!' The same message appears on the walls of the churches of San Pietro and Santa Croce, and [by the cemetery], for those going to the early Mass. In less time than it takes to retell, the word spreads, and hundreds of gathered women enter the town hall, chase out the administrators, and put the locks on the doors. They presided over the town hall for several days, in an apparently peaceful manner which however left no doubt about their firm determination, and that of their men [who were] also wary. The alarm reached the Prefecture and the Ministry of the Interior with lightning swiftness, and there was a great explanation of the [potential police action], but the authorities refrained from a trial of strength with Orgosolo. It revoked the decision that had been made, and 'the commons', the whole territory, was not touched. (Salis 1990: 119–20; my translation)

For Salis, this instance in history seemed to expose a moment when the 'true' cultural character of Orgosolo became apparent as a result of tense conflict with the state: residents were innately determined to protect the commons. Local historians like him have implicitly affirmed a rather mystical potency of the community, as a culture authentically rooted in the territory of the commons.

The local social memory of interdependence with the Orgosolo commons is evoked, shared, reshaped and made real by everyday work and hospitality and by a superabundance of historical narratives contained in murals, old photographs, festival celebrations, Sardinian poetry and even certain key works of anthropology and literature. The landscape itself is widely perceived by residents to be the ultimate visual text legitimizing local interpretations of history. The strongly imagined cultural protagonism of Orgosolo shepherds is attached to the symbolic potency of the commons. This communal territory is a *sine qua non* of local narratives about both the past and the future in Orgosolo. Various individuals' visions of local development may diverge to emphasize herding over forestry, tourism over environmental protection, or new measures of ecological and cultural management as a means of transcending dependence on marginal pastoralism and uncertain agricultural subsidies. Myriad potential futures are nevertheless embedded in a sense of positive, inherited, communal tradition. Nostalgic futures are literally grounded in Orgosolo's commons.

Landscapes of Memory

Memories of successful collective action affirmed that *su cumonale* (the commons) implied a unique heritage of social agency (Heatherington 2002). In the late 1960s, when the famous 'Battle of Pratobello' took place, Orgosolo's economy was still largely dependent on herding activities, and virtually every household included one or more herders. *Su cumonale* was a crucial economic resource to most, but it also constituted a symbolic focus for collective identity. The widespread, embodied male experience of hard pastoral work shaped perceptions of a cohesive, locally shared past and future tied to the communal territory. For example, old shepherds in Orgosolo acutely remembered the hard conditions of work they used to carry out in the highland countryside.

Banne Sio, an Orgosolo student of economics, in the mid-1990s undertook a number of interviews with retired pastoralists, who were once constrained to stay with the herds for weeks or months at a time. The chief tropes found in men's narratives of the pastoral past are those of 'suffering' and 'sacrifice', set in a landscape of isolation and exposure to the elements. Sio asked a man born in 1918 when he had begun herding, and the man answered, 'At eleven years [of age], with my cousins, [I was a] shepherd and in summer a pigherd. In November we left with the sheep and we came back in May, no pay, just food for the belly and some shoes, that's how it was' (Sio 1996–7: 146; my translation). Another man became a shepherd around age 10, and said that when he started in 1927, 'Before, when it snowed we slept outside... we were always wet for whole days... Before, there wasn't any work, it was a life of sacrifices because you were badly off, you ate badly, you had the same life as the sheep, you were worse off than a dog' (ibid.: 144). Such harsh, vividly embodied memories of the early to mid-twentieth century now represent a touchstone for the representation of 'traditional' life in Orgosolo.

These memories are significant, not only for the senior generations, but also for the young men and women who referred to the harsh lives of their parents when they spoke about their own perspectives on the problem of the Gennargentu National Park. The recounted experience of men during the 1940s, 1950s and early 1960s were strongly located outside the home and the town, especially in sites of pastoral work on the commons, but also connected to war and political exile. Women's memories of hardship were symmetrical to men's, confirming both a direct dependence upon the land and a commonality of experience linked to local-level identity. Their informal narratives highlighted tropes of 'sacrifice' and 'suffering' associated with daily work. Because the contemporary formal economy remains fragile, many local residents drew on narratives about work, suffering and personal sacrifice to establish the cultural continuity of past and present in Orgosolo. In the context of public discourses sustained by the Roman Catholic Church and its active congregations, this implied redemptive action in the face of ongoing social violence such as homicides. More importantly for residents' attempts to affirm the possibility of local-level environmental conservation, it contradicted visions of cultural decline following a shift towards 'modern' economic practices in the post-war era. Above all, it asserted the authenticity of cultural tradition, and legitimate, enduring connections to the local landscape of the commons.

Modelling Culture and Environment

Many people in Orgosolo explained to me that the freedom to make use of their territory as they saw fit was profoundly important to them. In Orgosolo, *su cumunale* commanded the emotional resonance of the sacred. Even the most environmentally minded or progressively minded individuals found it alarming to imagine severing the ties of moral and legal ownership between the communities and their territories, in order to create national parks. Why should this be so?

There are three possible alternatives of modelling human, cultural relationships with the Sardinian landscape, which imply quite different approaches to the role of emotion. First, we can analyse ways in which the Sardinian commons constitutes a productive resource. This is the usual approach taken in the literature on environment and development. The emotional charge of debates about a new park in central Sardinia seems to be intimately connected to a widespread perception of vulnerability to the loss of economic possibilities associated with landownership. Rural Sardinians depend upon their communal territories for economic survival and success. We could try to explain emotional attachment to the commons in terms of local dependency and aspiration, particularly given Orgosolo's structural marginality in the context of nation and region. The problem of a park might then be resolved, according to the universal logic of sustainable development, by an exchange of socio-economic programmes in return for the concession of the traditional commons.

This has in fact been a major thrust of negotiations for the new park throughout the 1990s, and these have met with some limited success. It is clear, however, that many rural Sardinians remain unwilling to bargain over communal ownership of land, even though pastoral activities are declining and land development in the area of the proposed park is already prohibited by national legislation. A more nuanced materialist analysis could certainly help us to interpret the reluctance of many working-class Sardinians to commit support to a project with few guarantees for their own access to new jobs and funds. The economic crisis experienced in Italy since the 1980s (which cut down government investment in public works as well as new job openings in most arms of the public administration) has merely enhanced the role of the informal economy in places like Orgosolo, making communal assets a vital form of insurance against uncertainty, particularly for those without university degrees and political patrons.

We meet the limits of the materialist perspective on the Sardinian commons, however, in learning to take seriously the affective discourses of rural Sardinians, not only for the landscape and its productive possibilities, but also for its aesthetic qualities, its history and its inherent relevance to social life. It should not be forgotten that economic possibilities are simultaneously also personal and collective stories that have been, or are yet to be, inscribed upon the landscape. Is it possible to explain the apparent sacredness of local connections to the commons in terms of symbolic resonance? A cultural approach highlights the importance of the landscape and pastoral traditions in the politics and economics of regional and local identity, and in structuring social relations within and between towns.

Shepherds and their work on the commons have been synonymous with highland Sardinia in the most positive cultural discourses about the area, including those devoted to tourism (see Schweizer 1988; Ayora-Diaz 1993; Satta 2001). While the land remains undivided and undeveloped common property, it validates a shared local past and many possible different futures. It symbolically defines and empowers the whole community in Orgosolo, notwithstanding growing fragmentation in occupation and cultural orientation. There is a romantic presumption of local agency that draws power from the historical examples of resistance against outsiders to protect the commons, so that recognized history shapes and gives force to collective endeavours in Orgosolo against the Park. This approach, however, still fails to understand the nature of affective ties, which entail more than economic calculations or intellectual, symbolic work. Discussion with Sardinians made me realize that everyday practice, experience and social memory shape political subjectivities that encompass both reason and emotion.

Senses of Belonging

In the town of Orgosolo, an *embodied* attachment to the land is perceived as inherent to cultural identity, economic futures and the persistence of community. Connections to the commons pervade the sensual experiences of material culture – the flavours, smells, touches and sounds of quotidian work and social life. Personal affection is expressed in the gift of a hand-made cheese, or home-baked bread, with textures, tastes and acts of sharing all redolent with histories of marginality, cooperation, hardship, devotion, celebration and survival. Pastoral heritage remains relevant to the daily life of the Orgosolo law student boarding in Cagliari, whose brother drops off a parcel of meat or sweets that will be divided happily with her new friends at university.

Similarly, pastoral pride remains relevant to the Orgosolo construction worker who ranges across the province to a job, and invites acquaintances from another town to come and enjoy *carne arrosto* (roast meat) with his friendship group at the foot of Monte San Giovanni, on the Orgosolo commons. Pastoral skill remains relevant to the Orgosolo bartender who leads his tall horse through crowded streets of tourists for the celebration of Ferragosto, and takes part in the traditional horse-back acrobatics held afterwards. Pastoral community remains relevant to the Orgosolo women who take charge of funeral processions and pilgrimages to the chapels on the commons, walking to the cadence of the rosaries they sing in vernacular Sardinian (Heatherington 1999). Interdependence with – and *belonging to* – the town commons is felt in the body and in the family. It is an object of ongoing 'love', nostalgia, passion, worry, grief and jealousy precisely because it is considered essential to the experience and agency associated with being both Sardinian and Orgolese.

Authentic Connections

Many Orgosolo residents were profoundly emotional about the politics of land management. Fiery ardour, expressed by raised voices, excited gestures and occasional self-references to the speaker's own state of mind, marked many conversations about the park, forestry projects, and land improvement works at Orgosolo. Public debates themselves became objects of memory and feeling. One friend, for example, told me she actually avoided going to the public assemblies about the park because they made her upset. She did not want to listen, she said, but rather to speak out, and she feared others would not wish to hear what she had to say. She explained to me, '*Per noi, queste cose sono brutte*' ('For us, these things [the assemblies and topics of land development] are ugly' [Italian]). Let me illustrate the depth and relevance of this comment by considering a conversation with two friends, Monica and Salvatore.

Late on an April evening in 1998, after I had been to a public meeting in the local auditorium about the Gennargentu Park, Salvatore invited me to come to visit him and his wife Monica. All three of us were tired, but I had been to their house many times before and the occasion was very informal. Monica brought out a tray of drinks as we talked. Salvatore informed his wife that the governmental accord to create the Gennargentu National Park had been signed in Rome the night before. This implied that local efforts to stop the park were probably in vain, and there had been considerable tension at the public meeting. Monica seemed visibly upset. A heartfelt debate about local politics and the park soon developed. Salvatore held a membership in the local Partito Democratico di Sinistra (PDS), and Monica irritably pointed out that the national and regional PDS had strongly supported the Gennargentu National Park as a regional development project. Both insisted that someone from outside Orgosolo could never understand the significance of the communal territory for the residents of Orgosolo, 'because it did not belong to them and they [had] not grown up with it'. I rejected this statement. I replied that the significance was obvious; the commons represented economic possibilities beyond the activities currently taking place there, independent of outside public assistance. I suggested that it represented a guarantee of minimum income, at least an informal one, in the event of crisis in the formal economy.

Both of them agreed with me. Salvatore affirmed, 'Yes, if you lose your job you know you won't go hungry because you can keep a couple of pigs on the territory.' Monica changed her definition of outsiders, adding that I had stayed there long enough and interested myself in the matter 'like a true Orgolese', but that 'some ignorant person from [the city], for example,' who had probably never been to Orgosolo, would have no idea how to read the ongoing events. My shared, first-hand experience of the community was taken to be key to my own comprehension of the role of the commons. It became evident, nevertheless, that I had so far grasped only part of the issue. There was far more at stake for Monica and Salvatore than economics. The two young people had salaried jobs with which to sustain themselves and help their families, and it was tacitly established that Orgosolo's territory meant far more to each of them than the baseline economic security of being able to keep 'a couple of pigs' ranging on its pastures.

We turned to talk about hunting, Salvatore's passion in sports, and one of the chief ways that he was able to enjoy time with both friends and the natural environment. Hunting associations in central Sardinian towns are made up of discrete groups of men who coordinate hunting parties in season on specific areas of local territory, monitored by the regional forest ranger service. Although not all men practise hunting, for those who do, it can provide a chance to enact identities linked to pastoral traditions and masculinity. The hardships entailed by rising as early as 3.00 a.m. to go stalking in the woods are often prized by them for the opportunity to appreciate healthy outdoor exercise, the aesthetics of the landscape and the conviviality of celebration that follows from a successful hunt. Salvatore claimed that local hunting companies had managed wildlife stocks with demonstrable success. The hunting associations, he said, were self-regulated and never in conflict with one another. He insisted that the merit for environmental conservation of the commons belonged to the community. Monica, who was exhausted from her work and little impressed by hunters, contradicted Salvatore irritably. Salvatore was still tense from the debate in the assembly. They began to argue. At last, Monica pretended to renounce the discussion, claiming sarcastically that she did not care if they created the park. Salvatore accused her a little angrily of never having been out to the territory; because she spent all her time in town, she would not know anything about the land. Monica looked annoyed, but responded to the implicit challenge that her personal tie to the commons was weak, by relenting that she might come to the next town meeting about the park.

This heated conversation demonstrated the role of emotion in the political subjectivities crafted by Orgosolo residents. The couple had quite different voting habits, jobs, personal and gendered visions of that landscape, yet both recognized the priority of maintaining ties to the landscape, whether through direct interaction with nature or a political commitment to maintaining the commons. The institution of a park would probably affect Monica and Salvatore, not only (or even primarily) at an economic level, but also at the levels of personal social life and community identity. The Orgosolo commons were central not only to many local livelihoods, but also to family excursions, religious pilgrimages, school trips and friendship group reunions. The symbolic and material products of the commons were consumed with appreciation at every meal, work party and special celebration, every exchange of hospitality and reciprocity. Emotions were a means of recognizing and communicating these shared bonds, encompassing histories, bodies, and families. It is this that defined the common ground of township, kinship and friendship.

'As if someone dear to me had died'

When they collaborated in affirming the authenticity of their emotions, residents like Monica and Salvatore transmuted their feelings of anger, mourning, vulnerability and love for the commons into the basis of a common political subjectivity. This stood in contrast to party politics, where the authority of textually produced meanings, of narrative and visual discourses over embodied actions, affirmed the power/knowledge of the educated and the media-savvy (Heatherington 2001b). Yet in the margins of party politics we may also discover alternative strategies of political practice, where moral authority to maintain control over key resources may be rooted in local discourses of embodied history, and emotions both naturalize and legitimize intimate connections between people and landscapes. The role of social memory, condensed and embodied as sensation or feeling, cannot be overlooked in attempting to interpret political action.

In an important comparative case, Aretxaga (1997) explored the role of emotionally potent personal memories, as well as expressions of pain and suffering, in constructing a new collective political subjectivity among working-class Catholic Republican women in Belfast. According to her, these women's preoccupations with the misery of sons, husbands and fathers in prison led them to dramatize the physical conditions of the prison protests in public. From their perspective, political change must follow from enabling the wider public to understand what was hidden from view, inside the prisons. They chose expressive and visual representations of prisoners to communicate their own direct, often shocking experiences of embodied suffering, humiliation and loss. Through 'the embodiment of emotion in social action' (Aretxaga 1997: 105) these women attempted to convey the experience of being Catholic Republican women in Northern Ireland.

Aretxaga's discussion is evocative in the context of Orgosolo, where women have sometimes brought particularly gendered discourses of social suffering, physical hardship and emotional anguish to bear on the matter of the park. During a town assembly, Zia Maria said that she found herself grieving for the impending loss of the communal territory as though for the death of a person she held dear. In a context where residential ties and familial relationships signified important social, economic and political collaborations, the implicit kinship metaphor was redolent with meaning. Thus her words, '*Eo appo sa sensatzione omente si fit morta una pessone cara*' ('I feel as if someone dear to me had died' [Sardinian]), unified fragmentary personal experiences and mobilized a framework of sentiment to support community political action.[4] The land itself, a cultural and economic space belonging to the community, was caught up in the natural, social bonds of a family defined by the boundaries of Orgosolo. What was for her as morally, experientially and emotionally compelling as a family tie must necessarily also become persuasive for outsiders, if only the depth and legitimacy of this communal feeling for the landscape could be articulated in political debate.

The essential difference between welcome guests and uncomprehending strangers consisted in recognition of the ways that relations of reciprocity bound the community to the past and future, and were rooted in the traditional commons.[5] Seremetakis (1994) has recalled attention to the role of commensality and material culture in constituting both historical consciousness and political subjectivity in rural Greece; I have followed her to suggest that embodied memories of reciprocity frame and inform political practice in Sardinia (Heatherington 2001b). Fieldwork should therefore entail attention to emotions and the senses as modes of meaningful social and political exchange. It was not only by virtue of my study and interviews that Orgolesi expected me to earn comprehension. Rather, they obliged me to learn firsthand what the words and statistics meant to them, through the indeterminate medium of shared experience with its inherently fluid social, gendered, spiritual, economic, meaningful, power/resistance-laden, passionate and sensual dimensions.

Although the cultural models of emotion proposed in the 1980s were limited by their conventional interpretive focus, and the clinging assumptions of bounded, stable symbolic systems, a key methodological contribution remains. Political-emotional subjectivities must still be encountered through exactly the kind of conscientious interpersonal engagement that feminist traditions in ethnography have championed. In Orgosolo, thinking, feeling, and social experience of the commons were bound together in the problem of a park. Zia Maria's public comment that new legislation made her feel 'as if someone dear to me had died' could be explained only by reflecting on local history encountered as embodied social experience.

Embodied Politics

As a notorious bastion of pastoral tradition in the central highlands of Sardinia, the townspeople of Orgosolo found it difficult to obtain legitimate political recognition of their opposition to the park. During the spring of 1998, anxiety over the commons had grown so tense in Orgosolo that the auditorium was packed full at public meetings about the park, and incidents of vandalism and political intimidation occurred. Although the perpetrators might have used these tactics intending to 'resist' the institution of a national park, the strategy backfired, at least in part. Higher levels of government refused to entertain the protests of the mayor of Orgosolo and her peers from nearby towns, and their administrative initiatives to block the legislation establishing the park were dismissed. Elected municipal authorities were presumed to act under threat and judged incompetent to represent local interests via normal political process. The Italian Minister of Environment cancelled meetings in Nuoro, and consulted with the forces of order instead. The political emotions of rural Sardinians were immediately ascribed to the domain of the dangerous.

These were the circumstances in which a grassroots, non-partisan, non-violent 'No-to-the-park' movement achieved widespread participation and support in Orgosolo and many of the other traditional herding towns whose lands were to be incorporated into the Gennargentu National Park. It was to the legitimacy of embodied emotions and embodied history that many rural Sardinians appealed when they organized a popular demonstration on the commons of Orgosolo in April 1998. The object of the rally was to protest the *legge regionale 394*, which defined the Gennargentu National Park. Between 3,000 and 5,000 people were estimated in attendance. Organizers from Orgosolo were volunteers from households dependent on either herding or forestry, conventionally associated with the commons. Long speeches by high-ranking, Italian-speaking politicians were eschewed as they sought to circumvent and transcend what they perceived as divisive and corrupt party politics.

Sardinian was selected as the primary language of the demonstration, to privilege the voices of authentic shepherds and ordinary townspeople. The material culture of local hospitality was featured prominently, both in the informal picnics that occurred on the periphery of the demonstration, and in the emulation of a folk festival with traditional poetry, music and dancing to follow the speeches. The embodied identities performed in this demonstration drew above all on strongly local models of experience and social reciprocity. The intimate and enduring connections between the landscape of the Sardinian '*Supramonte*' and a unique pastoral heritage were emphasized, above all by the location of the demonstration on the very site where Orgolesi had mounted their successful campaign against a NATO base in 1969. If one ignored the prominent presence of policemen and television cameras, the event resembled nothing so much as a kind of family reunion.

The subjective, personal experiences of participants mattered deeply to the re-enactment of historical resistance from the bottom-up.

Emotion is widely acknowledged to be a crucial aspect of political campaigns, and it is precisely the active and strategic interpretation of perceived biological states that grants meaning, force and legitimacy to certain political practices. As politicians manipulate and use local models of the family, they bring into play the gendered, cultural and developmental meanings commonly associated with emotions. In contrast to the embodied politics deployed by Italy's Northern League,[6] Sardinian political discourses of feeling and subjective experience were usually interpreted by the national media according to established perceptions of southern Italian backwardness and criminality. Widespread assumptions about the biology of gender, race and culture structured how expressions of political sentiment came to be interpreted by the Italian public.

It is important to recognize that attempts at 'objective' and 'scientific' discourses about the nature of political emotion are themselves entangled with established regimes of power/knowledge, not only within the academy but also in the world at large. Stereotypes of contemporary southern Italian backwardness have been rooted in nineteenth-century discussions of race, and the biological roots of criminality. The bifurcation of culture and development between north and south, used to explain the 'economic miracle' achieved by northerners after the Second World War, has deep roots in Italian social science discourses, as Schneider (1998) points out.[7] Sociocultural developmentalism reappears in the guise of Hobsbawm's (1959) theory about Sardinian banditry as a primitive form of political resistance. Hobsbawm portrayed the 'pre-modern' politics of rural Sardinians in opposition to the intellectually informed politics of a modern, European, civil society, making an implicit appeal to the Cartesian divide between feeling and thinking. Present-day Italian scholarly and public debates concerned with phenomena of mafia, patronage and banditry in various parts of southern Italy tend to reinforce notions of political practice – with a particular kind of 'hot' emotional inflection – as the direct outcome of virtually innate Mediterranean-style cultural-psychological dispositions. Anthropologists of Sardinia should reconsider the Cartesian legacies imbricated in these debates.

Conclusion

Political performances of cultural feeling for the traditional landscape remain salient for many townspeople in central Sardinia as they attempt to reappropriate spaces of action and discourse within the domain of environmental management. Disembodied, universalizing discourses of science currently define legitimate knowledge about 'global nature'. Yet local orientations and idioms of embodied history in Sardinia offer new ways of thinking critically about conservation and sustainable development. For now, the plan to create a Gennargentu National Park in Sardinia remains uncertain, though a bewildering variety of other environmental governance initiatives proceed apace. Creating opportunities for viable environmental partnerships must begin, however, with respect for expressions of local sentiment, and commitment to value local knowledge.

Acknowledgements

This chapter is developed from work undertaken for my doctoral dissertation at Harvard University, 1993–2000. Some elements of analysis presented here were developed from materials previously published in the *Irish Journal of Anthropology* (Heatherington 2002). I gratefully acknowledge research support from Fonds FCAR, the Wenner-Gren Foundation for Anthropological Research, the Krupp Foundation and the Mellon Foundation. I wish to thank the editors of this volume as well as the many teachers, colleagues and friends who contributed to this piece along the way; in particular, I wish to remember Begoña Aretxaga, whose work continues to inspire.

Notes

1. Later commemorated in poetry, murals and songs as the 'Battle of Pratobello', this effort to protect the commons drew media attention and support from all local political parties. See Haensch (n.d.), Circolo Giovanile di Orgosolo (1969), Muggianu (1999) and Heatherington (2000, 2002).

2. For critical discussion of the uneven impacts of the enclosure movement and anti-feudalism in highland central Sardinia, see Berger (1986).

3. Areas of oak trees in particular were sold off by many communities; these were valued for the production of railway ties and coal (Bodemann 1979: 35, 130). Orgosolo's forest, conserved not by the forestry service but by the municipality on its communal territory, has become a rare example of Mediterranean climax forest (see Heatherington 2001a).

4. The metaphor of a dead or dying beloved person also suggested an important political role for women. In Orgosolo, women generally care for sick members of an extended family and take on special roles to help and console the families of the deceased. In coordination with the priests, women manage all funerary rituals within Orgosolo. Women also manage most of the gift-giving; in some respects, we might see them as coordinating emotional ties within and between families, in that they mediate symbolic exchanges associated with kinship ties and social ties, including a discourse of feeling.

5. These relations of reciprocity could not be reduced to a Durkheimian model of solidarity, nor explained away as effects of a collective symbolic imagination.

Rather, as Mauss (1973[1935]) directed us from the beginning, reciprocity was profoundly embedded in bodily experiences.

6. Umberto Bossi's emotional, sexual, aggressive rhetoric was grounded in a vision of superior cultural progress associated with industrialization and economic growth in Northern Italy. See also discussions by Anna Cento Bull (1996).

7. For example, one can trace 'scientific' definitions of Sardinian cultural psychology from the work of the physical anthropologist Niceforo (1977 [1897]), who arrived in Orgosolo and a handful of other towns in central Sardinia at the end of the nineteenth century. He measured people's heads, seeking evidence for his theory that a predilection for banditry, as a *primitive* form of criminality, might be tied to the biological characteristics of race.

References

Abu-Lughod, L. (1986), *Veiled Sentiments: Honor and Poetry in a Bedouin Society*, Berkeley, CA: University of California Press.

Aretxaga, B. (1997), *Shattering Silence: Women, Nationalism and Political Subjectivity in Northern Ireland*, Princeton, NJ: Princeton University Press.

Ayora-Diaz, S. I. (1993), 'Representation and Occupations: Shepherds' Choices in Sardinia', PhD dissertation, McGill University, Montreal.

Berger, P. (1986), 'Cooperation, Conflict, and Production Environment in Highland Sardinia: A Study of the Associational Life of Transhumant Shepherds', PhD dissertation, Columbia University, New York.

Bodemann, M. (1979), 'Telemula: Aspects of the Micro-organization of Backwardness in Central Sardinia, PhD dissertation, Brandeis University, Massachusetts.

Bourdieu, P. (1977), *Outline of a Theory of Practice*, Cambridge and New York: Cambridge University Press.

Bull, A. C. (1996), 'Ethnicity, Racism and the Northern League', in C. Levy (ed.), *Italian Regionalism*, Oxford: Berg.

Cagnetta, F. (1975 [1954]), *Banditi a Orgosolo*, Rimini, Italy: Guaraldi.

Circolo Giovanile di Orgosolo (1968), *Orgosolo novembre 1968*, Milan: Feltrinelli.

Corda, E. (1989), *Storia di Orgosolo: 1937–1953*, Milan: Rusconi.

Csordas, T. (1990), 'Embodiment as a Paradigm for Anthropology', *Ethos* 18 (1): 5–47.

De Certeau, M. (1984), *The Practice of Everyday Life*, Berkeley, CA: University of California Press.

Del Piano, L. (1979), *Proprietà collettiva e proprietà privata della terra in Sardegna: Il caso di Orune (1874–1940)*, Cagliari, Italy: Della Torre.

Haensch, D. (n.d.), 'Sa lotta de Pratobello/La lotta di Pratobello/Der Kampf von

Pratobello 1969', unpublished manuscript.

Heatherington, T. (1999), 'Street Tactics: Catholic Ritual and the Senses of the Past in Central Sardinia', *Ethnology* 38 (4): 315–34.

—— (2000), *'As If Someone Dear To Me Had Died': The cultural politics of environmentalism in Sardinia*, PhD dissertation, Harvard University, Massachusetts.

—— (2001a), 'Ecology, Alterity and Resistance in Sardinia', *Social Anthropology* 9 (3): 285–302.

—— (2001b), 'In the Rustic Kitchen: Real talk and reciprocity', *Ethnology* 40 (4): 329–45.

—— (2002), 'Murals and the Memory of Resistance in Sardinia', *Irish Journal of Anthropology* 5: 8–25.

Herzfeld, M. (2003), *The Body Impolitic: Artisans and Artifice in the Global Hierarchy of Value*, Chicago: University of Chicago Press.

Hobsbawm, E. J. (1959), *Primitive Rebels: Studies in Archaic Forms of Social Movement in the 19th and 20th Centuries*, New York and London: W. W. Norton.

Jackson, M. (1983), 'Knowledge of the Body', *Man* (NS) 18 (2): 327–45.

Leavitt, J. (1996), 'Meaning and Feeling in the Anthropology of Emotions', *American Ethnologist* 23 (3): 514–39.

Lutz, C. (1988), *Unnatural Emotions: Everyday Sentiments on a Micronesian Atoll and their Challenge to Western Theory*, Chicago: University of Chicago Press.

Mauss, M. (1973 [1935]), 'Techniques of the Body', *Economy and Society* 2: 70–88.

Meloni, B. (1984), *Famiglie di pastori: continuità e mutamento in una comunità della Sardegna centrale, 1950–1970*, Istituto superiore regionale etnografico, Nuoro, Italy: Rosenberg & Sellier.

Merleau-Ponty, M. (1964), *The Phenomenology of Perception*, London: Routledge and Kegan Paul.

Milton, K. (1996), *Environmentalism and Cultural Theory: Exploring the Role of Anthropology in Environmental Discourse*, London and New York: Routledge.

—— (2002), *Loving Nature: Towards an Ecology of Emotion*, London and New York: Routledge.

Muggianu, P. (1998), *Orgosolo '68–'70: Il triennio rivoluzionario*, Nuoro, Italy: Studiostampa.

Niceforo, A. (1977 [1897]), *La Delinquenza in Sardegna*, Cagliari, Italy: Della Torre.

Rosaldo, M. Z. (1980), *Knowledge and Passion: Ilongot Notions of Self and Social Life*, Cambridge: Cambridge University Press.

—— (1984), 'Toward an Anthropology of Self and Feeling', in R. A. Shweder and R. A. LeVine (eds), *Culture Theory: Essays on Mind, Self and Emotion*, Cambridge: Cambridge University Press.

Salis, G. (1990), *Orgosolo tra Storia e Mito*, Cagliari, Italy: Ettore Gasperini.

Satta, G. (2001), *Turisti a Orgosolo: La Sardegna pastorale come attrazione turistica*, Naples, Italy: Liguori Editore.

Schneider, J. (1998), 'Introduction', in J. Schneider (ed.), *Italy's 'Southern Question': Orientalism in One Country*, Oxford and New York: Berg.

Schweizer, P. (1988), *Shepherds, Workers and Intellectuals: Culture and Centre–Periphery Relationships in a Sardinian village*, Stockholm: University of Stockholm.

Seremetakis, C. N. (1994), 'The Memory of the Senses Part II: Still Acts', in C. N. Seremetakis (ed.), *The Senses Still*, Chicago: University of Chicago Press.

Sio, G. F. (1996–7), *Gli Istituti Giuridici Tradizionali in Materia de Lavoro nella Pastorizia*, Tesi di Laurea, Università di Cagliari degli Studi.

Stoller, P. (1997), *Sensuous Scholarship*, Philadelphia, PA: University of Pennsylvania Press.

Strathern, A. J. (1996), *Body Thoughts*, Ann Arbor, MI: University of Michigan Press.

–9–

Love, Suffering and Grief Among Spanish Gitanos

Paloma Gay y Blasco

Introduction

In a recent volume on the emotions and aesthetics of community-making in Amazonia, Overing and Passes (2000: xi) explain as their main concern the exploration of the 'practices, notions and feelings relating to everyday communal life and ... the different ways of constructing, experiencing and embodying it'. Here I am engaged in a similar enterprise: I want to explore the role that emotions play in the construction of communities of particular kinds. More specifically, I want to understand how *el pueblo Gitano* (the Gitano people) or *nosotros los Gitanos* (us the Gitanos) as a lived reality and also as an imagined construct is brought about by the Gitanos of Villaverde Alto, a district in the south of Madrid. My starting point is the awareness that communal life has emotive as well as practical and imaginative dimensions and that communities do not have to be premised either on social cohesiveness or on feelings or ideals of harmony.

Both among the Gitanos of Villaverde and in the Amazonia described by Overing and Passes (2000), social life can be defined as structurally weak in classic anthropological terms; the relationship between the individual and the ideal of the group, the imagined community, is not seen as mediated by institutions such as kinship groups or corporations, and in fact the very concept of 'society' is absent from these peoples' self-representations. Indeed, in both cases responsibility for the creation of the community resides with the self, its attitudes, emotions and aesthetic inclinations. However, whereas in Amazonian contexts a group's sense of community is anchored in politico-moral notions to do with the collective good and the individual's subordination to it, notions of communal harmony and solidarity are very heavily downplayed in the Gitanos' accounts of themselves and in the feelings and practices that accompany them.

In this the Gitanos of Villaverde differ both from other acephalous minorities whose singularity and lifestyle survive under the pressure of dominant majorities, and indeed from some other Roma. The Hungarian Rom, for example, strive to transcend inequalities and achieve uniformity among themselves throughout multiple contexts – singing and drinking celebrations, exchanges of horses, dress, house decoration and so on. Their ideal is one of 'unity among brothers' and is threatened, not only by the non-Roma world, but also by the links of men to women and to their kinship groups (Stewart 1997). The Buid, shifting cultivators from the Philippines whose livelihood is jeopardized by settled Christian agriculturalists, similarly emphasize the subordination of the individual to the group. The Buid believe that 'life depends on the maintenance of solidarity' (Gibson 1986: 220) so that among them 'the idioms that dominate social life are those of community, companionship and sharing' (Gibson 1986: 218). Even among the Australian Pintupi, who lack a concept of an overarching 'society' or 'community' (Myers 1986: 257), it is the 'smoothly running, co-operative relations of mutual help that recognize shared identity' (Myers 1986: 256).

My concern in this chapter is with how in Villaverde 'the Gitano people' is created, sustained and reproduced as an entity that, by contrast to the cases just outlined, does not rely on feelings or ideals of community-wide harmony or cohesiveness as essential to 'the good life'. This entity is built instead on the expectation of conflict among non-kin, on moral mimesis among gendered Gitano persons, and on love towards relatives, dead or alive. In what follows, I concentrate on love towards kin and grief at the death of close relations, and on what these reveal about the particular Gitano way of linking the self and the group, and of positioning them in time and within the world at large – a world that, again as in Amazonia, is seen as including a large contingent of latent threats originating within and outside the Gitano collective.

Indeed, the Gitanos I met in Madrid most often described their relations with both non-Roma (called by the Gitanos *Payos*)[1] and unrelated Gitanos as strongly antagonistic. First, the power of social workers, doctors and teachers to harm the Gitanos is perceived as immense; they control the resources that the Gitanos need – housing, financial help, permits for selling in the streets or searching at the rubbish dump and so on – and they are often resisting, unyielding and unpredictable, and hence dangerous. Second, unrelated Gitanos present no smaller a threat; minor misunderstandings and falling-outs can very easily lead to more serious fighting and hence to injuries, deaths and feuding or, in other words, to major threats to the safety of substantial numbers of people.

Within a world populated by potential enemies close kin provide the Gitanos with a heaven. Love, born out of shared ancestry, shared experiences and intense day-to-day sociability among kin, is what binds relatives together, not only in the present but in the past too. Love towards deceased relations is described as extremely strong and, because they are no longer present, as extremely painful. The grief that these Gitanos experience upon the death of close kin is re-experienced through remembrance, and structured around elaborate practices of simultaneous private commemoration and public obliteration of individuals and events (see Gay y Blasco 2001). Most importantly, expressions of love towards kin, dead or alive, are essential to a mode of being in the world that purposefully disregards social cohesiveness as the domain where the togetherness or commonality of 'the Gitanos' or 'the Gitano people' originates.

A Fragmented Community

Villaverde Alto is very similar to other inner-city areas of Madrid: it has low standards of living and low life expectancy, and high poverty, unemployment and crime. Gitanos have been living there and in comparable lower-working class-districts since the 1950s, when they came to Madrid from the countryside as part of the massive rural exodus that swept across Spain in the late post-war period. They arrived and settled as they had lived until then, in clusters of patrilineally related kin – *razas* or patrigroups – who dealt with intra-community conflict through blood feuding and through the spatial separation of the parties involved. And, as they had done in the villages, these patrigroups continued to try to avoid impinging on each other's territory and resources and to disperse themselves as thinly as possible among the Payos (San Román 1994). Since the 1960s and up to the present, however, government policies have dictated the growing concentration of Gitanos in shanty towns, housing estates and even in Roma-only, purpose-built ghettos (Gay y Blasco 2003). This trend has made it difficult for patrigroups to scatter themselves among the Payos, and led, in the 1960s and 1970s, to high levels of *ruinas* (feuding) and later to the development of novel political institutions such as *caciques* and mafia-like networks (San Román 1994). Throughout the 1980s and 1990s, Gitanos from all over Madrid were resettled by the authorities in Villaverde, either in blocks of flats among the Payos or in Jarana, a physically isolated, Gitano-only estate built on the edge of the district to house those families perceived by local social workers and bureaucrats as most resistant to assimilation.

Although the frequency of violent conflict seems to have decreased significantly since the early 1980s or so (San Román 1994), the Gitanos of Villaverde continue to put much emphasis on the *leyes Gitanas* or 'Gitanos laws' that prescribe feuding and dictate that individuals' primary allegiance is to their *razas*. People who share the same *raza* affiliation also share juridical personality in the sense that they owe allegiance to each other in confrontations between Gitanos, and also that they are liable to be the object of retaliation when a patrilineal relative has offended or injured a member of another *raza* (see San Román 1976). Fear of feuding still retains a strong hold over the Gitanos' imaginations; Tía Tula, a woman from Jarana in her seventies, often described to me vivid nightmares in which she herself, or her children or grandchildren, were wounded or killed, and from which she would wake up screaming. The Gitanos of Villaverde always worry that even minor clashes will develop into fully fledged feuds, and act in consequence. They avoid unnecessary interaction with non-kin in daily life, they attempt to set mediation procedures in motion almost as soon as conflicts are sparked, and they pre-empt retaliation by fleeing their homes at the first sign of trouble. During March 2002, for example, I tried in vain to get hold of Sara, one of my closest friends, by phone. For weeks on end there was no reply and when I finally visited Villaverde in Easter, it was to find her and her family back in their flat after having just returned from hiding; a paternal cousin of Sara's had been involved in a shooting incident over drugs, and most of Sara's agnates, many with their spouses and children, had decided to abandon the area until the worst of the quarrel was over.

Feuding and fear of feuding are premised upon and reinforce links to paternal kin, and are essential in constructing an emotional universe where Gitano persons face a hostile world in which not only the threatening Payos, but also unrelated Gitanos, are potential sources of danger. In other words, feuding and fear of feuding go a long way towards displacing ideals and feelings of unity, harmony and cohesiveness to the margins of the Gitano imagined community (Gay y Blasco 1999). And yet in Villaverde the all-important agnatic ties around which feuding and its accoutrements revolve are balanced and complemented by other types of kinship connections that, in everyday life and outside feuding contexts, can be of equal or even greater importance. Love lies at the core of all these relations, whether paternal or maternal, or even in some cases affinal, and provides the centripetal counterpoint to feuding and to all its practical, imaginative and emotional ramifications. It is on the basis of love for close kin that the people of Villaverde are able to construct a refuge in the midst of a hostile environment, and it is love for kin that provides them with the actual day-to-day support and emotional and practical validation of the positive value of their difference from the Payos.

Love and Kin in Jarana

'To us Gitanos the family is the most fundamental thing, that is your father, your mother, your siblings, your family, your uncles, your everybody, it is the greatest [thing] there is'. This is how Clara, a woman now in her mid-thirties, described to me her feelings towards her relatives – sisters, parents, uncles and aunts, cousins and grandparents. Her vehement statement expresses the certainty that kin, especially those within the bilateral extended family, are the key element in the life of any Gitano, that for which the greatest *cariño* (love or affection) is felt. Physical links, the awareness of shared origins, lie at the core of these emotions; individuals share bodily substance with their relatives on the paternal and maternal sides, and this makes them love each other. So for example, explaining his love for his favourite nephew, Tío Juan told me that 'it is because we come from the same roots'. At the same time, he and his wife Tía Tula emphasized, although 'one is related to both sides' it is the 'seed', the male substance, that works as the activating principle, the source of life. In their account it is men who 'provide' or 'make' the child and it is because the father is the one who 'puts in' the child, whereas the mother 'is like the earth' who receives it, that he 'lifts (starts) the lineage' and that children inherit their father's *raza* affiliation over that of their mother.

Love of kin, both maternal and paternal, is therefore in part an inevitable consequence of their physical connection, and as such the people of Jarana and Villaverde consider it unavoidable and unproblematic: 'one loves one's kin'. At the same time, *cariño* towards relatives is said to grow through physical closeness and shared experiences. The sense that close relatives are, as Clara says, 'the most fundamental thing' feeds on the highly intense experience of spending daily life within a dense web of interactions with close bilateral kin, what I call endosociability. Time spent together, having lived nearby and especially *haberse criado juntos* (having grown up together) as part of the same household or in nearby ones are fundamental in strengthening relations between kin, making some extraordinarily deep.

Indeed, it is this daily endosociability that most clearly reveals that key role that relatives play in each other's social and emotional universe. Living as part of Clara's sister Sara's household for two months in 1993, I was struck both by how much the Gitanos of Jarana enjoyed the company of their close kin, and by how difficult it was to identify times in the day when a Gitano man or woman was not surrounded by them. At that time Sara was in her late twenties and lived in a high-rise flat in Villaverde with Paco, her husband, and their two young children. Sara and Paco sold textiles in five weekly markets in Madrid and every morning they left the house early with their merchandise and collapsible stall. They met Sara's father and two of her unmarried sisters at the market where they took up spaces side by side, Paco and his father-in-law Arturo setting up the stalls, and the women going for breakfast at a local bar. Throughout the morning Sara and her sisters would take breaks together or with other aunts and cousins, wives and children of Arturo's brothers, who were also working at the market. The men would do the same with their male relations. The younger people bantered with their cousins and in-laws of the opposite sex, and youthful female bottoms got pinched and male heads playfully bashed with loaves of bread. In between dealing with the Payo customers who thronged the market, Sara and her kin would shout news and jokes at each other or simply make eye contact. Unrelated Gitanos who passed by or who also worked at the market would be treated politely but coldly and Payos would be merely engaged to be enticed to stop at the stall and buy.

Some days, Sara and Paco would go back to their own flat for lunch. On other occasions, they joined Sara's parents. They had less contact with Paco's brothers, who lived in distant areas of the city; his parents had died some years previously. In the afternoon, Sara would take her children and walk to Jarana to watch the afternoon soap opera with her sister Clara and some of her aunts (FBsWs) and cousins (FBsDs) who lived in the ghetto.[2] Or else one or more of them would turn up at her flat for coffee and sweets. Later Sara would join sisters, cousins and aunts at the local Evangelical church, where they would sit nearby during the service. Dinner was again likely to be an endosociable occasion, with relatives popping in either to eat or for a cup of coffee. By contrast, Sara and her sisters rarely socialized with unrelated Gitanos. Even at the Evangelical church, which they all attended regularly and which strongly prohibits feuding and promotes relations among non-kin, these women tended to relate with their relatives. They would sit next to or near their female aunts and cousins, take cups of coffee with them at the church bar, team up to clean the church together, and so on. They would greet other Gitanos politely when they met them in the streets of the neighbourhood, at the health centre or at the market, but would not spend much time with them.

Sara and her sisters live within a sociable and emotive environment that is heavily dominated by their own – rather than their husbands' – paternal kin. In this, they are somewhat unusual in Jarana where, given the preference for virilocal and patrilocal residence, daily endosociability often strengthens ties to patrilineal relatives and is thus significant in giving experiential meaning to the obligation that individuals who share *raza* affiliation have to give support to each other during conflicts. Nonetheless, and because the Gitanos of Villaverde and Jarana much prefer to have their children marry close relatives – with a high incidence of first and second cousin marriage, both cross- and parallel- – individuals' consanguines are often also their affines and patrilineal kin are also maternally related. Take the example of Lola, Sara's sister. Lola married her paternal cross-cousin Juan. Juan's mother and Lola's father were children of Tío Sebas, who in turn was the son of a sister of Tío Juan, Juan's paternal grandfather. Juan married his MBD; Lola married her FZS; Juan's father married his FZSD; Juan's mother married her FMBS. Juan and Lola share a great-grandmother who was also Juan's great aunt (Tío Juan's sister). Lola's father and mother were unrelated, but Lola's mother was a patrilineal relative of Tío Juan's wife Tía Tula. If we go further back in time, we see that because Juan's and Lola's great-grandmother married a paternal parallel cousin, Juan and Lola share *raza* affiliation.

Similarly, constraints over choice of residence, dictated by state policies on Gitano housing (see Gay y Blasco 2003), mean that growing numbers of newly married couples are not able to live virilocally and that affines and maternal relatives, who may nonetheless be also patrilineally related, come to play a key role in the daily lives of women *and* men. Take the example of Tío Juan and his descendants. When Jarana was first built and the Gitano families about to be resettled there were given some choice over which houses to occupy, Tío Juan's four sons and two married grandsons with their wives took houses adjacent to the old man's. Of Tío Juan's three daughters, one came to Jarana and lives next to her brothers with her husband and children, and two live virilocally. The family continued expanding, however, and began to experience difficulties with space in 1993. Two more grandsons married that year, and had brick shacks built for them in their father's and brother's courtyards respectively – a common practice in Jarana where the council has forbidden the building of new houses and free-standing structures. Another grandson who married the following year was given a bedroom in his father's house; soon, he and his wife were sharing the cramped space with their two young children. By the time his younger brother married, however, there literally was no space for him and his wife and they, like other new couples, had to live uxorilocally. As the years go by and space in the estate becomes more and more restricted, young couples live where they can, often with or near the wife's parents.

As a result of these various constraints and practices, therefore, most people in Villaverde live within a tightly knight group of relatives to whom they are likely to be linked by multiple kinship ties. These are people to whom they feel emotionally very close and among whom conflicts would be very unlikely to escalate into fully fledged feuds. This group is called *familia* (family), a word the Gitanos use to refer to nuclear families, to patrigroups, and to the wider and bilateral *familia retirada* (distant family). Closeness and shared identity among members of the *familia* are reinforced by naming and godparenthood, and by forms of address. Thus, these Gitanos tend to choose very close bilateral kin – siblings, cousins or even their own parents or grandparents – as their children's godparents, and give them their names. Sara and her husband Paco, for example, are the godparents of little Sara, Lola's daughter. Sara's eldest daughter Nina was her deceased paternal grandmother's goddaughter and shares her name, and her brother Tomás is his maternal grandfather's godson, and shares his name. Lola in turn is the godmother of Sara's youngest child, baby Lola. Although not all children are named after their godparents – in particular among Evangelical Gitanos, who choose biblical names – a high proportion are. Through godparenthood the Gitanos acknowledge the given and unavoidable ties of shared ancestry while strengthening the ties of love and that unite close relatives.

Likewise, the people of Jarana refer to close kin as 'my' followed by their first names ('my Nina', 'my Tomás') and, in so doing, establish an emotive claim on each other. They are each other's because of the love that they share and because, I was told, they *sufren por ella/el* (suffer on behalf of) their close relatives, taking their troubles on and experiencing them as their own. What happens when a person has to be taken to hospital illustrates this very clearly. Whether somebody is undergoing a planned surgery or tests, or has been rushed to accident and emergency after some mishap, kin, both immediate and also more distant within the *familia*, hurry to hospital to *acompañar* (accompany) both the patient and their immediate family. Indeed, early afternoons in Villaverde are often taken up with hospital visits of one kind or another and it is very easy to come across groups of Gitanos in the waiting room in the local accident and emergency hospital, 'accompanying' the parents of a small child who needs stitches or an elderly man who has pulled his back.

After several years of illness, Sara's mother Elena died of breast cancer in January 2004. She had spent most of Christmas in and out hospital, in painful and drawn out agony but in full control of her mental abilities. Her husband, her daughters and her sons-in-law, as well as her parents and siblings and more distant relations like nieces and nephews, grandchildren, cousins, aunts and uncles and so on, spent days at a stretch in the hospital's waiting room. They slept on chairs, went unwashed, ate at the hospital's canteen and drank fizzy drinks from vending machines. Hospital rules allowed only one visitor at a time, and the daughters took turns to sit by Elena's bed. Other kin kept each other company, and attempted to reassure Sara and her sisters that their mother would soon recover. In the waiting room, a space shared with indifferent and ever-changing strangers, Elena's daughters cried intermittently, and had episodes of intensely displayed grief and worry when they would pace the room up and down, or leave the hospital altogether to cry loudly, rocking backwards and forwards and wringing their hands.

On one of the last occasions when Elena was taken to hospital, I arrived before she did and waited for the ambulance with her husband Arturo and other relatives. Arturo hugged me closely and cried in my arms, and I awkwardly did my best to do as I had seen others do, tell him that this was a minor hiccup, and that Elena would be back at home soon. When the ambulance finally arrived and they took Elena out on a stretcher, all the Gitanos who were waiting in small groups outside the hospital crowded around, smiling at Elena and wishing her well. I stood back, unsure of what to do, not wanting to interfere or push myself forward. Arturo later asked me why I had not approached the stretcher and when I replied that I had not wanted to disturb Elena or her close family, he said, 'Don't be silly, Palomi, she would have liked to have seen you were here, I'll sneak you into her room later on, she'll love to see you'. It became clear to me that 'accompanying' reassures the person who suffers and those who suffer on their behalf that they are not alone but surrounded by the protection of those who love them, in particular close relatives.

And yet, in spite of the closeness and strong affection that characterizes relations among close kin, the *familia* is by no means a wholly harmonious environment. Individuals often describe the tensions that result from conflicting demands from different relations and, in particular, how loving relationships with siblings and parents are often challenged by allegiances to spouses. At Easter 2003, almost a year before her mother's death, I met Sara in her flat in Villaverde. She was worried on behalf of her sister Clara, whose husband Lolo was dangerously ill in hospital. Sara explained how much she was 'suffering' on behalf of Clara: '*Sufro por ella. Es mi hermana, y lo que le pasa a ella es como si me pasara a mi, peor, lo sufro en mi propia carne'* ('I suffer on her behalf. She is my sister and what happens to her it is as if it happened to me, even worse, I suffer it in my own flesh'). Sara told me that Clara was having a very hard time, that she was completely devoted to her husband, and was hardly eating or taking care of herself and her appearance.

That afternoon we visited Clara and Lolo in hospital, and I was shocked to see how poorly and unkempt Clara looked. In her slippers, with dishevelled hair and obviously not having washed herself for some time, she was rocking to and fro in the corridor of the hospital, praying loudly while her husband underwent a blood test. She ignored Sara and me, and ran inside Lolo's room as soon as the nurses left him, leaving Sara's questions unanswered. In the hospital cafeteria Sara complained to me about Clara; it was obvious that she was extremely miserable and preoccupied, and Sara was distressed to witness this – *'se me parte el corazón de verla'* ('my heart breaks to see her like this') – and yet Clara refused to share her burden with her sisters or her parents. She had not even told them what Lolo had although he had been in hospital for over two weeks, getting worse by the day. They suspected AIDS and were worried that she too might be HIV positive. They felt left out, unable to comfort Clara but suffering on her behalf while watching her whispering in corners with her in-laws – who, Sara said, presumably did know what Lolo was suffering from. The following week Sara rang me to tell me that Clara had finally told their mother that Lolo had AIDS. For Lolo, a minister of the Evangelical Church, suffering from an illness that he had acquired as a young drug addict involved a huge loss of face. Indeed, it is common for families of AIDS sufferers to hide the disease from non-relations, and Sara told me she and her parents were heartbroken because for weeks Clara had treated them like non-kin. Clara had separated herself from her parents and siblings, choosing instead to align herself with her in-laws, and in the process undermined the strongest of bonds: that between people who, through their suffering, are able to claim each other as their own.

The Beloved Deceased

Given how intense in terms of both depth and frequency relations with close kin are in Villaverde, and given also the centrality of these relations to the Gitano social and emotive universe, it is not surprising that grief at the death of close relatives should be given a high degree of elaboration. Indeed, the Gitanos think of the dead as somebody's cherished kinsmen and women, calling them *los difuntos allegados* (the beloved deceased), and love is the pivot around which all relations between the living and the dead revolve. But, whereas in the case of relatives who are still alive, love is a source of joy, love towards the dead is a harrowing emotion because it cannot but remain unfulfilled. Once they have joined the ranks of the beloved deceased, worry, anxiety and suffering on behalf of close kin as well as regret at their absence can never be resolved and are described as the source of enormous grief.

Thinking and talking about the beloved deceased is therefore an unavoidably and intensely unhappy activity; many Gitanos cry when they speak about the dead and most appear visibly moved. Elsewhere (Gay y Blasco 2001), I have described how, in order to avoid the pain of loving and remembering, Gitanos try to avoid being reminded of the beloved deceased and how much of what these Gitanos do and say in relation to the dead seems aimed at erasing their memory. They explain that it is important to prevent the beloved deceased from appearing in the mind of the living (*que el difunto allegado no se represente*); talking about a cherished kinsman who is now dead, seeing somebody wearing his clothes, or hearing his favourite song, evokes the most powerful and distressing images and the resulting sadness is so overpowering that it is best avoided. Thus, because Paco's mother loved to sing, five years after her death Sara and his other kin still avoided singing the songs she liked best or even singing at all in his presence. They did not openly discuss their silence, but its reason was clear to those who had known the deceased and to them alone.

Hence, the dead should not be talked about and, when they are, it is never by their names but through kinship categories that are formalized and neutral but also subtly endearing ('Sara's poor little aunt, may she rest in peace'; 'My poor little brother, may he rest in peace'). Unhappy memories of the dead are often described by these Gitanos as triggered by visual reminders, such as photographs or the physical spaces where the dead spent time, which therefore have to be removed from sight or avoided. Thus the belongings of the beloved deceased are burnt or broken and thrown away shortly after the death; their photographs are hidden or destroyed; and their room or even their house remains locked, often for several years. After Elena's death, for example, Arturo left the flat they had shared for over a decade and moved in with his youngest daughter Lola. The flat was to remain empty and unused and Sara explained to me how 'when I went there to burn her clothes I saw her in every room, the feeling was too strong, I couldn't stand it. I don't think I could go back'.

The power of visual and other reminders to unlock sorrow is described by the Gitanos as enduring and even everlasting. I recall arriving one evening at the house of Sara's relative Tío Juan only to find him and his wife Tía Tula rummaging through a plastic bag holding old sepia photographs of kin deceased decades ago. Looking at one picture at a time, the couple were sobbing loudly and dabbing at their eyes with handkerchiefs. One photograph, in particular, made Tío Juan cry harder than the rest. It was very blurred and he, badly afflicted by cataracts, could barely distinguish a fuzzy human form; still, in that piece of worn paper lingered the image of the sister he had loved best, who died thirty years ago. When their grandson Alberto arrived on the scene, he scolded the old couple and blamed them for their unhappiness: 'One should not look at the photos of the dead; see what state you get yourselves in! You should have burnt them.'

It is as if the link between the living and the dead could never be completely broken, as if the love between the beloved deceased and their living relatives remained somehow not only in the latter's personae but also in the physical spaces and objects that surrounded the dead while they lived, and in the activities they carried out. It is, however, during the initial period after the death of a close relative – the weeks and months dominated by *luto* (formal mourning) – that the emotive presence of the dead among and in the living is most keenly felt and when the *familia* interacts most intensely. This is the time of deepest sadness, when relatives display their sorrow by dressing in black and when they 'accompany' the beloved deceased almost as if they were still alive. For over two months after Elena's death in early January 2004, her husband, daughters and sons-in-law, siblings and grandchildren spent every afternoon in the cemetery by her tomb. They would wrap up warm, for Madrid winters are windy and bitter, sit on folding chairs, and keep each other company while they cried or simply thought about Elena. Afterwards they would spend the evening together at Lola's house, chatting quietly around the wood-burning stove, never drinking alcohol or smoking, and without watching television or listening to the radio, activities that are considered *diversión* (entertainment) and a breach of *luto*.

It is only the immediate kin who 'accompany' the dead and each other in this way, and it is only they who are said to formally mourn. *Luto* lasts for varying periods of time, depending on the nature of the tie between the deceased and the mourner, and on the latter's emotional disposition. One mourns, Sara and her sister Clara explained long before their mother died, *hasta que te cumpla* (until one is fulfilled), that is, as long as one feels compelled to mourn, independently of others' opinions and pressures. The feelings that should trigger mourning, they stressed, cannot be imposed from the outside and taking on *luto* has to be a decision arising out of personal emotions that only the individual involved really knows. Fulfilment comes after months or years and, in the case of widows, should never be reached. Clara was adamant, if her husband Lolo died, she would mourn him until her own death. But mourning properly, she warned, is difficult and rather than doing it half-heartedly one should abstain from doing it at all: 'You'd rather wear *luto* short and good than long and bad'. When, after Clara's uncle Ernesto died the family found his drug-addict brother Pedro heavily stoned, his other brothers and nephews gave him a beating and removed his mourning clothes, effectively *quitándole* (taking away) his right to wear *luto*. Wearing *luto*, like refraining from talking about the dead or avoiding the foods and activities they liked, is an expression not only of love but, equally importantly, of respect towards them.

And yet mourning *llevarlo bien* (properly or well) is not simply an individual activity, or one shared by the immediate family, but one that depends on the support of both related and unrelated Gitanos who must also respect the *luto*. Displays of happiness and noise from entertainment – television, radio, spontaneous gatherings for dancing and singing in the street – in particular are considered disrespectful to people in mourning and must be avoided not only by them but also by Gitano neighbours and passers-by alike. Failing to respect the *luto* of others is an offence weighty enough to justify a full-blown blood feud and more minor disputes over *luto* are extremely common. Only Gitanos, however, are demanded to show this respect; Payos are considered to live outside the Gitano moral universe, and their overall lack of *conocimiento* (knowledge) and *entendimiento* (understanding) about what is right and wrong means that they are like small children or animals, from whom respect cannot be expected. So when Sara and Paco went back to selling at their weekly market stalls, they were extremely angry and upset when a distant cousin who sold cassette tapes would not turn down the loud music that advertised his wares, although he knew full well they were still in mourning and standing a mere 50 metres away. And yet, they only shrugged their shoulders when the Payo vegetable vendor whose stall was next to theirs turned on the radio.

Eventually feelings of sadness begin to subside or, as Sara explained, '*la pena se hace mas llevadera*' (become more bearable). After three or four months the younger family members are encouraged by their elders to stop mourning, and are pushed into enjoying themselves, going out to cafés or to the movies. 'We made them stop. They have worn it long enough', Sara told me after her younger sister Ana and her daughter Nina, both teenage wives, gave up their *luto* three months after Elena's death: 'They are too young for this, they need to go back to normal'. Slowly, everyday sociability becomes less sombre and the rules of mourning more flexible. An elaborate and very expensive tomb, commissioned from Payos carvers at the time of the death, is finally finished and adorned with hundreds of plastic flowers, and with marble jars and marble books with engraved messages from those left behind ('Father, we will never forget you'), as well as life-size statues of the deceased or of his favourite hunting dogs. The tomb embodies the love and care of the relatives who are still alive, it is the receptacle for their suffering on behalf of the beloved deceased. Recently Sara told me on the phone about her mother's tomb, how all the family had contributed financially, and how lovely it finally looked, covered in carved roses and doves, with two large vases and two open carved books with quotes from the Bible. They had hung on the tomb a little stained glass medallion, with a picture of a dove representing the Holy Spirit, that I had sent to Sara shortly after Elena's death thinking she would hang it in her own house. Like no other gesture or statement before this made me feel part of the family, the medallion turned by her daughters into a metonymic sign of my love for Elena.

After the early period of intense *luto*, visits to the cemetery become more spaced out but continue to take place several times per year and always during All Saints when the beloved deceased are once again accompanied as if they had only recently died. After the period of formal, openly displayed mourning is over, the silent and indeed private forms of avoidance and commemoration that I have described above take over, eventually leading to the invisibility of the dead in everyday, neighbourhood life. Ultimately, the dead should never be referred to by non-kin, who should not mention their names or even know about them. But when the dead have been removed from visible life in the neighbourhood, the cemetery remains the focus of emotive remembrance and intra-familial solidarity. Kin are buried nearby, ideally within sight of each other, in areas that become taken over by Gitano families with only the odd Payo tomb here and there. The physical space of the graveyard resembles a gathering of loving kin, and a relative sitting by the tomb of a wife or a father can see all around the statues and tombs of many other beloved deceased. When I visited Tío Juan's grave with María, his daughter-in-law, she indicated one by one all the tombs that surrounded it: his son Manuel was buried just two tombs away, his grave barely visible under a mound of red plastic carnations; his beloved nephew Sebas was just opposite, with a full-sized statue of the deceased as a young man; two sisters and another nephew were also buried next to Sebas, all in a row, and so on. '*Están todos juntos los pobrecicos*' ('They are all together, poor little them'), María told me. Even after death, she emphasized, the Gitanos should remain within the loving embrace of their kin.

Conclusion: Loving, Suffering, Grieving, and the Construction of a Fragmented Community

Like other Roma, the Spanish Gitanos face enormous and often overtly hostile pressures to assimilate into the dominant majority (Gay y Blasco 2003). They think of themselves as living under siege, surrounded by Payos with whom all interactions are negotiations, exchanges of goods and services in which it is essential to get the upper hand. And yet, they do not indiscriminately turn to other Gitanos for imaginative or practical support and, most importantly, do not think of *el pueblo Gitano* as a refuge from the threatening world outside. Instead they live strongly endosociable lives, where it is kin that shelter each other, and where unrelated Gitanos are almost as much potential enemies as the Payos. Links between close relatives are undeniably extremely strong, and are prolonged long after the death of particular individuals through elaborate if eventually private and silent mourning practices. These ties are also sustained at the cemetery, a space that is removed from the spaces of daily life but where the love and solidarity that should govern relations among kin is rehearsed by the living and re-created for the dead through the physical closeness of their tombs.

Elsewhere I have explained how the 'Gitano people' as an imagined community is built on centrifugal social relations shaped by dispersal, conflict and distrust of non-kin (Gay y Blasco 1999, 2001). I have also argued that, in spite of the radical fragmentation that characterizes Gitano communal life, the sense that the people of Villaverde have that they share who they are with each other and with Gitanos everywhere is extremely strong. If conflict, fragmentation and personal moral performance are one side of the coin that is Gitano life in Villaverde, cohesiveness, endosociability and emotional dependence upon kin is the other. The sense of commonality of the Gitanos of Villverde, however, is not anchored to an understanding of community comparable to those of the Payos, nor to the models that dominate anthropological theories of community-making; territory, history and attachment to a state, are all absent from the self-representations of these Gitanos as is the notion of an overarching society under which the individual might be subsumed. Most importantly, these Gitanos disregard any notion that parochial interests should or would work to the benefit of the group at large. 'Community', as an analytical translation for the Gitano concept of *pueblo* (people), has to refer not to 'communion' but to 'commonality' and 'the Gitano people' is premised on the belief that each Gitano man and woman upholds the Gitano morality in the here and now, or the there and then. This morality, as my ethnographic account has emphasized, is heavily emotive. At its core lies a series of strongly formalized rules that regulate interaction and conflict between patrigroups and, of equal significance, clear-cut expectations about the feelings that kin should have for each other and the actions that evidence these feelings. In other words, moral rules are strongly charged emotionally, and emotions are governed by clearly defined moral expectations. The quality of daily life in Jarana and Villaverde is shaped by this intertwining of emotions and moral expectations regarding what is of most importance to the Gitanos: their love for their kin, dead and alive.

Notes

1. The term Payo is strongly derogatory when used by Gitanos. However, it has entered the non-Gitano vocabulary and is commonly used by the non-Gitanos when referring to themselves in relation to the Gitanos. It is not derogatory when used by the non-Gitanos to refer to themselves.

2. These abbreviations are widely used in anthropology to refer to categories of kin. F = father, M = mother, D = daughter, S = son, Z = sister, B = brother. So FBsWs = father's brothers' wives, FZSD = father's sister's son's daughter, and so on.

References

Gay y Blasco, P. (1999), *Gypsies in Madrid: Sex, Gender and the Performance of Identity*, Oxford: Berg.

—— (2001), '"We don't know our descent": How the Gitanos of Jarana Manage the Past', *Journal of the Royal Anthropological Institute* 7 (4): 631–47.

—— (2003), '"This is not a place for civilised people": Isolation, Enforced Education and Resistance among Spanish Gypsies', in A. Bashford and C. Strange (eds), *Isolation: Practices and Places of Exclusion*, New York: Routledge.

Gibson, T. (1986), *Sacrifice and Sharing in the Philippine Highlands: Religion and Society among the Buid of Mindoro*, London: Athlone.

Myers, F. (1986), *Pintupi Country, Pintupi Self: Sentiment, Place and Politics among Western Desert Aborigines*, Washington, DC: Smithsonian Institution Press.

Overing, J. and Passes, A. (2000), 'Introduction', in J. Overing and A. Passes (eds), *The Anthropology of Love and Anger: the Aesthetics of Conviviality in Native Amazonia*, London: Routledge.

San Román, T. (1976), *Vecinos Gitanos*, Madrid: Akal.

—— (1994), *La Differencia Inquietant: Velles i Noves Estrategies Culturals dels Gitanos*, Barcelona: Alta Fulla.

Stewart, M. (1997), *The Time of the Gypsies*, Boulder, CO: Westview.

–10–

Maternal Feelings on Monkey Mountain: Cross-Species Emotional Affinity in Japan

John Knight

Introduction

The Japanese archipelago is home to two species of primate *Homo sapiens* and *Macaca fuscata* – human beings and Japanese macaques. Broadly speaking, these two primates occupy different parts of the land area: most of the humans inhabit low-lying areas, whereas most of the monkeys live in the mountains. The relationship between the two primates is a complex one. In my previous research on mountain villages, I examined the conflict between mountain villagers and crop-raiding monkeys from the mountain forest, a conflict that results in the culling of large numbers of monkeys each year (see Knight 2003: Chapter 3). In my present research I focus on another human–monkey interface in Japan: monkey parks. In contrast to forest-edge monkeys that threaten food crops and have to be forcibly resisted and driven back to the forest, these monkeys are lured out of the forest by the promise of food into clearings where the paying public can view them.

Monkey parks are popular visitor attractions in Japan. In this chapter I examine one aspect of their appeal – as sites of maternal sentiment. I shall draw a distinction between two aspects of the visitor's experience of these parks: as places for watching monkeys and as places for interacting with monkeys. As we shall see, in both these ways park visitors are emotionally engaged by the monkeys, but these forms of emotional engagement are very different.[1]

Monkey Parks

The 'Japanese monkey' (in Japanese, *nihonzaru*) is one of the many macaque species found in Asia. The Japanese macaque is a short-tailed, large-bodied monkey with reddish-brown to grey fur. It grows up to a metre in height and weighs up to 15 kilogrames, but is sexually dimorphic, with adult males having a larger body size than adult females. Japanese macaque troops have a multi-male and multi-female composition, though the number of adult females tends to be much greater than that of males because sexually mature males usually leave their natal troops, while females spend their whole lives in their natal groups. The Japanese macaque troop is clustered around reproductive females and is often described as matrilineal, with daughters acquiring their rank from their mothers and being ranked immediately below them. The usual habitat of the monkey is the mountain forest and until modern times they were rarely seen. But during the twentieth century monkeys became the most familiar of animals to the Japanese public due to their display in Japanese zoos and (after the Second World War) in monkey parks.

Commonly known as *saruyama* (monkey mountains), the parks are open areas, often scenically located, where free-ranging troops of Japanese macaques regularly gather. In the absence of physical confinement, the park authorities control the movements of the monkeys by means of daily provisioning at a fixed site within the park where the monkeys can be easily and clearly viewed by the paying public. The parks are sometimes called *shizen dōbutsuen* or 'natural zoos'. They are zoo-like to the extent that they are commercial visitor attractions which put animals on display to the public, but unlike conventional zoos, cages or enclosures are not normally used and usually visitors can walk freely among the monkeys. Originally, the parks allowed visitors to feed the monkeys, but while this is still found at some parks, many have stopped the practice.

The monkey parks have been places of scientific observation of monkeys by primatologists. Many of the parks were established by, or in collaboration with, primatologists who initiated or supervised the provisioning in the 1950s. Provisioning makes possible the individual identification of troop members and the detailed research on social relations among monkeys for which Japanese primatology is renowned.

Monkey parks are visitor attractions that can occupy an important place in the regional economy in which tourism is a major industry. The larger parks attract hundreds of thousands of visitors each year. Monkey parks tend to draw visitors from nearby holiday resorts (such as hot springs). In Japan many family holidays, club excursions and workplace outings take the form of overnight stays at hot-spring resorts. Typically, the parks offer such visitors the chance of an enjoyable outing the following morning (perhaps in conjunction with a visit to a scenic shrine or temple), before the coach or car ride back to the city. Although many of the tourists visiting the parks are first-time or one-off visitors, parks also tend to have a good number of regular visitors, usually people who live in the region and who are able to visit the park on a weekly or monthly basis, though some come from far away. Among the regulars there tend to be many photographers; amateur photography is hugely popular in Japan, and the monkey parks are a favourite destination for many who share this hobby. The parks are especially appealing to children, and many of the visiting parties are families with children, while on weekdays there are also parties of schoolchildren.

Visitors make certain basic distinctions among the monkeys of the park. The most prominent distinction is between the *bosu* (boss) monkey and the rest. There is a considerable interest among visitors in the boss monkey and on arrival at the park many visitors try to pick out or locate the boss monkey themselves or ask the keeper to pick him out for them. Much of the keeper's interaction with visitors is on the subject of the boss. In their commentaries to visitors, keepers often talk at length about the boss. Aside from the boss, the other main focus is on females and their young. If males – and especially the boss – often attract the visitor's attention, females and their young are more numerous, more observable (being located more centrally), and objects of fascination in their own right.

Devoted Monkey Mothers

Motherhood is a pervasive theme in the way female monkeys are represented. Adult female monkeys are routinely depicted as mothers, grandmothers or mothers-to-be. In Takasakiyama and other parks, keepers refer to the cluster of high-ranked females at the centre of the park as the *fujinkai* or 'Housewives' Association' and the highest-ranked female as the *fujinkai no kaichōsan* or 'Head of the Housewives' Association'. Female monkeys in the parks are usually portrayed as exemplary mothers devoted to their children. This is a common theme of keeper commentaries to visitors and in the conversations among regular visitors.

The Takasakiyama keeper Etō Junko gives visitors the following explanation of what she calls the *fukai haha no aijō* (deep mother love) to be found among the monkeys: 'As they only give birth to one baby at a time, female monkeys really dote on their own children. When the baby is crying in some place she cannot see, she understands what situation they are in from the way they are crying. If it doesn't seem normal, she will immediately rush over to find it.' This maternal sentiment is not confined to infancy, but – in the case of females who remain in the troop throughout their lives – extends to later years when the children reach sexual maturity. Etō Junko points out that a mother will do her utmost to protect her daughters throughout her life.

[This happens] even when the daughter has become older. When males come to them [her daughters] during mating season, her response to these males is always 'Don't touch my daughter!', and she fiercely chases them away so that they cannot get close to her. Even if it is the boss monkey, she is ready to confront him. Her attitude of trying to protect her children does not change throughout her life. As a mother, her view is that her children are always her children, no matter what age they become, and anyone who comes to attack them is an enemy.

This maternal love and protection extends to the children of her children. The Takasakiyama keepers illustrate the point by recalling a famous incident in which a young monkey was left behind in the centre of the park after its troop had left and one of the other troops had entered the area. On account of the tensions between troops, this was a very dangerous situation for the young monkey now surrounded by hostile monkeys from another troop, and it was the grandmother of the stranded youngster who came to its rescue.

Most parks seem to have stories about exemplary maternal monkeys. One narrative of maternal love is to be found in the Jigokudani park. In the 1970s a female monkey was born without hands or feet. Despite this severe physical handicap, the female monkey not only survived, but went on to become a mother. The story of this monkey, named Mozu, is told in a small booklet sold at the inn next to the park.

> In monkey society, where there is a fierce struggle for survival, it is said that the fate of an infant with such a handicap is to be abandoned by its mother, but Mozu's mother was different. Overcoming all sorts of difficulties, she raised Mozu admirably ... When Mozu was seven she had a daughter whose name was Momiji [Maple]. Now, herself taking the role of mother, Mozu, with her disabled body, had to raise Momiji. Feeding would not be easy, as she had to feed Momiji as well as herself.

Overcoming her deformity, Mozu managed to raise her baby successfully. In fact, she went on to raise five offspring of her own and lived to the age of 26 (she died in 1997). Mozu's story has attracted considerable media interest in Japan. In addition to the numerous newspaper and magazine articles, a number of television documentaries have been made about Mozu, including footage of her raising her young. As a result, Mozu became well known, not only among park visitors, but also among the wider Japanese public. In fact, many of the visitors to Jigokudani in the 1980s and 1990s knew of Mozu's story in advance and on arrival at the park would expressly ask keepers to point her out for them.

There are also, from time to time, infertile females who do not have the chance to be mothers. Until recently, it was believed that one such example in Takasakiyama was a monkey named 'Get' in C troop. She was known for adopting stray baby monkeys and trying to raise them herself. However, as she was unable to suckle the babies herself, they tended to die within a few days. This happened a great many times with Get (and this is the origin of her name). However, much to the delight of the keepers, Get did eventually give birth herself and was able to raise a healthy baby of her own.

The theme of maternal devotion is evident in some of the souvenirs sold at the parks. A striking example of this is the *hahakosaru* (mother-and-child monkeys) figurines sold in the Kawaguchikō park. The figurine (which costs ¥1,700) takes the form of a mother monkey carefully holding – and being tightly held by – her baby. A notice next to the figurines reads as follows:

Mother-and-child monkeys. The mother of a monkey always holds her child wherever she goes, and doesn't let go. For its part, the baby monkey never falls off no matter how much the mother jumps and leaps around. This image is a symbol of the love between mother and child [*oyakoai no shōchō*]. This mother-and-child monkey ornament can serve as a protective charm [*omamori*] in child-raising.

To the side of this text is an inset photograph of a mother monkey holding an infant next to her chest, indicating that the figurine is representing an actual mother–child pose. As the notice states, the figurine is not just an ornament, but is supposed to be an *omamori* that has protective power for human mothers and their children.

In general, references to maternal behaviour of park monkeys are extremely positive and praiseworthy, with the monkeys appearing models of maternal devotion and self-sacrifice. But there is also criticism of excessive maternal devotion among monkeys. One example of this from Takasakiyama involves a monkey called Chiyomi from C troop who is characterized by keepers as a *kahogomama* (overprotective mother). An issue of the park newsletter describes Chiyomi's overprotective behaviour in the following way:

In front of the storehouse in the park centre 3-year-old male monkeys play together by wrestling each other.[2] Close by is another 3-year-old male monkey who has submerged himself in his mother's chest where he is drinking her milk. This is a rather ridiculous scene, and one that is rare. For a 3-year-old to still want to drink his mother's milk appears a shameful state of affairs, but the problem actually lies with the mother who is giving the milk. This mother monkey is called Chiyomi. Chiyomi is a gentle, warm monkey who belongs to a high-ranking lineage in C troop, though she is not from one of the top lineages. In fact, Chiyomi is the mother of Zoro, the eighth boss of C troop and of fifth-ranking Zorome of C troop. Usually, boys leave their natal troop before they attain maturity, but neither Zoro nor Zorome have left the troop in which they were born. We think that the reason that they have not separated themselves from their parent is because of Chiyomi's overprotectiveness towards them. (Takasakiyamadayori no. 63)

As this indicates, Chiyomi's overprotective manner of child-rearing is said to have had a lasting influence on the behaviour of her adult sons, including the C troop boss, Zoro, who, on account of the fact that he has remained in his natal troop, is sometimes actually described by keepers as a *mazakonzaru* or 'a mother-complex monkey'! I have heard similar comments in other parks, such as in Iwatayama where the son of the highest ranked female of the leading Mino lineage has stayed in the troop rather than leave it as sexually mature males are supposed to.

The context of these various maternalistic representations of monkeys is the strong preoccupation with motherhood in contemporary Japanese society. In Japan particular importance is attached to motherhood and to maternal ties. Motherhood has long been represented as a woman's destiny, with women expected as a matter of course to marry and become mothers soon afterwards. Yet in contemporary Japan rising levels of education and occupational ambitions lead more and more women to defer marriage and motherhood or even forgo them altogether, a trend which makes a significant contribution to the decline in the Japanese birth-rate (Natsukari 1994: 139). The falling birth-rate is seen as threatening the future existence of the nation. Concerned about declining national fertility, some commentators even speculate on the demographic disappearance of the Japanese people at some point in the future. 'There will come a time when the [Japanese] people [*minzoku*] will no longer exist, when they may well vanish from the face of the Earth' (Yamamoto 1998: 45). As well as this concern about too few mothers, there are qualitative concerns about child-rearing among those women who do become mothers. Younger mothers are often deemed deficient in the attributes that define a good mother. There are growing numbers of younger mothers who find difficulty coping with the various demands of motherhood, a situation which invites moral condemnation on the grounds that these women are unable or unwilling to sacrifice themselves for their children as earlier generations of Japanese mothers did (Jolivet 1997: 32).

On the other hand, there is a concern with what we might call maternal excess. Japanese maternal care is known to have a number of distinctive characteristics, including prolonged breast-feeding, co-bathing, co-sleeping, communicating physically rather than verbally, carrying the child on the mother's back, and toilet training the child by holding it above the toilet (Miyake et al. 1986: 243). Japanese mothers exercise a particular mechanism of control over their children, raising their children in a way that creates a strong mutual attachment. This is achieved by maintaining intimate physical contact and minimal separation, the effect of which is to create a strong affective dependence on her: 'The mother's devotion and indulgence evoke a strong sense of dependence in the child; he or she senses what pleases the mother and behaves accordingly' (Azuma 1986: 7). But this maternal indulgence is not unconditional; the mother is ready to withdraw her indulgence in order to control extreme behaviour in her child. The sheer scale of this maternal devotion and indulgence makes the mother emotionally indispensable to her children.

In post-war Japan child-rearing practices have been extensively discussed and debated, and there is much criticism of its excesses. Commentators refer to the 'overprotectiveness' of parents toward their children (Yamamura 1986: 36). It is suggested that the traditional tendency for Japanese parents and especially mothers to become obsessed with their children – captured variously in terms such as *kobonnō* or (child passion) and *kodakara* (child treasure) – has become even more pronounced in present-day Japan (Yamamura 1986: 34). The maternal bond is viewed as excessively intense; in the present era of fewer children, this leads to problems of 'overinvolvement' of mothers who 'exhaust themselves psychologically in their maternal role' and who create overdependence in the children they raise (Iwao 1993: 131). Maternal commitment is held to reach the point of pathological excess in the figure of the obsessive 'education mother' who exerts intolerable pressure on her children to succeed at school – leading, according to some critics, to a generation of spoilt, egotistical and even maladjusted Japanese youth (Jolivet 1997: 100; see also Lebra 1984: 195–202). This maladjustment of youth finds its most extreme expression in the phenomenon of domestic violence by children, especially sons against mothers, including attempted matricide (Kawai 1986).

The existence of this wide-ranging debate on motherhood in Japanese society forms the context of many representations of the monkeys in the parks – such as 'overprotective mothers' and 'mother complex monkeys', terms which are normally applied to human mothers. This of course suggests that the debate about human motherhood in contemporary Japan serves as the lens through which people make sense of maternal behaviour among monkeys. But, in addition to this kind of human-to-monkey metaphorizing, reverse interpretation also occurs whereby monkey maternalism evokes a wider context in which to understand current trends in human maternalism. At one level, the maternal monkeys of the monkey park serve to rhetorically naturalize the devoted mother archteype – by seemingly expressing some elemental truth about child-rearing and the necessity of maternal devotion and self-sacrifice. Yet the park monkeys can give expression to the dangers of excessive maternal sentiment and attachment – as in the example of the 'overprotective' Chiyomi.

As fellow primates faced with the same imperatives of protracted rearing of dependent offspring, humans have a ready fascination with how monkeys raise their young. Most primate mothers rear their young on their own. Primates are known for the strength of the mother–infant bond and the prolonged period of infant dependency. Primates also carry their young with them as they move around foraging. Maternal ties offer a ready focus for the imaginative identification with primates. Aware of this, the monkey parks rhetorically foreground this maternal aspect of the monkey mountain – describing not only the dedication and devotion of monkey mothers, but also their trials and tribulations. This maternal emphasis will have a resonance for all human societies, as the experience of maternal care is a human universal. But in Japanese society, where we find an especially strong cultural emphasis on the devoted mother, we can expect this resonance to be all the greater. A self-consciously maternalistic society is all the more likely to be moved by the apparent maternalistic virtues of monkeys. Through their capacity for maternal love and devotion, monkeys give expression to a human ideal.

The parks are not, however, simply places where visitors observe maternal devotion among the monkeys. They are also places where maternal sentiments are aroused among the visitors themselves. Park monkeys do not, in other words, simply demonstrate or illustrate maternal affect; they also elicit it among the humans who come to watch them. Monkey parks are the site of the *crossover of maternal affect* between humans and monkeys, whereby baby monkeys become the object of human nurturant interest and affection.

Responsive Young Monkeys

There is a sense in which park monkeys are viewed as children or childlike figures. Monkeys tend to be characterized as cute. They are represented as child-like figures by the parks on pamphlets, logos, signs, noticeboards and gift-wrapping. Takasakiyama employs a boylike monkey mascot, known as 'Takkey', who wears a football strip. Many monkey parks actually resemble children's playgrounds and are equipped with, among other things, swings, slides and climbing frames, pools and suspended tyres. In fact, playfulness tends to be confined to young monkeys and is not ordinarily evident among adult monkeys.

In present-day monkey parks there tend to be many young monkeys about. Regular provisioning of the park monkeys leads to greater numbers of young monkeys. This is because the extra nutrition available at the monkey park greatly increases levels of monkey fertility, so that female monkeys who, under natural (non-provisioned) conditions, would give birth every two or three years, instead give birth every year. This leads both to a change in the population profile of the park monkeys, as the young monkeys make up a much higher proportion of the total population, and to proliferating numbers overall. This trend in park monkey demography is in marked contrast to the trend among the human population of Japan, which is experiencing ageing and the prospect of a long term decline in numbers.

The sight of young monkeys playing together on slides and swings is entertaining and amusing to visitors. One is struck by the fact that these transplanted children's playgrounds really do work as monkey playgrounds. The fact that the fixtures of the children's playground are re-created in the *saruyama* for use by monkeys is an indication of the degree of behavioural continuity between humans and monkeys. This impression is only reinforced when one observes how much young children visiting the park – who invariably notice the swings and climbing frames – are attracted to these fixtures themselves. Indeed, so inviting are they, that some children want to play on them. I recall one occasion in the Chōshikei park on Shōdoshima when a young boy asked his parents in front of the keeper if he could have a go on the swing – the keeper duly let him and his parents took him over and pushed the swing for him. The scene clearly demonstrated that the *saruyama* is potentially a *trans-species playground* that can allow humans as well as monkeys to play in it. This accords with the representation of the parks as places where people can play with monkeys. The verb *asobu* (play) is often used to characterize the normative interaction between visitors and monkeys.

Newborn and infant monkeys hold a special appeal for visitors. Baby monkeys are one of the most popular attractions in the monkey parks. Parks often point out to visitors that the summer is a good time to visit because of the appearance of newborn monkeys at this time. During a visit to the Kawaguchikō park in December 2003, I recall a notice on the wall, pointing out to winter visitors that the monkeys give birth between May and August and that the park will be 'full of cute babies' at this time. Many parks carry photographs of the newborns on their websites to appeal to the public to come and visit, and during the summer reports of newborns – accompanied by appealing photographs – appear in newspapers or even on television.

Young monkeys hold a special appeal for the visiting public. Visitors commonly refer to young monkeys as 'children', with a variety of Japanese terms being used, including *aka-chan*, *kodomo* and *bebii* (English loanword used). Keepers are asked lots of questions about the infant monkeys, especially by women visitors. How old is this or that 'child'? How long will it cling to the chest of its mother? When will it start walking? How long will it suckle for? How dangerous is it for the infant clinging on to the mother's chest or back (and does it fall off)? When will it start playing with other young monkeys? Does the mother give it solid food? Is there such a thing as *shitsuke* (upbringing) among monkeys? What role do male monkeys play in raising the young?

Young monkeys are icebreakers. As they become more mobile in their first year, they roam around more and tend to be much less inhibited in their approaches to visitors than are older monkeys. Whereas adult monkeys appear indifferent to visitors, young monkeys often look directly at visitors (as they have yet to learn that direct looking or staring is a sign of aggression). They delight visitors when they hold on to a trouser-leg, sit on somebody's shoe, play with somebody's shoelace, or come and sit next to a visitor on a bench and touch their arm or leg (though they can also annoy visitors when they hold the hem of a skirt or touch clothes with muddy hands). The appeal of baby monkeys appears especially strong among young women. I have seen infant monkeys virtually surrounded by groups of admiring young women repeating loudly the word *kawaii* (cute) and/or trying to take a picture of the infant. Sometimes the women want to have their picture taken next to the baby monkey.

Monkeys occasionally groom visitors. Visitors tend to characterize monkey grooming as *nomitori* (flea-catching) or *shiramitori* (lice-catching), but keepers usually inform visitors that grooming is a kind of *sukinshippu* (skinship) among monkeys, which has to do with developing and maintaining relationships. In Isegatani the monkey Keiko was known for trying to groom the heads of visitors when she was young. She was tied to a tree near the entrance hut and would sometimes alight on visitors seated on nearby bench. According to Itani Chizuyo, Keiko's grooming was very popular with visitors, especially children, who would queue up to get their heads groomed. However, as Keiko grew, visitors started to become uneasy (especially when she snatched their spectacles) and Chizuyo had to stop Keiko's grooming of visitors. In Takasakiyama too young monkeys some-times jump onto the shoulders of visitors to groom their heads. The Takasakiyama newsletter has featured photographs of this. In 2000 the newsletter carried one such photograph, of a young boy getting his scalp groomed by a young monkey. In the adjacent text it was pointed out that the park staff have no idea how monkeys choose which visitors to groom, but went on to mention that such incidents are considered by some people to be auspicious. The brief article ends with an invita-tion to readers to come and visit the park to see if the monkeys choose to groom them: 'If you are lucky, they may well groom you!'

In addition to these one-off instances of monkeys grooming visitors, there are regular grooming interactions between monkeys and visitors. In Iwatayama one old man who has been visiting the park for decades told me proudly that he used to be groomed by the present boss Doron when he was a young monkey. Doron would jump on his shoulder and groom his head. Another example from Iwatayama involves a visitor from Nagoya who claims that Hiruko, his favourite monkey, often grooms him – both his arms and his head. Monkey grooming of vis-itors is exceptional because grooming presupposes a high degree of familiarity between groomer and groomee, and most visitors are not regular enough to assume such a status. The Nagoya man is obviously very proud of this degree of intimacy with the monkeys, which is achieved by few other visitors.

In parks which allow visitors to feed monkeys, visitors often try to give their food to the younger, smaller monkeys, rather than the more strident adult monkeys. Of course, the young monkeys usually have their mothers nearby, but apart from suckling, mothers do not feed their young and the young monkeys have to compete for food with the other monkeys. This is something that strikes some visitors to the *saruyama* as at odds with proper maternal behaviour, and may well prompt them to raise this issue with keepers. Keepers usually make the effort to correct this interpretation, reminding visitors that the reason monkeys do not give food to their young is because young monkeys must learn how to fend for them-selves, and that the apparently selfish behaviour of the mother monkey is therefore actually in the interests of her young. In making this point to visitors, one Takasakiyama keeper uses the phrase *esa o ataenai no ga aijō nandesu* ('not to give feed is what love is'), and goes on to emphasize that it is human society which is in error because human parents nowadays give children anything they want and spoil them; he uses the expression *ningen no oya wa ko ni ataesugi* ('human parents give too much to their children') (NNS 2004). But park visitors are more likely to be left with the impression that young monkeys cannot even depend on their mothers for nurturant feeding and are therefore in need of whatever food they can get. This is why – in those parks that allow visitors to feed the monkeys –

visitors may well come to see themselves as supplementing the diet of young monkeys by giving them the food they believe they need to grow up strong.

This alloparental disposition towards the park monkeys among visitors becomes all the more marked when a young monkey is orphaned, following the death of its mother (or occasionally, after being disowned by its mother). The effect of being orphaned is to weaken the status of the young monkey in the troop, as it no longer has a mother to protect it. Indeed, an orphaned monkey may well die (or disappear) soon afterwards. But even if it is old enough to survive, it will usually be very low ranked, and dominated by other monkeys in the troop whose lineage associations make them strong. Such orphaned monkeys often attract the attention of regular visitors, who endeavour to get to them the food that their lowly status otherwise denies them. The plight of monkey orphans is a particularly heart-wrenching one. No matter what their individual merits, they are condemned to be dominated by other monkeys. For such monkeys, life is a struggle to get by; they survive only by enduring great hardships arising from their lowly status. Some of the human observers of this monkey drama naturally seek to intervene – to offer help to monkeys condemned by fate to a life of hardship.

I recorded an example of this from Iwatayama in 2000. Shiro is a female monkey born in 1985. In the 1990s Shiro's mother died and she became isolated in the troop thereafter. A number of regular visitors to the park tried to support Shiro, as they did other isolated and low-ranking, 'bullied' (*ijimerareta*) monkeys. Despite her isolation and lowly status, Shiro managed to become pregnant and in 1996 gave birth to a daughter. For both keepers and regular weekend visitors, the birth of Shiro's daughter was a source of great joy, an instance of this monkey over-coming adversity to produce a family. However, the daughter was weak and sickly. Over the following months keepers and regular visitors made a special effort to get food to her, to try to boost her diet and improve her health, but in 1999 the 3-year-old daughter finally passed away, leaving Shiro, now aged 14 years, childless once more.

In an interview with me, Asaba Shinsuke, the then deputy head keeper at Iwatayama, referred to some of the regular visitors to the park who are in the habit of picking out small, weak monkeys to feed.

Everybody especially likes the small monkeys. They feel sorry for them. They feel sorry for them especially if they see that they don't seem to be growing up well and getting bigger. When the big monkeys come along they tell them to 'go away' or when overbearing monkeys come along they tell them to 'go away'. They seem to have those sorts of feelings. They decide that 'I will bring up this monkey myself'. The Kimuras [pseudonym used] are like that. They believe that if it wasn't for them this or that weak monkey would suffer and become even weaker. Thinking like this, they do their utmost to come up here and give [food] to the weak monkeys. You hear them say things like, 'So and so has become a lot bigger, hasn't he!'... The way they think is that 'he has gotten bigger thanks to me and thanks to the feed I've been giving him'. They see themselves as doing their best to help raise them.

The Kimuras, a couple in their forties, visit at weekends, usually very late in the afternoon. They buy large quantities of food and always carefully direct their food to their favourite monkeys. Both keepers and other regular visitors pointed out to me, as if by way of explanation, that the Kimuras are a childless couple – and that, by implication, they have in effect adopted some of the young park monkeys as surrogate children.

Much of this visitor intimacy towards young monkeys is of course likely to be dangerous because of the potential defensive reaction of the nearby mother at the sight of humans approaching her infant. Young women may well ask the keeper if it is all right to approach a young monkey and have their photograph taken with it (or indeed to get the keeper to take their photograph next to it), but the keeper usually advises them against it. Or again, when curious young monkeys come up to visitors and sit next to them or touch them, many visitors tend to reciprocate by touching the monkey, at which point the young monkey may well react with a cry, causing the mother to come to its defence and threaten the visitor. Thus while cute baby monkeys are a major attraction for young women, there are limits to the degree of intimate interaction these women can have with them, as the mother may well mistake their interest in her young as a threat.

Maternal aggression is also directed to other monkeys attempting to handle infants. These non-mother infant handlers are usually immature and subadult females, which has led to the suggestion that such behaviour is a means by which these immature females gain valuable experience of infant handling and learn to develop maternal skills prior to motherhood – the so-called 'learning-to-mother hypothesis' (Schino et al. 2003: 628). Interestingly, an alternative interpretation of such infant handling is a manifestation of the 'cute hypothesis' – that is, that 'infant handling is the non-adaptive by-product of selection for maternal attraction to one's own infant' (Schino et al. 2003: 628). In other words, among monkeys too the babies of others hold an instinctive attraction to other females. Maternal aggression caused by infant handling by other monkeys is especially frequent in the early stages of lactation when the infant is still very young, but becomes less frequent as the infant ages (ibid.). Non-mother monkeys that handle infants risk incurring an aggressive response from the infant's mother – they may be chased or physically attacked. Moreover, the mother's concern over such infant handling by other monkeys is not unfounded. Although other monkeys generally do not harm the infant, there are occasional instances where such handling results in harm. Cases of infant kidnapping have been recorded among captive Japanese monkey populations (Schino et al. 1993), which can result in the death of the infant. Thus, when humans show an interest in a baby monkey, the mother is already disposed to be wary and defensive. When the mother monkey reacts aggressively to visitors' interest in her infant, she would appear to be transferring to humans behaviour normally directed to other monkeys.

In the above, we can distinguish between *two* kinds of human emotional engagement with the park monkeys: indirect or vicarious in relation to (loving) mother monkeys, and direct in relation to the (lovable) young monkeys. Adult monkeys are usually not responsive or at least not noticeably so, as they pointedly do not look directly at visitors.[3] I would suggest that this apparent indifference to visitors does not actually mean that visitors cannot engage emotionally with these monkeys. They do so, but in a vicarious way, by observing the emotional engagement among the monkeys themselves – this is possible because monkey sociality has this (partially) transparent quality that allows people to look into it. Arguably, this is especially the case when humans see a mother and her offspring together. We believe we recognize the intimate sociality *among them*, even if this intimacy is not extended to us. This is why monkey 'mothers' and 'babies' tend to attract so much human attention in monkey parks. On the other hand, direct emotional engagement is possible in the case of young monkeys. These monkeys do respond to the presence of visitors. In her book *Loving Nature*, Kay Milton has argued that the responsiveness of animals to us is a key criterion of their personhood (Milton 2002: 50, 86). Accordingly, young monkeys, by virtue of their obvious responsiveness, would tend to strike visitors as person-like.

Conclusion

This chapter has looked at maternal sentiments in Japanese monkey parks and the relationship of the visitor to these sentiments. The chapter showed that monkeys manifest maternal sentiments in the interactions with each other that visitors watch. The chapter also looked at the ways in which visitors themselves become involved in intimate maternal interactions with young monkeys. In contrast to the former relationship of detached observation, this latter, active engagement with the park monkeys is significant in that monkeys acquire some of the attributes of personhood. Perhaps this accounts for the special appeal of monkey parks as visitor attractions in Japan, and why they have lasted more than fifty years. The 'natural zoo' format permits a special kind of intimate interaction between visitors and monkeys that is not possible in the classical zoo where animals are physically separated from visitors. It is this potential for cross-species proximity and contact which can make the experience of the park so special – as we find among many of the regular visitors.

However, the cross-species intimacy offered by the monkey park remains limited and should not be exaggerated. The examples of human intimacy with monkeys described here do not compare with the manifest monkey-to-monkey maternal intimacy in the form of suckling, carrying, grooming, huddling and so on. The monkey park may claim to be the site of visitor–monkey intimacy, but in fact the park visitor largely remains a spectator of monkey intimacy rather than a party to it.

Notes

1. This chapter is based on visits to monkey parks across Japan between 1997 and 2003, including the Jigokudani park in Nagano Prefecture, the Isegatani park in Tsubaki, Wakayama Prefecture, the Iwatayama park in Arashiyama, Kyoto Prefecture, the Awajishima park in Hyogo Prefecture, the Chōshikei park on Shodoshima, and the Takasakiyama park in Oita Prefecture.

2. Usually when keepers point to such late examples of weaning, they convert the age of the monkey to a human scale by multiplying by three – so revealing that Chiyomi's 3-year-old represents an unweaned nine-year-old in human terms!

3. This is now the case in most parks. But the situation is different in those few parks which still allow visitors to hand-feed monkeys in the park grounds. Where such hand-feeding is allowed (which was once the case at all the parks), monkeys tend to follow visitors around and persistently 'beg' for food (see Knight 2005).

References

Azuma, H. (1986), 'Why Study Child Development in Japan?', in H. Stevenson, H. Azuma and K. Hakuta (eds), *Child Development and Education in Japan*, New York: W. F. Freeman.

Iwao, S. (1993), *The Japanese Woman: Traditional Image and Changing Reality*, New York: Free Press.

Jolivet, M. (1997), *Japan: The Childless Society?* London: Routledge.

Kawai, H. (1986), 'Violence in the Home: Conflict between Two Principles – Maternal and Paternal', in T. S. Lebra and W. P. Lebra (eds), *Japanese Culture and Behaviour: Selected Readings*, Honolulu: University of Hawaii Press.

Knight, J. (2003), *Waiting for Wolves in Japan: An Anthropological Study of People–Wildlife Relations*, Oxford: Oxford University Press.

—— (2005), 'Feeding Mr Monkey: Cross-species Food Exchange in Japanese Monkey Parks', in J. Knight (ed.), *Animals in Person: Cultural Perspectives on Human–Animal Intimacy*, Oxford: Berg.

Lebra, T. S. (1984), *Japanese Women: Constraint and Fulfillment*, Honolulu: University of Hawaii Press.

Milton, K. (2002) *Loving Nature: Towards an Ecology of Emotion*, London: Routledge.

Miyake, K., Campos, J., Bradshaw, D. L. and Kagan, J. (1986), 'Issues in

Socioemotional Development', in H. Stevenson, H. Azuma and K. Hakuta (eds), *Child Development and Education in Japan*, New York: W. F. Freeman.

Natsukari, Y. (1994), 'A Structural Study of Spouse Selection in Japan', in L-J. Cho and M. Yada (eds), *Tradition and Change in the Asian Family*, Honolulu: East-West Center.

NNS (*Nishi Nippon Shinbun*) (2004), 'Takasakiyama no gaidoreki sanjūnen – Matsui Takeshi' (Thirty Years as a Guide at Takasakiyama: Matsui Takeshi), 1 February 2004.

Schino, G., Aureli, F., D'Amato, F. R., D'Antoni, M., Pandolfi, N. and Troisi, A. (1993), 'Infant Kidnapping and Co-mothering in Japanese Macaques', *American Journal of Primatology* 30: 257–62.

Schino, G., Sperenza, L., Ventura, R. and Troisi, A. (2003), 'Infant Handling and Maternal Response in Japanese Macaques', *International Journal of Primatology* 24 (3): 627–38.

Yamamoto, H. (1998), *Shōshi bōkokuron – teishusseiritsu shakai o dō norikiruka (The Thesis of Falling Fertility and National Demise: How Do We Manage the Low Birthrate Society?)*, Tokyo: Kanki Shuppan.

Yamamura, Y. (1986), 'The Child in Japanese Society', in H. Stevenson, H. Azuma and K. Hakuta (eds), *Child Development and Education in Japan*, New York: W. F. Freeman.

–11–

The Politics of Chosen Trauma: Expellee Memories, Emotions and Identities

Maruška Svašek

On Sunday, 17 July 1945, at eleven o'clock at night, four Czech partisans (two civilians, a man in a Czech uniform, and a man in a Russian uniform) broke into the bedroom of my twenty-five year old daughter, Angela Schreier, in order to rape her. She resisted. Furious at this, one of the partisans levelled an army pistol at her and fired. She died after a few minutes … In the same bed with my daughter when she was murdered was her child, Ingrid, born on 15 March 1943, who was also hit by a shot in the spine, and has been paralysed ever since. (Schreier 1953 [1950]: 233)

This horrifying report was written (in German) by the Sudeten German expellee Franz Schreier. It formed part of *Documents on the Expulsion of the Sudeten Germans,* a collection of official documents and personal reports about the mistreatment and killing of tens of thousands of Sudeten Germans in Czechoslovakia after the ending of the Second World War. The collection was put together and translated into English by the Association for the Protection of Sudeten German Interests, Arbeitsgemeinschaft zur Wahrung Sudetendeutscher Interessen, which was established by Sudeten German expellees after their arrival in Germany. The publication included 116 accounts of beatings, killings and suicides – a selection of the total number of reports that had been collected. Headings such as 'Joachimsthal: house searches, brutal ill-treatment, public executions' and 'Tschachwitz in the district of Kaaden: several murders of Sudeten Germans in June 1945' give some indication of their content, and suggest why many expellees were traumatized after their forced migration to Germany.

This chapter will take an anthropological approach to terror and trauma, and will criticize medical/psychiatric models of trauma that have focused solely on the clinical condition of individual bodies and minds. As demonstrated by various authors, such models have ignored the social and political dimensions of trauma (Volkan 1999; O'Nell 2000; White 2000; Fierke 2002; Svašek 2002c; Cappelletto 2003; Kidron 2004), and have disregarded the fact that trauma itself is a culturally and historically specific interpretation of human suffering (Young 1995; Antze and

Lambek 1996; Kenny 1996; Leys 2000). In line with this critique, the main aim of this chapter is to show how extremely shocking experiences such as those described here have been made politically relevant through the politics of 'chosen trauma', a concept that was introduced by the psychiatrist Vamik Volkan in 1999 to analyse the intergenerational transmission of trauma. This chapter will examine the ways in which proclaimed trauma victims – both survivors of terror and people who claim to have been indirectly affected – have used discourses and practices of collective victimhood in an attempt to gain political influence and claim compensation for their suffering.

Referring to the factual unreliability of social memory, Volkan argued that chosen trauma 'is, of course, more than a simple recollection; it is a shared mental representation of the event, which includes realistic information, fantasized expectations, intense feelings and defences against unacceptable thoughts' (Volkan 1999: 46).[1] As we shall see, the politicization of emotional dynamics is inherent in this process of remembering and forgetting.

Rejecting the notion of emotions as primarily evolutionary or intrapsychic phenomena (Svašek 2002b: 10), the analysis will regard emotions as embodied experiences and discursive practices which, on an analytical level, blur the boundary between body and mind. Arguing that emotions should not be regarded *solely* as cultural constructions as the cultural relativists would have it (see, for example, Abu-Lughod and Lutz 1990), I will stress that to be able to understand how 'past suffering' can gain social and political significance, it is necessary *also* to examine processes of social and bodily interaction (Lyon and Barbalet 1994) and sensual perceptual experience (Csordas 1990).

As Thomas Csordas convincingly argued, the textual turn in anthropology has wrongly disregarded bodily experiences by analysing human experience in terms of discourse and representation. Inspired by phenomenology, he suggested an alternative approach which acknowledges that 'language itself is a modality of being-in-the-world' (Csordas 1994: 11). In this perspective, the experiential, perceptual process of being-in-the-world is as important as representational practice.

To explain how personal traumas can be shared and politicized, this chapter will also address the debate about individuality, sociality and selfhood (Cohen 1994; Morris 1994; Overing and Passes 2000; van Meijl and Driessen 2003). Analysing the intersubjective dynamics of Sudeten German suffering, it will explore the emotional and political potential of interactions with 'internalized presences' which have objectified trauma as a collective experience. The politics of chosen trauma will also be examined in the analysis of trauma transmission through expellee poems and commemoration rituals.

The Sudeten German case: Violence as Revenge

The maltreatment and killing of the Sudeten Germans in the post-war period has to be put in historical context. When Czechoslovakia was established in 1918, the Sudeten Germans were the second largest ethnic group whose members lived mainly in the Moravian, Bohemian, and Silesian border areas. In 1938, the majority supported Hitler and welcomed the incorporation of the Sudetenland into the Third Reich. In 1939, many enthusiastically supported the Nazi occupation of the remaining parts of Moravia and Bohemia. The Sudeten German cooperation with the Nazis and the post-war revelations about the Holocaust fuelled the already existing Czech anti-German sentiments. These feelings were not only felt by 'ordinary' Czechs, but also shared by members of the post-war Czechoslovak government. Soon after the liberation, President Beneš signed a number of decrees on the basis of which the Sudeten Germans lost their citizenship rights and most of their property. In accordance with the Potsdam agreement, the majority of the over 3 million Sudeten Germans were subsequently expelled to Germany and Austria, and allowed only a minimum amount of luggage.

As Schreier's and other reports testify, large numbers of Germans never made it to the border. Especially during the first post-war months, Czechs, Russians and others – both civilians and members of the liberating forces – took revenge on the German population whom they regarded as collectively guilty of the Nazi crimes. From May till November 1945, they maltreated and brutally killed many Sudeten Germans during the *wilde Austreibung* (wild expulsion) which was followed by the less brutal *geregelte Vertreibung* (organized expulsion) in 1946. According to Sudeten German sources, around 250,000 people lost their lives. Czechs have insisted on the much lower number of between 20,000 and 40,000 victims (Staněk 1991; Hamperl 1997; Svašek 1999; Cordell and Wolff 2005).

Not surprisingly many expellees were traumatized when they arrived in post-war Germany. According to the physician Wolf-Dieter Hamperl, himself an expellee from the Bohemian district of Tachau, '[m]any expellees who experienced such excesses can even now, after fifty years, not talk or think about their experiences because the shock was too great' (Hamperl 1996: 228, my translation). Most Sudeten Germans I spoke with in 1997, 1998 and 1999 were still emotionally affected by the loss of their homeland and the experience of terror.

In 1997 and 1998 I attended the Sudetendeutscher Tag, an annual gathering of Sudeten Germans organized by the largest expellee organization, the Sudetendeutsche Landsmannschaft. The two-day event usually takes place in a large conference centre in Nuremberg or Munich, and attracts tens of thousands of expellees and a wide variety of expellee associations. The event was first organized in 1949, and can be regarded as a complex ritual of social, cultural, and political belonging, during which expellees transform the centre into an emotionally charged memorial space.

In 1997, I met an elderly couple while having a coffee in one of the restaurant areas. When asked for their personal reasons to participate in the event, the husband said that he often still felt like a 'foreigner' in Germany, and was happy to be surrounded by other expellees and regain some sense of *Heimat* (homeland).[2] When talking about his experiences during the expulsion, he recalled how a number of inhabitants from his home village had been killed during the first chaotic post-war months. Half-way through his story, he suddenly stopped, looked away and began to cry. His wife said that I was not to blame: 'It's not your fault, he often cries when talking about the past. He just can't help it'. On other occasions, other expellees I talked with also broke down in tears or told me that they were still regularly haunted by nightmares.

Interestingly, the topic of Sudeten German trauma has recently regained political significance.[3] After the end of the Cold War and in the context of discussions about the Czech Republic's entrance into the European Union (realized in May 2004), several expellee organizations have intensified their call for *Heimatrecht*, a legal right claimed on the basis of collective Sudeten German suffering. Depending on the political views of the individual expellee, the right to *Heimat* can mean anything from the more radical 'right to return to the lost homeland' or 'right to regain stolen property' to a more moderate claim for financial compensation for past suffering.

Trauma and Suffering: Memory and Self

Several questions are crucial when examining the issue of trauma politics. Can traumatized persons *objectively* reconstruct traumatic events? How are their individual experiences objectified as a marker of *collective* suffering? In asking these questions, it is not my aim to deny the fact that Sudeten Germans have suffered. Instead, I am interested in the ways in which embodied memories and narratives of trauma have been politicized in local, national and transnational contexts. In other words, I am interested in the interplay of history, memory, emotions and politics.

Various assumptions have underlined trauma theory throughout its history. In the 1860s, the physician John Erichsen introduced the term 'trauma syndrome' in a study of victims of railway accidents who suffered from extreme fears, and argued that their anxiety was caused by physiological shock. During the late nineteenth century, the meaning of 'trauma' shifted from the physiology of shock to the psychology of mental afflictions (Kenny 1996: 152–3; Young 1996: 90; Leys 2000: 3–4). Over the following century various researchers focused on historically situated groups of trauma victims, and proposed different causal explanatory models which centred on the nature of trauma recollection. They were engaged (like myself) in 'memoro-politics': 'a power struggle built around knowledge, or claims to knowledge' about the functioning of memory (Hacking 1996: 69).

Generally speaking, trauma victims are people who suffer physically and mentally because they find it difficult to come to terms with extremely shocking past experiences, either by integrating and thus normalizing them into their life stories, or by forgetting them altogether (Herman 1994; Caruth 1995; Leys 2000). Medical and psychiatric studies have pathologized this type of human suffering through more particular forms of labelling (Kleinman and Kleinman 1991: 170). Discourses of 'hysteria', 'shell-shock', 'combat-fatigue' and 'post-traumatic stress disorder' have suggested a diversity of therapeutic cures for what has generally been described as a characteristic feature of traumatic suffering: the confrontation of individuals with 'indelible and distressing memories – memories to which the sufferer [is] continuously returning, and by which he [is] tormented by day and by night' (Janet 1984[1919–25], vol. 2: 205, quoted by van der Kolk and van der Hart 1995: 158; see also Cockerham 1981: 49–50; Tedeschi and Calhoun 1995: 26).

Psychiatrists and pschychoanalysts have focused their attention on 'abnormal' processes in trauma patients, including numbing, compulsive re-enacting and splitting. 'Numbing' refers to the inability to remember or reconstruct traumatic events in narrative form.[4] 'Re-enactment' refers to intrusive, destabilizing re-experiences of the traumatizing episode. 'Splitting' is a defence mechanism in which victims dissociate from parts of their selves during the traumatizing event, and continue to feel estranged afterwards (Klein 1975: 144). In a critical analysis of the genealogy of trauma, Leys (2000) argued that all theories of trauma paradoxically contain contradictory 'mimetic' and 'antimimetic' perspectives.[5] Therapists who have emphasized the antimimetic paradigm have argued that the factual narrative reconstruction of trauma events is crucial to the healing process. By contrast, those who have stressed the mimetic paradigm have claimed that the objective representation of trauma experiences is impossible because the victims' cognitive and perceptual capacities are shattered during traumatizing incidents. In their view, guided unconscious re-enactment and emotional catharsis are essential to the healing process. Leys (2000: 307) stressed that treatment should not be limited by theoretical models but be led by pragmatism and that, in some cases, it would be necessary to 'verify by documentation or other independent means the reality of past traumas'. By pointing out that trauma victims are able to construct images of self that do not necessarily reflect earlier experiences, she acknowledged that memory is not 'the pregiven object of our gaze', and that memories of trauma must at least partially be regarded as products of *present-day* contextual practice (Antze and Lambek 1996: xii; see also Leydesdorff 1992). As we shall see, this means that people who share a past of suffering, but who are not necessarily all traumatized in the medical sense of the term, can all be actively involved in trauma politics.

Emotions: Evoked, Remembered, Re-experienced

In an earlier publication (Svašek 2000), I distinguished the terms 'evoked', 'remembered' and 're-experienced' emotions to analyse the Sudeten German claims to collective victimhood. 'Evoked emotions' are the more or less immediate emotional reactions to current events. This term describes the feelings of shock, fear, anger and hatred felt by the expellees at the time of the expulsion. By contrast, 'remembered emotions' are *memories* of past emotions that do not cause a similar emotional reaction in the person recalling them. 'Remember how afraid I was?', somebody might say with a smile on his face, clearly being emotionally detached from the earlier experience of fear. Alternatively, 're-*experienced* emotions' are past feelings that are remembered *and* re-experienced in the present. In the case of trauma, these memories may be highly selective and compulsory, as when trauma victims are constantly haunted by a single horrifying moment, and forced into a state of extreme anxiety or of social paralysis. Yet re-experienced emotions may also empower victims to take measures to protect themselves (Winkler 1994), or to identify themselves with other victims and form political action groups (Svašek 2000).

The adjective 're-experienced' in 're-experienced emotions' does not imply that people experience and interpret their feelings in exactly the same way as they did in the past. Even though feeling and thinking bodies may be affected by past emotions, they exist in the present as 'beings-in-the-world' (Merleau-Ponty 1962), and are therefore partially influenced by present-day predicaments. These may include, for example, changing locality and social networks, altering physical conditions as one moves from childhood to old age, shifting personal interests, and, crucial to this chapter, political and religious engagement.

Even when victims are confronted with memories of traumatic episodes, their re-experiences cannot be considered exact relivings of the original event (Kramer, Schoen and Kinney 1984; Leys 2000: 232–9; Svašek 2000: 114). Caruth's (1995: 152–3) claim that re-experienced emotions are 'literal registration[s]' or reproductions 'in exact detail' of the emotions originally felt during the traumatic event is therefore unsubstantiated. Her assertion that trauma victims are 'possessed by the past' (Caruth's (1995: 151) is similarly misleading because it produces the image of passive sufferers who live outside history within the confinement of timeless bodies and minds. This image leaves no room for political agency.

Suffering and the Political Potential of Internalized Presence

The phenomenon of trauma takes place in a dialectical space between individuality and sociality. Even though traumatized individuals may withdraw within themselves (Erikson 1995: 186), the image of isolated sufferers who are locked within their own bodies and minds, is problematic. The notion of the detached individual has been reinforced by dichotomous theories of selfhood that have made clear-cut distinctions between 'individual/society', 'internal selves/external environments' and 'public/private dimensions of self' (Tonkin 1992: 102; Cohen 1994: 2; Overing and Passes 2000). Yet from an experiential perspective, 'self/other' distinctions are always blurred because 'mind is fashioned from without – known from without via identifications with others' (Casey 1987: 244–5). Identifications with close relatives, ethnic groups or religious movements are often central to self-experience. Emotional interaction – the creation of trusting and loving relationships with a selective group of people – is crucial to this process.

This does not mean that people have no emotional experiences outside social contexts, or that emotional dynamics can be fully understood through a focus on their sociogenesis (see Milton, Chapter 1 in this volume). Yet frequent social interaction is vital to the process of embodiment in which emotions are learned, felt and interpreted, and in which emotional ties are formed with relevant others. After all, people cannot survive, at least during early childhood, without contact with others. This means that 'other (s) act as a template for further development thanks precisely to identification, *which establishes these other(s) as active internalized presences*' (Casey 1987: 244, my italics).

The dynamics of internalized presence can be regarded as a force that bridges the domain of the individual and the social, and undermines the Cartesian split of body and mind. Even more important, it demonstrates how internal and external emotional dynamics are intertwined, and how intersubjectivity can politically motivate human beings. The following imaginary case scenario is based on several conversations with Sudeten German expellees about the ways in which memories of the expulsion affected their lives. It illustrates the more general point that remembering involves identification and dialogue with internalized presences, a process which may in individual cases activate personal involvement in the politics of trauma.

Years after the expulsion, an expellee who settled in Munich meets a person in a bar who reminds him of his best friend, who was killed by Czechs. If the expellee suffers from extreme trauma, the confrontation may numb him or cause a debilitating emotional reaction. In either case, it is impossible for him to identify or communicate more 'freely' with his friend in his imagination. The situation is rather different when the expellee was not or is no longer traumatized. In this case, he may recall how he and his friend used to drink beer together in the old village pub. The process of selective remembering and imagining may produce different inner dialogues and emotional responses. Recalling a particularly happy occasion, for example, his attention focuses on three different internal presences, namely 'himself in the pub', 'his friend in the pub' and 'himself in the present', as a spectator of the imagined scene. Identifying with the two friends, the remembering expellee unconsciously smiles, 'sharing' their cheerful mood. As a spectator he possibly feels nostalgia ('Look how happy we were'), grief ('I miss him, why did he have to die?') and hatred ('I abhor those who killed him'). These emotional shifts may be marked by internally felt or outwardly observable physiological changes: an increased heartbeat, tears in his eyes. In the process, he may objectify his thoughts and sensations as a 'proof' of injustice, and a morally justified urge to fight for political redress: 'I feel miserable. Like my dead friend, I am a victim of terror. We, all Sudeten German expellees, need compensation for our collective suffering!' In this not uncommon case scenario, remembered and re-experienced emotions are translated into a politically highly relevant discourse of shared victimhood.

Multiple Identification and the Suffering Self

'Identification as co-victims' is only part of a multiple identification process in which individual expellees define themselves in various ways as they move through changing social settings, in terms of both expulsion and non-expulsion experiences (Svašek 2002a: 514). A dynamic theory of self-consciousness and intersubjectivity which, on the one hand, acknowledges that '[t]he self provides experiential continuity throughout a life' (Cohen 1994: 68), but which, on the other, defines the self as a multiplicity of I-positions among which dialogical relationships are established, provides a good analytical model that 'offers the possibility to situate the study of the multiple self in socio-cultural practice' (van Meijl and Driessen 2003: 24). Such an approach also helps to clarify why people may have seemingly contradictory feelings, such as love and longing for the homeland *and* satisfaction with their new place of residence. A focus on multiple identification also explains how expellees may have feelings that are politicized *only* in certain settings. Individual expellees may, for example, feel nostalgic and sentimental while remembering their childhood in the Sudetenland. This mellow form of nostalgia may be 'translated' into a political, angry form of yearning when participating in public expellee events that call for *Heimatrecht*.

The phenomenon of multiple identification and shifting emotions also explains why expellee communities of suffering do *not only* include heavily traumatized victims of terror. In fact, the majority of the expellees know only indirectly about the severe maltreatment and killings of their countrymen and women through documentaries, photographs and victims' testimonies. Yet the widespread availability of representations of terror that show death and destruction in expellee networks has strongly motivated their identification with these victims, and processes of imagination (as opposed to personal memory) have transformed these 'horror images' into more permanent internalized presences that, in certain contexts, generate intense feelings of anger and distress. As such, 'traumatized wounds inflicted

Trauma as culturally specific

on individuals can combine to create a mood, an ethos – a group culture – that is different from (and more than) the sum of the private wounds that make it up' (Erikson 1995: 185).

Instead of 'group culture', I prefer the notion of 'shifting communities of memories and emotions' which allows for a more dynamic analysis of contextual identification processes, in terms of both actual and imagined encounters. As noted at the beginning of this chapter, the concept of 'chosen trauma' is also extremely useful to explain how individuals define themselves, at certain moments more emphatically that at others, as co-victims (Svašek 1999: 46). Despite the obvious difficulties one may have with the verb 'chosen' (after all, nobody chooses voluntarily to become a victim of terror), it does point to the fact that direct victims and their descendants may, consciously or unconsciously, *choose* to make a traumatic experience the centre of collective identification (see also Kidron 2004). The rest of this chapter will demonstrate that particular discursive practices and regular bodily co-presence have been crucial to the Sudeten German politics of chosen trauma.

The Lost Homeland: Intergenerational Projection of Loss and Suffering

How have memories of Sudeten German suffering been shared intergenerationally? Many expellee children were simply too small to remember directly the people who had lost their lives during the expulsion. Not pretending to give a full answer to this complex question, I would like to focus here on the emotional and political potential of images of 'the lost homeland'. In this context, it is important to note that expellee internalized presences that objectified 'painful loss' were not just other human beings, but included all sorts of objectifications, such as lost property (the family house), property lost but saved (artefacts taken to Germany and exhibited in expellee museums), lost access to emotionally evocative places (relatives' graves) and – of major importance – the overall category of 'the lost *Heimat*', the Sudetenland as a space of collective Sudeten German belonging (Svašek 2002a).

The following poem by Ferdinand Roth (1949) demonstrates how he, like many of his contemporaries, tried to reproduce feelings of suffering in his children by attempting to evoke feelings of regret and longing for the lost Sudetenland.

To my Children[6]

Children, look East across forest and barren fields!
Open your eyes, unlock the heart!
Today is an important day for you,

You're looking homeward.
The dilapidated houses, that hamlet between the trees,
It is your homeland and also mine!

Look at the ruins, that's where you were born.
It is our father's house that we lost
And it remains your father's house
For ever and ever!

In that small church over there, it is true,
Your parents stood in front of the altar once when they got married.
You both were once baptized there,
Never forget it!

Silently the cemetery lies under the green hill
Our ancestors have rested there for a long, oh, long time.
God's peace they have and rest …
Ourselves, never, never!

Children, raise your hand and take the holy oath:
'Homeland, we shall remember you always!'

The references to buried ancestors, identity-forming rites-of-passage (birth, baptism and marriage) and shared belonging were clearly intended to emotionally engage the next generation, not in the form of debilitating traumatic suffering, but as part of an identity politics of shared victimhood. In that perspective 'the lost homeland' was an important emotional presence to think and feel with, and 'remembering the homeland' constituted a cross-generational moral and political duty (see also Passerini 1992: 12).

Obviously, not all parents expected their children to identify themselves with the expellee cause, especially when the unfolding Cold War complicated the chance ever to return to the Sudetenland. Indeed, many expellees concentrated on their integration in Germany and elsewhere, and some totally dissociated themselves from their Sudeten German identity (Svašek 2002a). The experience of the expulsion has, however, remained an important motor of expellee identity politics (Wolff 2000: 229–30).

Social Interaction and Time/space Dimensions

Examining the pragmatics of identity politics, it is crucial to realize that people interact with internalized presences in real time and space. Emotional processes *within* individuals are influenced by interpersonal dynamics, and vice versa. In the example of the remembering expellee, though occupied with his own thoughts, the expellee is still sitting in the pub, and his attitude may generate reactions in others who may say, 'Why are you so quiet?' He may, in turn, respond by saying, 'Leave me alone' and keep his focus on the internalized presences. Alternatively, he may say, 'It's nothing, let's get another drink', and turn his attention to those around him. In another case scenario he may tell somebody that he is distressed by the memory of his deceased friend, and discover that the person has also lost Sudeten German friends or relatives. Their mutual empathy and shared suffering may create an emotional bond between them, and potentially, create a common political goal.

From an experiential point of view, identification with remembered or imagined others radically differs from social interactions with persons who are physically present. The obvious point of difference is that physically present persons share time and space, relate to each other in terms of bodily interaction, and communicate verbally. As will become clear in the rest of this chapter, in the Sudeten German case, bodily co-presence has been vital to the politicization of suffering.

Various studies have shown that sharing time and space after a traumatic event can be of major importance to individual victims, and that sharing thoughts and feelings about the traumatic past may produce a strong sense of collective identity. In different contexts, victims of a wide range of calamities (including incest, rape, street crime, natural disasters and war-related experiences such as the Holocaust) have formed networks and organizations in an attempt to find mutual support, and to strive for financial or other forms of compensation. This agrees with Erikson's claim that that even though '[t]rauma is normally understood as a somewhat lonely and isolated business because the persons who experience it so often drift away from the every day moods and understandings that govern social life ... paradoxically, the drifting away is accompanied by revised views of the world that, in their turn, become a basis for communality' (Erikson 1995: 198).

In the Sudeten German case, large organizations such as the Sudetendeutsche Landsmannschaft and the Bund der Vertriebenen, as well as numerous smaller associations of expellees, have been established that have created links among victims of the expulsion on the basis of pre-expulsion residence, post-expulsion residence, religious orientation, political orientation or particular cultural activities. In some of these organizations, 'shared victimhood' forms the main raison d'être, whereas other organizations are focused on shared interests, such as folk dancing or genealogical research. Yet 'collective suffering' has been an important source of identification for *all*, and bodily co-presence during ritual re-enactments of suffering has been a significant defining experience.

Collective Suffering and Bodily Co-presence

The annual Sudetendeutscher Tag, referred to at the beginning of this chapter, formed a social setting in which shared victimhood was both discursively reproduced and physically enacted. The commemoration for those who had died at the hand of the Czechs, attracted tens of thousands of expellees and their relatives. The whole set-up, the large crowd of serious and sad-looking people, the tears and handkerchiefs, and the solemn words by the religious leaders, produced feelings of communality – even if these lasted only as long as the ceremony for some.

Physical co-presence was important in a number of ways. First, direct and indirect embodied memories of maltreatment and displacement produced bodily changes, especially in those expellees who were still heavily traumatized. An elderly woman told me that she always found it difficult to breathe during the ceremonies, imagining all those who had suffered and died. Second, sharing time and space in a highly orchestrated ritual context caused and required habitual changes – culturally specific bodily movements, internalized through repetition and routinization (Connerton 1989: 59; see also Whitehouse, Chapter 5 in this volume). During the ritual, the participants took on particular postures that expressed deep sorrow, and respect for the ritual authorities. They folded their hands and closed their eyes during prayers, and many were visibly affected by each other's emotional displays, a phenomenon known as emotional contagion.[7]

The first time I attended the commemoration ceremony, even I, an unrelated stranger, felt the urge to cry. My grief was partly caused by empathy through active identification with the mourners, and partly resulted from the multisensual experience of the ritual itself. My reaction demonstrated that physical co-presence not only influences 'informants' but also affects fieldworkers like myself, engaging them in processes of emotional intersubjectivity (see Tonkin, Chapter 3 in this volume), and setting in motion particular dialogues with internalized presences. As with the conversations I had with expellees about the commemoration ceremony, my own feelings unveiled a process of shifting, multiple self-identitication that was influenced by the powerful context of the ritual.[8] Interestingly, like myself, some expellees had mixed feelings about Sudeten German victimhood, and were critical of the one-sided emphasis on Sudeten German suffering. The difficulty of observing such intrapsychic contradictions in others during ritual commemorations demonstrates the political potential of rituals: their capacity to create the illusion of collective emotional unity (Kertzer 1988).

Chosen Trauma: Rhetorical Strategies

The following describes how, in 1998, a religious ritual was used to politicize memories of Sudeten German suffering. The analysis focuses not only on bodily co-presence, but also on discursive practice, reinforcing Casey's (1987: 235) observation that 'almost every public ceremony that is commemorative in character brings together the impelling corporeal movements of the participants with the equally urgent authority of a text'.

In May 1998, the Suffragan Bishop Gerhard Pieschl, representative of the German Episcopal Conference for the Spiritual Welfare of Refugees and Expellees, preached at the Sudetendeutscher Tag in Nuremberg, during the Roman Catholic Mass that always takes place on the festival of Whitsuntide. Pieschl began by addressing his audience, an impressive gathering of thousands of expellees, as 'Brothers and Sisters in the communal belief in God the Father, Jesus Christ and the Holy Ghost, beloved compatriots!' Having stressed their relatedness, he used further rhetorical means to take the members of the audience back to the time of the expulsion by reflecting on his own, personal memories.

> Looking back, memories are evoked. I remember Whitsuntide 1945. We were fleeing, and had only just escaped from the partisans and the low-flying aircrafts. We, a mother and three young children, made our way back to our Moravian homeland. Afraid and totally exhausted, we reached the farm of relatives who lived away from the Russian advance.

No doubt his reminiscences made many members of his audience remember their own fear and confusion. Obviously, their present emotional reactions were directly affected by Pieschl's narrative performance. As Brian Parkinson (1995: 225) indicated, 'the performance of getting emotional is often shaped dynamically by the unfolding structure of the interpersonal situation rather than run off in accordance with a prespecified internal script'.

Pieschl depicted the Sudeten Germans as a group of collective victims who had continued to suffer after their expulsion.

> Our Sudeten German ethnic group ... has the experience of the unauthorized creation of chaos, disunity, and confusion: first of all the expulsion itself, the loss of our fatherland, the distress caused by flight and displacement, the uncertainty about the fate of one's closest relatives and friends, the separation from land and people. Then follows the building of a new life in a new homeland, the difficulties of finding one's way in a strange environment, among people with another mentality, and other dialects and habits.

Conversations with numerous expellees clarified that, coming from a highly respected church official (as well as on other occasions from influential politicians, such as Edmund Stoiber, see Svašek 2002b, 2002c), his words influenced expellee self-perception. Pieschl also defended the demands for *Heimatrecht*, and noted that the claims had recently been supported by transnational authorities.

With justification, in 1997 a subcommittee of the United Nations pointed out that expulsion lasts as long as the expellees are denied the right to their homeland – which confirmed statements made by our Pope. Therefore, the fact that the expulsion cannot be regarded as past history but still continues, is central to the Sudeten German question.

Presenting it as a more general human rights issue, he further stated that the expellees wanted reconciliation with the Czechs, but that this was possible only if injustice was acknowledged through compensation:

We want compensation and reconciliation for all people and peoples. We want to outlaw expulsion, so that future generations will be spared our own fate. We want the reappraisal of the past on the basis of the historical truth. We want to reach an atonement with those who expelled us which is reasonable for all parties, and to make clear that expulsion is not worthwhile. Injustice cannot become justice in the course of time.

The above again clarifies that the image of 'shared suffering' was of central importance to expellee politics. As with expellee poems and other commemoration rituals, the Mass constructed the audience as a united group of victims – both through the dynamics of bodily co-presence and the rethorics of collective suffering. As proclaimed by Pieschl, this united group of victims had one major political aim: to gain compensation for their past and present distress. It may be clear that in his account of moral and political injustice, the distinction between trauma 'patients' and others who actively associated themselves with Sudeten German suffering was irrelevant.

Conclusion: The Politics and Dialectics of Individual and Social Suffering

In this chapter I have argued that, in order to examine the political dimensions of traumatic suffering, 'trauma' must neither be reduced to individual psychobiological malfunctioning, nor be simplified as a purely sociocultural phenomenon. Using Volkan's (1999) concept of 'chosen trauma' and Csordas' (1994) view that human experience cannot be solely understood as discursive practice, I have further argued that, to be able to examine the politics of trauma, it is necessary to analyse interrelated processes of bodily interaction, perceptual experience and meaning construction.

The perspective of 'internalized presences' meant to point out that individuals, as thinking and feeling bodies, are inherently social beings, since ongoing social experiences influence their self-experience and self-judgement. The dynamics of intersubjectivity, understood in this chapter as the emotional engagement and identification of shifting selves with remembered, imagined and physically present others, bridges the domain between the individual and the social. In the Sudeten German case, the category of emotion-evoking 'others' has included a wide variety of phenomena, including (memories of) other people, artefacts and localities, as well as parts of multiple selves. These phenomena have partly merged into each other through dynamic association, for example when grief for a dead friend was experienced as grief for the suffering self, and objectified as an identifying experience of Sudeten German victimhood.

The notions of internalized presence and 'chosen trauma' helped to explain how trauma has been shared, intergenerationally transmitted and politicized. While the direct confrontation with terror has had a numbing effect on numerous Sudeten German trauma patients who have found it hard to talk about their experiences, others have told their personal stories of terror in public, producing them as 'accessible' narratives that have subsequently acted as internalized presences to other people (see also Cappelletto 2003: 250). Collected and published by expellee organizations, these accounts have been transformed into politically significant symbols of collective Sudeten German victimhood.

The two internalized presences of 'the expellee co-victim' and 'the lost homeland', have been particularly evocative in expellee politics. As objectifications of collective victimhood, they have been 'good to think and feel with', both for the survivors of terror and for those who have identified themselves with Sudeten German suffering. As the analysis of the expellee poem demonstrated, 'the lost homeland' has been reproduced as a continuous source of Sudeten German distress, even to those born after the expulsion. The analysis of the expellee commemorations showed how orchestrated bodily interactions and well-thought-out discursive strategies have produced feelings of collective suffering in a ritual context.

In conclusion, the concept of 'chosen trauma' served well to explain how, in the Sudeten German case, many direct and indirect victims of the expulsion and their religious and political representatives, have chosen to form a fluid community of memories and emotions, calling for compensation for what they see as a gross political injustice. The selective recollection of past emotions and their incorporation and translation into powerful discursive practices and (re)experiences of suffering has been vital to these politics of chosen trauma.

Acknowledgements

I would like to thank Kay Milton, Elizabeth Tonkin, Paul Antze, Jan Eelman and Roberta McDonnell for their helpful comments on an earlier draft of this chapter, and Volker Ellerbeck for his assistance with the translation of the poem.

Notes

1. In the Sudeten German case, the most painful unacceptable thought – fiercely criticized by many expellees – is that the Sudeten Germans deserved to suffer because many were actively involved in the Nazi system of oppression which caused death and destruction. Even though, in the light of post-Cold War reconciliation politics, several expellee organizations have raised the issue of Sudeten German guilt, critical reflections on their own role in causing the suffering of other peoples (Jews, Roma, Czechs) were tellingly absent in expellee life stories (Svašek 2002a).

2. See Svašek (2002a) for a more detailed discussion of the concept of *Heimat*.

3. The increased interest of many expellees in their (traumatic) past can also be explained by the fact that many have reached retirement age. In a study of Holocaust survivors, Krystal (1995: 78) noted that the need to come to terms with earlier, traumatic experiences often becomes more urgent when people reach old age and look back at their lives.

4. For a discussion of 'numbing' in connection with Holocaust victims, see for example Laub (1995). See also Daniel (1994) who, taking a Peircean perspective in a study of Tamil victims of torture, argued that memories of intense suffering can be expressed only when the unmediated, prereflective qualisigns of pain enter a process of signification.

5. According to the *antimimetic* paradigm, trauma is an external incident that happens to a fully constituted subject who keeps a sense of integrated self. This perspective reflects a belief in the reliability of memory, and argues that traumatic pasts can be traced back through therapy and value-free scientific research. It also projects the image of contained selfhood in which the self is an integrating centre of awareness, emotion, judgement and action. By contrast, the *mimetic* paradigm contends that victims are not able to process traumatic experiences in the normal memory system because their cognitive and perceptual capacities have been shattered, and they have lost their sense of integrated self. This view also projects the image of a self that is integrated under 'normal' conditions, but argues that disintegration occurs as a result of trauma. The knowing self becomes blind to the trauma experience, and thus, trauma accounts are unavoidably untrustworthy.

6. Kinder, nehmt den Blick nach Osten über Wald und öde Fluren hin! / Machet groß die Augen, schließet auf das Herz! / Heute ist ein großer Tag für Euch, / Ihr schauet heimatwärts. / Die zerfall'nen Häuser, jenes Dörflein zwischen Bäumen drin, / Es ist Eure Heimat, und sie ist auch mein! // Sehet Ihr die Ruine, dort seid Ihr gebor'n, / Unser Vaterhaus ist es, das wir verlor'n/ Und es bleibt Euer Vaterhaus … / Für immer, immer! // Dort in jenem Kirchlein drüben, fürwahr, / Standen Eure Eltern einst am Traualtar. / Beide wurdet Ihr einst dort getauft … / Vergeßt dies nimmer! // Stille liegt der Friedhof dort am grünen Hang,/ Uns're

Ahnen ruhen dort schon lang, ach lang. / Gottes Frieden haben sie und Ruh' ... / Wir nimmer, nimmer! // Kinder, hebt die Hand und tut den heil'gen Eid: / 'Heimat, wir gedenken deiner allezeit!'

7. The term 'emotional contagion' has been used to describe how people unconsciously synchronize their feelings (Meltzoff and Moore 1977; Hatfield, Cacioppo and Rapson 1992), and how they, more consciously, 'jointly negotiate emotional meanings' (Parkinson 1995: 183; see also Casey 1987: 221).

8. In my case, the involuntary sensations in my body set in motion a telling process of internal reflection. Feeling a lump in my throat, I immediately distanced myself from my own distress ('this can't be me') and objectified it as 'overinvolvement'. Judging from another I-position, I almost automatically accused myself of 'mourning for the old enemy'. The latter reaction can be explained by the fact that I am of Dutch-Czech descent, a factor that has unavoidably produced latent anti-German sentiments. I immediately responded to these feelings by moral self-accusation, telling myself that it was highly inappropriate and politically wrong to think in terms of negative stereotypical images, especially after having talked to so many expellees, having gained a more nuanced view of Sudeten German history. Their voices, or – theoretically more apt – my own interpretation of our interactions, had clearly affected my views, yet without (I must admit) fully eliminating anti-German feelings.

References

Abu-Lughod, L. and Lutz, C. A. (eds) (1990), *Language and the Politics of Emotion*, Cambridge: Cambridge University Press and Paris: Editions de la Maison des Sciences de l'Homme.

Antze, P. and Lambek, M. (eds) (1996), *Tense Past: Cultural Essays in Trauma and Memory*, New York: Routledge.

Cappelletto, F. (2003), 'Long-Term Memory of Extreme Events: From Autobiography to History', *Journal of the Royal Anthropological Institute* (NS) 9: 241–60.

Caruth, C. (ed.) (1995), *Trauma: Explorations in Memory*, Baltimore, MD: Johns Hopkins University Press.

Casey, E. (1987), *Remembering: A Phenomenological Study*, Bloomington, IN: Indiana University Press.

Cockerham, W. C. (1981), *Sociology of Mental Disorder*, Englewood Cliffs, NJ: Prentice Hall.

Cohen, A. P. (1994), *Self Consciousness: An Alternative Anthropology of Identity*, London: Routledge.

Connerton, P. (1989), *How Societies Remember*, Cambridge: Cambridge University Press.

Cordell, K. and Wolff, S. (2005), *A Triangle of Fate: A Comparative Study of Czech–German and Polish–German Relations*, London: Routledge.

Csordas, T. J. (1990), 'Embodiment as a Paradigm for Anthropology', *Ethos* 18 (1): 5–47.

—— (ed.) (1994), *Embodiment and Experience: The Existential Ground of Culture and Self*, Cambridge: Cambridge University Press.

Daniel, V. (1994), 'The Individual in Terror', in T. J. Csordas (ed.), *Embodiment and Experience: The Existential Ground of Culture and Self*, Cambridge: Cambridge University Press.

Erikson, K. (1995), 'Notes on Trauma and Community', in C. Caruth (ed.), *Trauma: Explorations in Memory*, Baltimore, MD: Johns Hopkins University Press.

Fierke, K. M. (2002), 'The Liberation of Kosovo: Emotion and the Ritual Reenactment of War', *Focaal: European Journal of Anthropology* 39: 93–116.

Hacking, I. (1996), 'Memory Sciences, Memory Politics' in P. Antze and M. Lambek (eds), *Tense Past: Cultural Essays in Trauma and Memory*, New York: Routledge.

Hamperl, W. (1997), *Vertreibung und Flucht aus dem Kreis Tachau im Egerland: Schicksale in Berichten, Dokumenten und Bildern*, Altenmarkt: Published by the author.

Hatfield, E., Cacioppo, J. T. and Rapson, R. (1992), 'Primitive Emotional Contagion', in M. S. Clark (ed.), *Review of Personality and Social Psychology* 14: 151–77.

Herman, J. L. (1994), *Trauma and Recovery*, London: Pandora.

Janet, P. (1984[1919–25]), *Les Médications Psychologiques*, 3 vols, Paris: Société Pierre Janet.

Kenny, M. G. (1996), 'Trauma, Time, Illness and Culture. An Anthropological Approach to Traumatic Memory', in P. Antze and M. Lambek (eds), *Tense Past: Cultural Essays in Trauma and Memory*, New York: Routledge.

Kertzer, D. (1988), *Ritual, Politics, and Power*, New Haven, CT and London: Yale University Press.

Kidron, C. A. (2004), 'Surviving a Distant Past: A Case Study of the Cultural Construction of Trauma Descendant Identity', *Ethos* 31 (4): 513–44.

Klein, M. (1975), *Envy and Gratitude and Other Works: 1946–1963*, London: Hogarth Press.

Kleinman, A. and Kleinman, J. (1991), 'Suffering and its Professional Transformation: Toward an Ethnography of Interpersonal Experience', *Culture, Medicine, and Psychiatry* 15: 275–301.

Kramer, M., Schoen, L. S. and Kinney, L. (1984), 'The Dream Experience in Dream-Disturbed Vietnam Veterans', in B. van der Kolk (ed.), *Post-Traumatic Stress Disorder: Psychological and Biological Sequelae*, Washington, DC:

American Psychiatric Press.

Krystal, H. (1995), 'Trauma and Aging: A Thirty-Year Follow Up', in C. Caruth (ed.), *Trauma: Explorations in Memory*, London: Johns Hopkins University Press.

Laub, D. (1995), 'Truth and Testimony: The Process and the Struggle', in C. Caruth (ed.), *Trauma: Explorations in Memory*, London: John Hopkins University.

Leydesdorff, S. (1992), 'A Shattered Silence: The Life Stories of Survivors of the Jewish Proletariat of Amsterdam', in L. Passerini (ed.), *International Yearbook of Oral History and Life Stories, Volume I, Memory and Totalitarianism*, Oxford: Oxford University Press.

Leys, R. (2000), *Trauma: A Genealogy*, Chicago: University of Chicago Press.

Lyon, M. L. and Barbalet, J. M. (1994), 'Society's Body: Emotion and the "Somatization" of Social Theory', in T. J. Csordas (ed.), *Embodiment and Experience: The Existential Ground of Culture and Self*, Cambridge: Cambridge University Press.

Meltzhoff, A. N. and Moore, M. K. (1977), 'Imitation of Facial and Manual Gestures in Human Neonates', *Science* 198: 75–8.

Merleau-Ponty, M. (1962), *Phenomenology of Perception*, trans. J. Edie, Evanston, IL: Northwestern University Press.

Morris, B. (1994), *Anthropology of the Self*, London: Pluto

O'Nell, T. D. (2000), '"Coming Home" among Northern Plains Vietnam Veterans: Psychological Transformations in Pragmatic Perspective', *Ethos* 27 (4): 441–65.

Overing, J. and Passes, A. (eds) (2000), *The Anthropology of Love and Anger: The Aesthetics of Conviviality in Native Amazonia*, London and New York: Routledge

Parkinson, B. (1995), *Ideas and Realities of Emotion*, London and New York: Routledge.

Passerini, L. (1992), 'Introduction', in L. Passerini (ed.), *International Yearbook of Oral History and Life Stories, Volume I, Memory and Totalitarianism*, Oxford: Oxford University Press.

Roth, F. (1949), 'An meine Kinder!', *Heimatbote für die Bezirke Tachau-Pfraumberg und Bischofteinitz* 4–5: 23.

Schreier, F. (1953 [1950]), 'Tschirm in the District of Troppau: Murder of my Daughter on June 17, 1945', in Arbeitsgemeinschaft zur Wahrung Sudetendeutscher Interessen (eds), *Documents on the Expulsion of the Sudeten Germans*, Munich: University Press.

Staněk, T. (1991), *Odsun Němců z Československa*, Prague: Akademie naše vojensko.

Svašek, M. (1999), 'History, Identity and Territoriality: Redefining Czech–German Relations in the Post-Cold War Era', *Focaal: Journal of Anthropology* 32: 37–58.

—— (2000), 'Borders and Emotions: Hope and Fear in the Bohemian–Bavarian Frontier Zone', *Ethnologia Europaea: Journal of European Ethnology* 30 (2): 111–126.

—— (2002a), 'Narratives of "Home" and "Homeland": The Symbolic Construction and Appropriation of the Sudeten German Heimat', *Identities: Global Studies in Culture and Power* 9: 495–518.

—— (2002b), 'The Politics of Emotions: Emotional Discourses and Displays in Post-Cold War Contexts', *Focaal: European Journal of Anthropology* 39: 193–6.

—— (2002c), 'Gewältes Trauma: Die Dynamik der Erinnerten und (Wieder) Erfahrenen Emotion', in E. Fendl (ed.), *Zur Ikonographie des Heimwehs. Erinneringskultur von Heimatvertriebenen. Schriftenreihe des Johannes-Künzig-Instituts für ostdeutsche Volkskunde* 6, Freiburg: Johannes-Künzig-Instiut für ostdeutsche Volkskunde.

Tedeschi, R. G. and Calhoun, L. G. (1995), *Trauma and Transformation: Growing in the Aftermath of Suffering*, London: Sage.

Tonkin, E. (1992), *Narrating our Pasts: The Social Construction of Oral History*, Cambridge: Cambridge University Press.

Van der Kolk, B. A. and van der Hart, O. (1995), 'The Intrusive Past: The Flexibility of Memory and the Engraving of Trauma', in C. Caruth (ed.), *Trauma: Explorations in Memory*, Baltimore, MD: Johns Hopkins University Press

van Meijl, T. and Driessen, H. (2003), 'Introduction: Multiple Identifications and the Self', *Focaal: European Journal of Anthropology* 42: 17–29

Volkan, V. (1999), *Bloodlines: From Ethnic Pride to Ethnic Terrorism*, Boulder, CO: Westview.

White, G. M. (2000), 'Emotional Remembering: The Pragmatics of National Memory', *Ethos* 27: 505–29.

Winkler, C. (1994), 'Rape Trauma: Contexts of Meaning', in T. J. Csordas (ed.), *Embodiment and Experience: The Existential Ground of Culture and Self*, Cambridge: Cambridge University Press.

Wolff, S. (2000), 'German Minorities in East and West: A Comparative Overview and Outlook', in S. Wolff (ed.), *German Minorities in Europe: Ethnic Identity and Cultural Belonging*, Oxford: Berghahn.

Young, A. (1995), *The Harmony of Illusions: Inventing Post-Traumatic Stress Disorder*, Princeton, NJ: Princeton University Press.

—— (1996), 'Bodily Memory and Traumatic Memory', in P. Antze and M. Lambek (eds), *Tense Past: Cultural Essays in Trauma and Memory*, New York: Routledge.

Afterword

Kay Milton

Anthropologists are professional observers of human situations, and emotions are present in everything they observe. In Liberia, a group of children amuse themselves by mocking the gait of the visiting anthropologist, provoking indignation, but also understanding. In a gallery at the Alexandros Papachristophorou Church for Missing Persons in Cyprus, an elderly woman gazes at a painting of a mother and her daughter carrying a cross, and contemplates the cross that she herself must bear: the burden of fear, sadness and the remnants of hope that survive after the disappearance of her son some thirty years before. In Sardinia a young man describes the excitement of hunting in the early morning in the woods near his home town, and the intense attachment to the land that is born of such excitement. In Madrid an elderly couple rummage through their family photos and cry over the images of relatives who died long ago.

Emotions need not be intense or lasting to be significant. Resentment can be mild and brief, happiness can pass in a moment, annoyance may be dismissed with a smile. But whether they erupt in vivid public action or remain the hidden property of those that feel them, emotions define the quality of our lives. Given their centrality to human well-being, it is surprising that emotions remained marginal for so long, in the work of anthropologists and other scholars of the human condition.

The contributors to this volume have each sought to understand something about the role of emotions in human lives. The majority (Gay y Blasco, Heatherington, Josephides, Knight, Lysaght, Sant Cassia, Svašek) have focused on events observed in the field and shown how an understanding of emotions helps to throw light on the discernible patterns of social and cultural life. Some (Bowler, Milton, Whitehouse) have considered the role of emotions in theoretical ideas about how human beings operate, while others (Josephides, Tonkin) have addressed the role of emotion in the anthropologist's encounter with the field and in the production of ethnographic understanding. It would be superfluous, in this concluding chapter, to try to summarize the arguments of each contribution, so I shall focus instead on a few common and overlapping themes, and comment on their implications for the research agenda in anthropology. In doing so, I have selected what I find particularly important and interesting; what follows is therefore self-consciously interpretative and subjective, in the sense that a different author might draw out different themes and make different suggestions.

Emotions Connect

Perhaps the most pervasive theme running through this volume is the idea that emotions build connections, between thoughts and actions, between individuals, between species. Knight's contribution (Chapter 10) takes up the inter-species theme by showing how visitors to Japanese monkey parks respond to perceived displays of emotion by the monkeys. In particular, Japanese women identify strongly with behaviour which they interpret as expressions of maternal love (mother monkeys protecting their young, struggling in difficult circumstances to rear them successfully, and so on). In the context of a culture in which motherhood is changing, monkey mothers have come to represent a particular kind of traditional ideal, demonstrating what is good and 'natural' about maternal emotions.

For Darwin, emotions were an important part of our biological nature, something we hold in common with our nearest non-human relatives, linking us to the rest of the animal kingdom. His contemporaries and successors preferred to ignore such connections (Bowler, Chapter 2), being more concerned to establish what 'raised' human beings 'above' their animal past rather than dwelling on what was, at the time, an uncomfortable reality. The stigma was not fully left behind until the 1970s, when psychologists, in particular, began to take Darwin's ideas on emotions seriously, and research on emotions in non-human animals became a serious pursuit. The question of whether human emotions are part of a biological heritage, whether they are innate, 'natural' phenomena, has now become embedded in the continuing nature–nurture debate, in which a major concern has always been to identify a line between biology and culture. Even though this is now widely considered a gross oversimplification, the 'selectionists', as Ingold (2000) called them, still present persuasive images of human beings as largely genetically determined. The study of emotion, in human and non-human animals would seem to offer real possibilities of elucidating this complex area of debate and offering ways out of the dualistic thinking that created the nature–nurture impasse.

It was with this in mind that I suggested, in Chapter 1, that emotions connect individual organisms (human and non-human) to their environment, that they are ecological mechanisms through which we, as individuals, engage with our surroundings (human and non-human; see also Milton 2002). As such they enable us to learn (see Whitehouse, Chapter 5) and so lay the foundations of our role as producers of culture. The ecological function of emotions, which is implied in Damasio's (1999, 2003) theory of consciousness, is already an important topic of investigation in neuroscience and evolutionary psychology, but without an input from anthropology, this work tends to assume, and therefore reinforce, an understanding of emotions, their meanings and modes of expression as innate, universal, and immune to cultural variation. The challenge for anthropology is to engage with this research to build an understanding of how we develop as emotional beings in cultural contexts. The cultural constructionist tradition did this at the expense of effectively denying the physical nature of emotion. The challenge issued by Leavitt (in 1996) still remains: to develop an understanding of emotion that takes account of its dual character, as both physical feeling and cultural meaning. The idea of emotion as an ecological mechanism is a step towards this, but it is just a beginning. In Chapter 1, I have pointed to three possible areas of investigation: how people in different cultures learn what and how to feel about what (cf. Hochschild 1983, 1998), how they learn to perceive specific bodily sensations as particular feelings, and how they learn whether and how to express or suppress those feelings.

A concern with how emotions operate as ecological mechanisms is likely to encourage a greater emphasis on what is rather clumsily called 'methodological individualism' – focusing on the personal life stories of individuals and using them as a basis for (cautious) generalization. This is for two reasons. First, it is individuals who experience and express emotions, and second, ecology has to do with the relationship between an entity and its environment, and a society or group is rarely sufficiently corporate or self-contained to be said to have an 'environment'. An individual's environment, on the other hand, clearly includes all the social, cultural and non-human phenomena with which that individual engages. The study of emotion in this context should thus enable us to explore the relationship between 'the individual' and 'society', by examining the emotional dynamics that operate between individuals and their human associates. But it is important to recognize that an ecological approach encompasses rather than privileges social relations, by treating them as just one category of ecological relations. Relationships with non-human phenomena may be more emotionally compelling and have more influence over someone's actions than many of their social relationships, as I found when I investigated the motivations of environmentalists (see Milton 2002). There is always the danger, in an academic world dominated by a respect for quantification and scientific rigour, that a focus on individual lives, to say nothing of a focus on emotions, will lead to anthropology being regarded as more impressionistic, more humanistic, less scientific. So be it. We need to recognize that different kinds of understanding come from different kinds of approach; Jane Austen, after all, taught us a great deal about the culture of early-nineteenth-century England by describing the innermost thoughts of imaginary characters. Surely anthropologists can provide similar insights into contemporary cultures by exploring the emotional experiences of their real members.[1]

In arguing that emotions can usefully be understood as ecological mechanisms, I am not intending to diminish their social importance, and it is on this area, not surprisingly, that most of the contributors have focused their attention. Emotions operate in interpersonal contexts; they connect individuals to each other, and so help to constitute groups and 'communities', because they are effective means of communication. As Josephides put it, 'emotions link people in understanding'. They appear to do this routinely, if not always reliably, within cultural milieux, in the processes of everyday life, and across cultural boundaries. Both Josephides and Tonkin describe how emotions communicated to them within the field shaped their ethnographic knowledge. Tonkin's emphasis on co-presence as the essential basis for ethnographic understanding helps to elucidate the nature of anthropological research. The favoured model for research in anthropology remains the lone scholar engaged in participant observation and other forms of qualitative research over extended periods. In other words, the favoured approach is one that creates precisely those conditions necessary for emotional understanding, which suggests that such understanding has long been important in anthropology, even though it has rarely been made explicit. I shall return to this point in the following sections.

Emotions as Internal

The opposition between public and private has been almost as pervasive in the study of emotions as the opposition between nature and culture. The assumption that emotions are private, internal phenomena had the effect, for many years, of rendering them inaccessible to cultural analysis (since what is cultural was considered, by definition, public and shared), and consigning them to the realm of psychology rather than anthropology (see Lutz and White 1986). Several contributors to this volume dwell, implicitly or explicitly, on the internal nature of emotions; not only Josephides, for whom the 'innerliness' of emotions is central, but also Gay y Blasco, Heatherington, Lysaght, Sant Cassia and Svašek. It is the acknowledgement of the importance of the internal nature of emotions that takes the perspectives employed in these chapters beyond the traditional cultural constructionist perspective. Without being powerful motivators from within human minds and bodies, emotions would not be capable of shaping public social life. The same goes for ideas, norms, values, all of which are most often studied as cultural constructs. Phenomena constructed through social discourse do not lead to actions without a degree of internal processing, contemplation, interpretation, feeling.

Thus it is important, for the Sudeten German cause of *Heimachtrecht*, that yearning for the lost homeland be felt, as an aching or emptiness in the heart, not only by those who directly experienced the horrors of the expulsion, but also by their descendants, who must be taught how to feel it (see Svašek, Chapter 11). Belfast's urban space is composed of segregated areas bounded by dangerous interfaces. It is constructed and maintained as such by the actions of residents who, driven by an internally experienced fear of sectarian violence, follow safe routes and avoid dangerous ones (Lysaght, Chapter 7). The internal suffering caused by the death of a close relative among Gitanos becomes an important factor in how the bereaved are treated by their associates. It is not just the recognition of another's internal state that produces the observable patterns of bereavement, but the ability of others to feel (internally) *for* the bereaved, and to respect their suffering (Gay y Blasco, Chapter 9).

Emotions and Memory

The relationship between emotions and memory runs through several of the chapters. Memories and emotions mutually influence each other. A period of excessive stress may leave a long-lasting imprint on somebody's feelings and thoughts. Strong emotions in the present may distort memories, as when homesickness, for example, generates brightly coloured, purely positive memories of home. The smell of a flower may evoke romantic feelings because it reminds somebody of an earlier romantic occasion. A person may feel a tightening of the stomach when remembering a fearful past event. In my own chapter (Chapter 1) and that written by Whitehouse (Chapter 5), the impact of emotions on the functioning of memory is discussed. In a very broad sense, I argue, emotions affect how and what we learn, and therefore what we remember. At a fundamental level, interest (or anticipation, expectation), which psychologists have identified as a basic human emotion, is necessary for us to receive information from our environment. But other emotions (joy, sorrow, fear), when experienced in varying degrees of intensity, can affect the extent to which we remember things.

This idea is central to Whitehouse's discussion of how religious knowledge is sustained and transmitted. Religious rituals that are repeated frequently tend not to be emotionally arousing; they are remembered simply because of the frequent repetition. Rituals performed only occasionally, perhaps once in a lifetime, incorporate emotionally powerful experiences to ensure that what is learned through them will be remembered. This seems to be particularly so for initiation ceremonies, in which important knowledge about adult responsibilities is imparted, and in which young people may be exposed to frightening or otherwise powerful images and sounds (see, for instance, Turner 1967; Bloch 1992). In the Kenyan community where I did my doctoral fieldwork in the late 1970s, I was told that boys' initiation rituals, which had not taken place for many years, used to be accompanied by a terrifying sound like a lion's roar. Even those who had not passed through initiation themselves, but were old enough to remember the ceremonies taking place, could recall the sound, which had made them shiver in their beds at night.

If emotional experiences create and fix memories, it is also well established that memories generate emotions. It is for this reason, for fear of causing emotional pain to the bereaved, that Gitanos avoid talking about their 'beloved deceased', that they burn their clothes and other possessions (Gay y Blasco, Chapter 9). The Gitano reaction to memories of deceased relatives is an example of what Svašek calls 're-experienced emotions' (Chapter 11). The memory recreates the sadness of bereavement, even though the death may have occurred many years ago. Svašek's distinction between 're-experienced' and 'remembered' emotions is important in analysing the effect of the past on the present. While people remain traumatized by highly emotional events, their memories will continue to evoke 're-experienced emotions'. When the trauma subsides, they may still remember what they felt without feeling it, and being troubled by it, again.

Emotions and Community

Several contributions discuss emotions which are, in some sense, communal (Gay y Blasco, Heatherington, Lysaght, Sant Cassia, Svašek). It is difficult to express what is meant by this. Just as thoughts are located in individual minds, so emotions (as physiological processes, perceptions, thoughts, meanings, however they might be conceptualized) are located in individual minds/bodies. There is no communal mind/body, no entity which can hold communal feelings, and the contributors to this volume are not suggesting that there is. They are suggesting, rather, that emotions, as phenomena experienced and expressed by individuals, help to constitute communities in a number of ways.

The directness of emotional communication, discussed by Josephides, means that one can receive signals indicating another's resentment, anger, sorrow, happiness. Just as sights, sounds, scents and memories can affect how we feel, so the signals of another's mood can affect our own moods. This does not mean that emotions are 'shared'. After all, the mood provoked may not be the same as that which provokes. My sorrow can provoke your irritation, or even your pleasure, if you dislike me enough to enjoy my suffering. But often the infectiousness of emotion, whether communicated through mood signals or through speech and gestures, can create a community united in feeling. Catholics and Protestants in Northern Ireland are united against each other partly through fear and distrust (Lysaght, Chapter 7), while the relatives of missing Greek Cypriots are united in their continuing trauma (wound), born of a sense of absence which cannot be fully experienced as a loss (Sant Cassia, Chapter 6).

The unity born out of the experience of similar feelings can be a springboard for political action. The attachment felt by residents of Orgosolo to the common land around their town is grounded in personal life histories (Heatherington, Chapter 8). The commonality of this attachment generates indignant protest when regional and national authorities threaten to restrict their access to and control over this land. Conversely, the perceived need for political action, to keep alive a claim for compensation, for instance, can be an incentive to maintain the intensity of feeling in oneself and others. Thus it is important that the new generations of Sudeten Germans feel the loss of their homeland as their parents and grandparents did; emotions must be kept alive so that justice can be pursued.

A different sense in which emotions can help to constitute a community is demonstrated by Gay y Blasco (Chapter 9). Gitanos feel loyalty only towards their own kin, and hostility towards unrelated Gitanos and non-Roma. They do not think of themselves, the Gitano people, as a community with common interests. Nevertheless, their expectations of fellow Gitanos, whether or not they are kin, are different from their expectations of non-Roma. Gitanos experience a deep and enduring sense of loss for their own kin and so are expected to respect the suffering of the bereaved. Anyone who fails to do this, by talking about the deceased or through loud behaviour during the mourning of others, is failing to live by Gitano standards. There is thus a 'moral universe', grounded in common emotions if not a sense of commonality, that separates Gitanos from non-Roma.

Emotions and the Self

Several chapters touch on the importance of emotions in constituting a sense of personhood or selfhood. In Knight's analysis (Chapter 10), this takes place across the species boundary. It is clear that the visitors to Japanese monkey parks think of the monkeys as 'persons' with motives and feelings which, in many ways, resemble human persons. What seems to engender and reinforce this understanding is the manner in which the young monkeys, in particular, respond to the visitors who pay them attention. They look directly at the visitors (something adult monkeys have learned not to do), come up to them and touch them, just as human children might do. The manner in which the monkeys interact with each other, not just mothers with their young, but generally within the troop – playing, fighting, comforting, bullying – suggests that they each experience a human-like inner world of feelings, ideas, grudges and expectations. Thus they are perceived as having the kinds of characteristics that humans perceive in each other and which are fundamental to social interaction.

The contribution of emotions to one's own understanding of oneself as a person comes across particularly strongly in Josephides' contribution (Chapter 4). She concludes that resentment is the mode of constructing the self everywhere, not just among the Kewa. The causes of resentment and its behavioural consequences are clearly culturally variable, but the feeling of resentment might, in all human societies, be the signal that the self has been violated, defining the limits of acceptability in terms of personal insult or injury. A sense of personal attachment to the common land around Orgosolo is part of Orgolese selfhood (Heatherington,

Chapter 8). When external authorities threaten that attachment, they strike at the heart of what it means to be 'a true Orgolese', and the response, not surprisingly, is angry resistance. In the case described by Sant Cassia (Chapter 6), violation of the self extends to deep trauma, from which neither the political authorities nor orthodox Christianity offer any hope of emergence. Instead, Sant Cassia argues, popular art expressing the personal emotions of the traumatized self can, in the manner of a myth (Lévi-Strauss 1963) at least address irresolvable contradictions and help people to live with an unbearable reality.

The internal nature of emotions, together with their role in the constitution of self and community, has implications for the way anthropologists and other social scientists study and conceptualize identity. In the constructionist tradition in anthropology, identity, be it communal/group identity (a shared understanding of who and what we are) or personal identity (a sense of who or what I am), has been treated, like other cultural products, as emerging out of social discourse. The emphasis has been on identifying and analysing the discursive practices through which people construct an understanding of themselves as groups or individuals. Much of this has focused on cultural markers that set one group off from another, such as food (Wilk 1988) or language (O'Reilly 1999). If emotions are important in the constitution of personal and communal identity, then this process must have dimensions which are not amenable to discourse analysis. In a recent study of Muslims in Northern Ireland, Marranci found that established sociological models of identity, which tend to depend on the identification of differences among groups, did not fit the personal experiences of those whose lives he studied. As he put it, 'To know what I am, I do not need to know that you are different'. [2] He found, instead, that people's understandings of themselves arose out of their primary emotional commitments. It is what I *feel* I am that determines my identity for me, regardless of how others, engaged in countless public discourses around the use of cultural markers, might perceive me.

Emotions and Anthropology

This brings us back to the question of how we know, or come to know, what people feel. In the constructionist and interactionist traditions, which have dominated social and cultural anthropology in recent decades, the inner world of thought and feeling has been acknowledged but not explored. The practicalities and technicalities of fieldwork have dictated this. You cannot, literally, read people's minds, so you have to infer their thoughts from their actions. If thoughts have been treated as inaccessible, feelings have been more so. And yet, as Leavitt (1996) pointed out, some ethnographers, in defiance of the strictures of general theory, have presented emotionally rich and sensitive accounts of the cultures they have studied. He cites Rosaldo (1980) and Feld (1982) as examples, but others could be added: Briggs

(1970), Jeffery (1979), Sansom (1980), Abu-Lughod (1986). These monographs are memorable, I suggest, because they convey a vivid sense of what it feels like to belong to the societies they describe. How is this kind of understanding developed in the course of fieldwork?

Josephides (Chapter 4) describes the 'maelstrom of human passions' which surrounded her in the field and through which she began to understand the Kewa. In her experience, empathy, the recognition of feelings in others, proved to be an important research tool, offering insights beyond what could be learned purely from the observation of what people say and do. But Tonkin (Chapter 3) gives examples of 'cross-cultural dissonance' (a shake of the head that means 'Yes', a body stance which misleadingly conveys aggression) through which we come to misunderstand others' internal worlds. Clearly, the recognition of others' feelings is not always straightforward; we often get it wrong. For this reason, it would be naïve simply to advocate the wider use of empathy as a tool in fieldwork. On the other hand, it would be going too far if we were to abandon the attempt to recognize emotions across cultural boundaries. Since we routinely read each other's feelings in everyday life, and often do so accurately, there seems no obvious reason why we should not learn to do so in other cultural contexts; if we can learn another society's language and codes of behaviour, then why not their 'feeling rules' (Hochschild 1998) and how they express their emotions. As Leavitt pointed out, 'The problem with empathy is not that it involves feeling but that it assumes that first impressions are true' (Leavitt 1996: 530). It is, he argued, a matter of translation. Just as an anthropologist in the field will examine and revise their own interpretations of words and gestures in the light of new knowledge gained, so they can examine and revise their own empathic reactions as they gradually get to know what the people they are studying feel about what, and how those feelings show themselves in postures, inflections of the voice, facial expressions.

Whatever the ease or difficulty in reading others' feelings, the contributions to this volume demonstrate that it is both necessary and worthwhile if we want to explore what shapes people's thoughts and drives their actions, a quest which is surely more urgent now, in a globalized and politically volatile world, than ever before. Understanding why people act as they do requires an understanding of how they feel, how they develop the emotional commitments that motivate their actions. Anthropology is not the only discipline that can advance this understanding, but it has a vital role to play.

Notes

1. For excellent examples of individualistic, humanistic anthropology, see Rapport (1997, 2003).
2. Gabriele Marranci, personal communication, February 2003.

References

Abu-Lughod, L. (1986), *Veiled Sentiments: Honour and Poetry in a Bedouin Society*, Berkeley, CA: University of California Press.

Bloch, M. E. F. (1992), *Prey into Hunter: Politics of Religious Experience*, Cambridge: Cambridge University Press.

Briggs, J. L. (1970), *Never in Anger: Portrait of an Eskimo Family*, Cambridge, MA: Harvard University Press.

Damasio, A. (1999), *The Feeling of What Happens: Body and Emotion in the Making of Consciousness*, London: Heinemann.

—— (2003), *Looking for Spinoza: Joy, Sorrow and the Feeling Brain*, London: Heinemann.

Feld, S. (1982), *Sound and Sentiment: Birds, Weeping, Poetics and Song in Kaluli Expression*, Philadelphia, PA: University of Pennsylvania Press.

Hochschild, A. R. (1983), *The Managed Heart: Commercialization of Human Feeling*, Berkeley, CA: University of California Press.

—— (1998), 'The Sociology of Emotion as a Way of Seeing', in G. Bendelow and S. J. Williams (eds) *Emotions in Social Life: Critical Themes and Contemporary Issues*, London and New York: Routledge.

Ingold, T. (2000), 'The Poverty of Selectionism', *Anthropology Today* 16 (3): 1–2.

Jeffery, P. (1979), *Frogs in a Well: Indian Women in Purdah*, London: Zed Books.

Leavitt, J. (1996), 'Meaning and Feeling in the Anthropology of Emotions', *American Ethnologist* 23 (3): 514–39.

Lévi-Strauss, C. (1963) *Structural Anthropology*, New York: Basic Books.

Lutz, C. A. and White, G. M. (1986), 'The Anthropology of Emotions', *Annual Review of Anthropology* 15: 405–36.

Milton, K. (2002), *Loving Nature: Towards an Ecology of Emotion*, London and New York: Routledge.

O'Reilly, C. (1999), *The Irish Language in Northern Ireland: The Politics of Culture and Identity*, London: Macmillan.

Rapport, N. (1997), *Transcendent Individual: Towards a Literary and Liberal Anthropology*, London and New York: Routledge.

—— (2003), *I am Dynamite: An Alternative Anthropology of Power*, London and New York: Routledge.

Rosaldo, M. Z. (1980), *Knowledge and Passion: Ilongot Notions of Self and Social Life*, Cambridge: Cambridge University Press.

Sansom, B. (1980), *The Camp at Wallaby Cross: Aboriginal Fringe Dwellers in Darwin*, Canberra: Australian Institute of Aboriginal Studies.

Turner, V. W. (1967), *The Forest of Symbols: Aspects of Ndembu Ritual*, Ithaca, NY and London: Cornell University Press.

Wilk, R. (1988), 'Beauty and the Feast: Official and Visceral Nationalism in Belize', *Ethnos* 53 (3–4): 294–316.

Index

Aborigine studies 8
absence/loss 117–18
Abu-Lughod, L. 1, 9, 79, 146, 196, 223
affects 2–3, 8, 16, 62, 152; maternal 186
aggression 12, 187, 223; maternal 190
Alexandros Papachristophorou Church for
    Missing Persons, Nicosia 113–14, 215
Alor community (Dutch Indies) 6
Amazonians 97, 163, 164
anaesthesia, emotional 113, 120
anger 29, 34, 74, 83, 85–6, 93, 146, 220;
    as expression of grief 110; and political
    subjectivity 155
animals: behaviour 43, 44, 45, 47; and
    emotions 45, 50; instincts 51, *see also*
    monkey behaviour
annoyance 187, 215
anthropology: approach to terror and
    trauma 195–209; challenges 217; cross-
    cultural research 79–80, 93, 223;
    cultural 6, 47, 222; encounters and key
    informants 58, 63–4; methodology
    55–67; narrations 65–6;
    physicalist/culturalist approaches to
    emotion 78; studies/theories of emotion
    78–80, 222–3, *see also* communication;
    fieldwork
Anthropology Today 38
anthropomorphism 46, 47, 52
anticipation 33–4, 36, 121, 132, 219
Antze, P. 195, 199
anxiety 9, 12, 36, 71, 118; in grief and
    trauma 118, 172, 198, 200
Apostoleris, N. H. 36
apprehension 60, 71
Aretxaga, B. 145–6, 155–6
Aristotle 2, 85, 109, 111, 122, 123
art: analysis of Cypriot murals 114–16; as
    emotional representation 110–12,
    113–15, 121–4; painting an aporia
    113–15, 118, 121; and religion 120, 121,
    122

Atkinson, P. 14
Atran, S. 97
attention 33, 66, 221
Ayora-Diaz, S. I. 152
Azuma, H. 184

Bain, Alexander 50
Bakhtin, M. 67
Barbalet, J. M. 12, 196
Barkow, J. 61
Barnett, S. A. 45, 52
Barnouw, V. 6, 7
Barrett, J. L. 104
Barth, F. 62, 98
Bartlett, J. C., 34
Basten, A. 136
Bataille, G. 118
Battle of Pratobello 150
behaviour: animal 43, 44, 45, 47; human
    12, 36, 46–8, 51, 52, 61; instinct and
    innate 48; patterns 94, *see also* monkey
    behaviour
behaviourism/behaviourists 47, 51, 52
being-in-the-world 13, 85, 196
Belfast: case study of fear management
    129–40; as a divided city 128–9, 135–9,
    218–19; living with feared violence
    129–34; sectarianism 128–38; social
    scripts of fear 135–9; women and social
    suffering 155
Bell, Charles 45
Benedict, R. 6
Beneš, President Eduard 197
Berlin, I. 3
Blackburn, S. 3
Bloch, M. E. F. 91, 219
Bock, P. K. 6, 7
body: behaviour and reactions 12, 36; and
    emotions 12–13, 14, 26, 36, 128; hexis
    concept 12; language 56, 83, 223, *see*
    also mind–body dichotomy
boredom 14, 57